Pulpit Fiction

How the Modern Church Is Endangering the Eternal Destiny of Its Followers

Galatians 5:16
This I say then, Walk in the Spirit, and ye shall not fulfil the lust of the flesh.

GREGG POWERS AND ED NOLAN

Copyright © 2018 Gregg Powers and Ed Nolan.

All rights reserved. No part of this book may be used or reproduced by any means, graphic, electronic, or mechanical, including photocopying, recording, taping or by any information storage retrieval system without the written permission of the author except in the case of brief quotations embodied in critical articles and reviews.

This book is a work of non-fiction. Unless otherwise noted, the author and the publisher make no explicit guarantees as to the accuracy of the information contained in this book and in some cases, names of people and places have been altered to protect their privacy.

All scripture quoted within this book is from the King James Version of the Bible but is not meant in any way to be an exclusive endorsement of that version. All efforts invested in this book are to encourage men and women who have taken the first step in accepting Jesus Christ as their Lord and Savior to build a closer relationship with God, not primarily dependent on other men. We would like to thank our wives, Lois and Naomi, for their patience and support during the development of this work. Proceeds to the authors from this book will go to support the work of the Lord. May this book bring glory to our God.

THE HOLY BIBLE, NEW INTERNATIONAL VERSION®, NIV® Copyright © 1973, 1978, 1984, 2011 by Biblica, Inc.® Used by permission. All rights reserved worldwide.

Scripture taken from The Message. Copyright © 1993, 1994, 1995, 1996, 2000, 2001, 2002. Used by permission of NavPress Publishing Group.

WestBow Press books may be ordered through booksellers or by contacting:

WestBow Press
A Division of Thomas Nelson & Zondervan
1663 Liberty Drive
Bloomington, IN 47403
www.westbowpress.com
1 (866) 928-1240

Because of the dynamic nature of the Internet, any web addresses or links contained in this book may have changed since publication and may no longer be valid. The views expressed in this work are solely those of the author and do not necessarily reflect the views of the publisher, and the publisher hereby disclaims any responsibility for them.

Any people depicted in stock imagery provided by Getty Images are models, and such images are being used for illustrative purposes only. Certain stock imagery © Getty Images.

ISBN: 978-1-9736-3490-4 (sc)
ISBN: 978-1-9736-3489-8 (hc)
ISBN: 978-1-9736-3491-1 (e)

Library of Congress Control Number: 2018908729

Print information available on the last page.

WestBow Press rev. date: 10/03/2018

Contents

Introduction vii

CHAPTER 1: BIBLE VERSIONS AND READING THE BIBLE 1
CHAPTER 2: THE NATURE OF GOD 12
CHAPTER 3: LISTENING TO MAN AND NOT GOD, FALSE PROPHETS 28
CHAPTER 4: THE LAW 64
CHAPTER 5: SALVATION AND ETERNAL LIFE 73
CHAPTER 6: FAITH AND WORKS 92
CHAPTER 7: SINNING AND OBEDIENCE 109
CHAPTER 8: FORGIVENESS OF SINS 137
CHAPTER 9: GOD'S PROMISES 151
CHAPTER 10: THE SOVEREIGNTY OF GOD 162
CHAPTER 11: ONCE SAVED, ALWAYS SAVED (OSAS) 180
CHAPTER 12: THE TEMPORAL VERSUS THE ETERNAL:
  THE PROSPERITY GOSPEL 259
CHAPTER 13: CALVINISM AND ITS IMPACT ON THE
  MODERN CHURCH 271
CHAPTER 14: THE HEART FOR OUR GOD 283
CHAPTER 15: THE FOUNDATION OF FAITH 288
CHAPTER 16: SAVING FAITH 293

Closing Thoughts 307
About the Author 309

Introduction

The Modern Church and many of its congregants are in trouble. When we say Modern Church, we are referencing, as a group, primarily evangelical churches in America but also in any other place where the body of Christ has had scriptural truths watered down or simplified to dangerous levels to accommodate the world and the desires of men.

There are many differing doctrinal beliefs preached to Christians in different churches in America today. However, conflicting doctrine is not an outcome of Holy Spirit, but of men. The Holy Spirit does not lead us into different doctrinal truths. Truth is not relative, and only one interpretation of a Bible passage can be correct, that being what the Holy Spirit intended that passage to mean: "Knowing this first, that no prophecy of the scripture is of any private interpretation. For the prophecy came not in old time by the will of man: *but holy men of God spake as they were moved by the Holy Ghost*" (**2 Peter 1:20–21**). We regularly see evidence of the Modern Church's increasing tolerance of sin and errant doctrine.

Errant doctrines taught in the Modern Church promise believers that no matter how much sin they engage in, no matter how much about self they are, no matter what they believe in, no matter how they act, they remain saved. People, based on such errant teachings, live the life they want, not the life that God has called them to. Professing Christians in today's churches often don't have the Holy Spirit inspired conviction to avoid sin. Doctrines taught from the pulpit often reinforce this. This is totally contrary to what Christ did for us and what Christ taught us. This tolerance of sin, indeed the expectation of sin, has worked its way into the Modern Church. Under the guise of grace, many are living in rebellion against what God teaches.

The teachings of the Modern Church tend to have the effect of causing people to be lukewarm towards God because it turns the truth into a somewhat unimportant component of our relationship with our Creator. In some modern movements, truth is even acknowledged as unobtainable. Portions of the Modern Church focus more on aligning Christianity with American culture rather than having the culture submit to God.

This has happened because Christianity has fallen into the same trap that Judaism and other religions have. For example, Judaism has the Talmud: books with lots of different rabbinical interpretations or extensions of scripture espousing different truths. Instead of relying on the Jewish Bible (our Old Testament) alone, many practicing Jews rely on the rabbinical writings as well. Jesus gave examples of such error when He confronted the Pharisees. The frequency with which Christians quote other men instead of scripture is appalling. In modern Christian literature we have many different authors, some that espouse different truths. Consequently, Christianity has become a religion not unlike Judaism, Islam or a number of other man-made religions.

Jesus condemned the same in His day because the teachings of men exposed a heart apart from God. It is exactly what Jesus condemned when He taught, "This people draweth nigh unto me with their mouth, and honoureth me with their lips; *but their heart is far from me. But in vain they do worship me, teaching for doctrines the commandments of men*" (**Matthew 15:8–9**). We have developed a similar orthodoxy today which is built on the rules of men and which often does not result in the right heart towards God. This orthodoxy conflicts with many scriptures and yet is taught throughout much of the Modern Church. It focuses primarily (and mistakenly) on teaching the minimum that one needs to do to be saved and that is exactly what many try to do. This demonstrates neither a heart for God, or consistency with scripture.

In this era, we are creating too many individuals who have an intellectual awareness of Christ, but who do not truly follow Him or have a true relationship with Him. Statistically, the problem is getting worse. We preach doctrines that allow people to live in sin, to live in the flesh, to disobey and are telling them such behavior cannot affect their salvation. The essence of modern day doctrine and teaching, which are only partially scriptural, builds the Laodicean Church because it encourages people to be lukewarm in spite of what Christ taught.

In America and in other places, Christianity has become too much a religion and a business. It is evolving into something that is less about a relationship with Christ than it is about a relationship with a church or other people. Spiritual integrity is on the wane. We, as God's people, often spend far too little time in the Word of God, even though it should be the single most important writing in our life.

God's Word tells us that Paul reasoned from scripture in explaining why Jesus was the Christ (or the Messiah). We are to use the scriptures to reason, not simply to quote sound bites out of context. But through these simple sound bites, many are misled. Yet by the same token, we are not to take scripture and try to find logic to invalidate that which God commands. Too often we have such a high view of other men's teaching that we do not spend the time in the Word of God needed to ascertain the truth. The relationship is supposed to be first and foremost about us and our Creator, not us and other men.

Although new people are coming to Christ all the time, the focus on maturing existing Christians has taken a back seat to filling pews and building earthly churches. As such, our churches are filled with immature and often lukewarm Christians unable to discern right from wrong or spiritual truth from false doctrine. This builds the Laodicean Church which Jesus rebuked in Revelation 3. Instead of a passion for holiness and for acting correctly, we have a passion for all sorts of earthly pleasures. Our focus is far too weighted on getting people to accept Christ and far too little on helping them to grow as Christians. Our doctrines at times lead people away from, rather than to, Jesus Christ. But that is not what the Bible teaches.

Many Christians mistakenly accept that there are different truths, yet make little attempt to get to the real truth. We hear in Bible studies often "this is what this passage means to me" or "this is what this person says it means" as if individual interpretation is okay. We accept that different church leaders teach different things and we put up with this. But at its core, this is relativism. It denies the absolute truth of God's Word. Church leaders are often fine with different interpretations of scripture.

Yet we know God does not lead men into different (a.k.a. opposing) doctrinal truths. God is not divided. The Bible was not designed to be a relative truth work. Christians willingly accept all sorts of different doctrine as though it makes no difference. It was our Lord's will that we be unified, and that we be unified *in the truth*. Paul expressed his dismay in 2 Corinthians 11 that those in the Corinthian Church were willing to put up with a different Jesus, a different spirit, or a different gospel.

In fact, the Bible calls us to come out (separate ourselves) from false teachers. Because we spend too little time with God, too little time listening to the Holy Spirit, we have a proliferation of religions and denominations all segregated under the umbrella of Christianity. Too many brothers and sisters, and even church leaders, refuse to examine scripture, instead trusting in what other men tell them. Most of the time we have discussions with those espousing errant doctrine, they refuse to go to scripture and instead quote men. We have come to a time where we are either unable or unwilling to discern false teachers from true teachers.

The problem with this is clear. Some leaders are being led by the Holy Spirit and some are not. The fractionalization of Christianity, in our humble opinion, is not the work of the Holy Spirit, but the evil one. The Holy Spirit does not lead men into different truths. He does not lead men to divide. The church (that is, the body of Christ) is increasingly falling into the same moral relativism that permeates the secular world.

The great human experiment with liberal theology is destroying the Modern Church and Christians with it. Francis Schaeffer wrote about this in The Great Evangelical Disaster, where he warned about evolving doctrine. Many members of Christ's church refuse to earnestly contend for the faith. Compromise is the order of the day. Indeed this is what scripture warns about near the end times: "For the time will come when they will not endure sound doctrine; but after their own lusts shall they heap to themselves teachers, having itching ears" (**2 Timothy 4:3**).

Many Modern Church doctrines appeal to the flesh and our sinful nature. These doctrines which appeal to the flesh allow and even encourage individuals to live the way they think right (Judges 21:25) because many claim there are no eternal impacts to one's salvation. The evidence of what these doctrines produce in some should convict us they are incorrect. But we are challenged in the ability to recognize compromised doctrine because we don't spend enough time in God's Word, and because we want to believe the lies which appeal to the flesh.

Unfortunately, many of the compromised doctrines in the Modern Church, like everything Satan tries to manipulate, are not fully lies. He is the master of mixing truth and false doctrine. As such, many doctrinal errors occur where man has taken a simple truth and extended it to much more than it was ever intended and in doing so have created scriptural conflicts. This is a misuse of scripture which those with biblical knowledge and a heart for God are able to discern.

We are warned about this when we are told: "As also in all his epistles, speaking in them of these things; in which are some things hard to be understood, which they that are unlearned and unstable wrest, as they do also the other scriptures, unto their own destruction. Ye therefore, beloved, seeing ye know these things before, *beware lest ye also, being led away with the error of the wicked, fall from your own stedfastness*" (**2 Peter 3:16–17**).

So where is modern Christianity heading? It seems that we are headed for the same place that Israel went many times. The problem in America is not with unbelievers, but with Christians. At one time, this country was more than 90% Christian. Consider the behavior of modern "believers." We arrived at our current state because we refused to stand for what is right. We have allowed our culture to take precedent over our relationship with our God. Our attention has been diverted from scripture to scrip (money). Even more disconcerting is that we are continuing further down that path.

What is the evidence?

Evidence shows that America is still a largely "Christian" country. About 73% of the adult population of the United States still self-identify as Christian (*State of the Church 2016*, Barna, September 2016). Other studies show a slightly higher number. We set this as a baseline because if 73% of those in this country (and again the number may be higher) are Christian and if the Modern Church is doing its job, we would expect to see commensurate levels of belief about what God teaches. Yet here is what we find:

- Among all Americans, only 19% of those contacted said that their relationship with God was their most important relationship (*Americans Identify Their Most Important Relationships*, Barna, March 2008). Think about this for a moment. This means greater than 50% of those self-identifying as Christian say their relationship with God is not their most important. The actions of many American Christians bear witness to the truth of this statistic.

- Only 45% of Americans attend church regularly (*State of the Church 2016*, Barna, September 2016). But other studies (Olson, *The Journal for the Scientific Study of Religion*, 2005) show the number attending church on any given week at about 17.7%.
- 55% of Americans agree somewhat or agree strongly that good works will reserve them a place in heaven (*State of the Church 2016*, Barna, September 2016).
- Only 15% of Americans actually believe in all four cornerstones of evangelical beliefs which are: 1) The Bible is the highest authority for what I believe, 2) It is very important for me personally to encourage non-Christians to trust Jesus Christ as their Savior, 3) Jesus Christ's death on the cross is the only sacrifice that could remove the penalty of my sin, and 4) Only those who trust in Jesus Christ alone as their Savior receive God's free gift of eternal salvation (*Evangelical vs. Born Again: A Survey of What Americans Say and Believe Beyond Politics*, Christianity Today, December 2017).
- 75% of American Christians don't take their faith seriously based on a study by Lifeway Research (*Survey Finds Most American Christians Are Actually Heretics*, The Federalist, October 2016). Here are some of the heretical teachings Christians believe
  - 70% believe Jesus was the first being God created.
  - 60% believe everyone goes to heaven but of that number, about 50% of them also said they believe that only those who believe in Jesus will be saved.
  - 56% believe the Holy Spirit is an impersonal force, not a being of the Trinity.
  - Almost 50% believe that "God accepts the worship of all religions including Christianity, Judaism, and Islam."
- Born again Christians struggle mightily with the truth (*Where Born-Against are Missing the Mark*, American Culture and Faith Institute, May 2017). We find that:
  - Only 52% believe Jesus lived a sinless life.
  - Only 47% believe in absolute moral truth.
  - Only 42% believe Satan is real.
  - Only 73% believe you can't earn your way to heaven.
  - Only 34% believe we have a responsibility to share the gospel.

- With respect to Bible reading, only 11% of Americans have read the entire Bible (*Americans Are Fond of the Bible, Don't Actually Read It*, Lifeway Research, April 2017).
- 80% of Christians don't read their Bible daily (*80% of Churchgoers Don't Read Bible Daily, LifeWay Survey Suggests*, Christianity Today, September 2012).
- Only 80% of self-identifying American Christians believe in the God of the Bible (*20 Percent of Christians Say They Don't Believe in the God of the Bible*, PJ Media, April 2018).
- The younger the age group and the more educated that a person is, the less they believe in the God of the Bible (*When Americans Say They Believe in God, What Do They Mean?*, Pew Research, April 2018). The more educated the individual, the less chance is they believe in the God of the Bible exactly as our educational system desires. Specific findings include:
  - 48% of Americans believe that God determines what happens to them all or most of the time; 72% of evangelical Christians believe so
  - 45% of American college graduates believe in the God of the Bible.
  - 43% of Americans under the age of 30 believe in the God of the Bible.
- Christians today donate only 2.5% of their income compared to 3.3% during the Great Depression (*What Would Happen if the Church Tithed?*, Relevant Magazine, March 2016).
- A tad over 37% of those having abortions are Protestants; another 28% are Catholic meaning 2 in 3 of those undergoing abortions believe in Jesus Christ (*Characteristics of Abortion Patients*, Guttmacher Institute, May 2010).
- Our children, who should be one of our highest priorities, are often shipped off to ungodly institutions whose efforts to eliminate God from their lives are front and center of their programs. These schools manipulate the minds of our children against God, and we gladly accept that as a part of the educational experience. It is having its effect. The greater the education level, the less our children believe in the God of the Bible.

- Obedience and holiness, a theme throughout the Old and New Testament, has been relegated to an afterthought (or worse), replaced by mistaken doctrine that obedience is works, or that as long as we love others, we can disobey God. We have accepted adultery, greed, abortion, pre-marital sex, and homosexual behaviors. We in America are too committed to engaging our flesh.
- We discount our God-given ability to choose as shown in the Bible, and hence we often discount our ability to, with the Holy Spirit's help, resist sin even though scripture teaches otherwise. Christians tell other Christians "I sin all the time," not truly understanding or appreciating what Christ went through for them or what scripture really teaches.
- Moral relativism is growing; that which is right for me may not be right for you or that a given Bible verse means this to me, not that. This view ignores the absolute nature of God's truth. This is also starting to happen more and more within the church. The fact that we have differing doctrines across Christianity emphasizes this relativism. We welcome differing viewpoints in bible studies as if the Holy Spirit leads men and women into different truths, re-enforcing the idea there is no absolute truth.
- We see voters rationalizing support for candidates who squarely set themselves up against God, not realizing that they are also endorsing their ungodly policies when they vote for them.
- We sit in church and listen to church leaders preach "easy Christianity" or "cheap grace," the notion that if we "believe" we can do whatever we want.
- We see those in the Modern Church preach various degrees of the prosperity gospel, not recognizing there are those giving their very lives and the lives of their families for Christ. Scripture teaches that those rich in faith (the most important thing) are often poor and persecuted. In some places, our riches are viewed as the level of acceptance of us by God because of the blessings He has provided. The message of prosperity through the gospel whether directly or indirectly taught, has distracted many from Christianity's central truths. How sad.

- Knowledge of the scripture is lacking, and so the ability to challenge errant doctrine is disappearing. The desire to spend time with the Lord is diminishing. Milk is the staple of the day; the desire for the meat of the Word has long since passed for many followers.
- Repentance, baptism, and truly following Christ by denying self are often relegated to non-essentials of the faith (or are eliminated from the teaching of the truth), when in fact they are a central part of the salvation process biblically.

Many of the statistics above clearly show that Christians are committed to living a life apart from God; that is, not living with true faith. They don't have a Christian world view. Others reflect woeful disconnects from scriptural teachings. These statistics within the Christian Community clearly demonstrate the effect that errant doctrines of the Modern Church are having on those that claim Jesus Christ as Lord. These are exactly the types of statistics we would expect to find when we have corrupted doctrine in many churches.

In short, we are the proverbial frog in the pot of water that is slowly being heated to boiling, and now true Christianity is slowly dying out in America. Successive generations are less, not more, likely to follow Jesus Christ. We see clearly the evidence of a lukewarm church where actions are said to mean nothing to one's salvation, producing in many cases, the fruits of unrighteousness. As you consider the issues discussed in this book, remember the evidence presented above of what is actually happening in Christianity; this is not evidence of a healthy church, at least from a scriptural perspective. We see very clearly that a time is coming when the idea of actually acting consistent with our faith is abhorrent to "believers." This is a part of the errant message coming from the pulpit today and its adoption is only gaining steam.

The millennial generation knows and understands this hypocrisy; they see many Christians as hypocrites because they do not live what they claim to believe. In some places Christianity is seen as a means to worldly gain. We see more and more people leaving God and church. God's Word is used as a source to discredit American Christians. American Christianity, in many places, has morphed into something that is so inconsistent with the first century church it is largely unrecognizable.

Many church leaders in today's pulpits reassure believers with false doctrines, resulting in the building of the Laodicean church. The Laodicean Church is condemned in scripture:

> "And unto the angel of the church of the Laodiceans write; These things saith the Amen, the faithful and true witness, the beginning of the creation of God; I know thy works, that thou art neither cold nor hot: I would thou wert cold or hot. *So then because thou art lukewarm, and neither cold nor hot, I will spue thee out of my mouth.* Because thou sayest, I am rich, and increased with goods, and have need of nothing; and knowest not that thou art wretched, and miserable, and poor, and blind, and naked: I counsel thee to buy of me gold tried in the fire, that thou mayest be rich; and white raiment, that thou mayest be clothed, and that the shame of thy nakedness do not appear; and anoint thine eyes with eyesalve, that thou mayest see. As many as I love, I rebuke and chasten: be zealous therefore, and repent. Behold, I stand at the door, and knock: if any man hear my voice, and open the door, I will come in to him, and will sup with him, and he with me. To him that overcometh will I grant to sit with me in my throne, even as I also overcame, and am set down with my Father in his throne. He that hath an ear, let him hear what the Spirit saith unto the churches" (**Revelation 3:14–22**).

Doctrines in the Modern Church make it very comfortable for God to be a part of a one's life, just not the paramount part. They make it very easy to be lukewarm or even rebellious towards God. In fact the very doctrines the Modern Church embraces and teaches create too many lukewarm followers of Jesus Christ. So we have a problem here in America, but the problem also exists within the Modern Church throughout much of the world.

Before moving on, a word on the simplicity of faith may be helpful. Faith should not be complicated. We complicate and compromise our faith by our desire to place our desires ahead of God's and then try to use God's Word in a way that supports or justifies those desires. Nor is faith some purely intellectual exercise. True faith is a mixture of unified beliefs and actions. This is what true faith is. The teaching of Hebrews 11 is clear; we use our faith in God to produce actions as those commended by God did.

There are those, especially in other countries, who readily accept the gospel. Because they have a heart for God and are earnestly seeking the truth, it becomes unnecessary to explore the issues within this book since they come naturally to the truth by faith. They do not suffer from the culture of abundance that we have here and as such their devotion to, and dependence upon God, is often more natural.

They understand the importance of the message that this life is not the focus of the gospel. Jesus Christ came to rescue us in the next life. Indeed, their hope is in the next life because this life is hard for them. We, on the other hand, are busy trying to reconcile God's teachings with our society because we are too focused on our desires and pleasures in this life. Our wealth is a terrible distraction and we must constantly be on guard against the charges levied by God against the Laodicean church.

Within this book, many of the simple sound bites that can mislead people are examined. To this end, this book has been arranged into different subject matter sections. Within the heading of each section is a list of sound bites, which when used out of context, can mislead people. The goal of each section is to examine those sound bites against the broader range of scripture to either clarify or refute those isolated sound bites using a broader range of scripture. At the end of each section is a "Key Thoughts" section designed to summarize the points of the section.

This book is a call for us all to return to Biblical Christianity through frequent reading of the Word of God *as it is* and not as we want it to be. We invite you, as you read through this book and the scripture therein, to compare teachings in the churches you attend with what the Bible actually says to see if the teachings heard in churches truly align with all of God's teachings. Hopefully it will motivate all of us to return to the source of real truth – God and His Word as aided by the Holy Spirit.

We have all been told things by friends, church leaders, and preachers and commentators on radio, television, and the Internet, and yet none of these are the canonical source of truth. As we consider the doctrinal positions we hold, we should ask ourselves: are the positions we hold for our will or God's will, for our pleasure or for His pleasure? Do they engage our spiritual nature or our sinful nature? Everything in this book is designed to draw us all closer to Jesus Christ.

As you consider the words of this book there is a question you should contemplate. If the doctrinal teachings of the Modern Church were fully correct, would the statistics presented above, given by Christians themselves, be the same? There is little doubt there will be many that will try to attack this book on a doctrinal level, yet it is the Modern Church's doctrine which is building the Laodicean Church; a church condemned by Jesus Christ and about to be spit out of His mouth. When we see the truth consistently preached from the pulpit, we will begin to realize a change in the impact we have and we will see significantly less claims of "hypocrite" from those outside the church.

Before reading this book, we urge you to spend time in prayer with the Lord. We also counsel you, the reader, to the degree possible, to leave any preconceptions behind. This can be one of the single largest problems in understanding scriptural truths. Ask God for understanding of truth as you read His Word. Too much of what we believe today is what we *want* to believe, not necessarily what God teaches.

Finally, the subject matter of this book is challenging for two reasons. First, as mentioned above, this book examines scriptures which may challenge your understanding of what the Bible says about salvation. Second, the depth and scope of the subject matter is extensive. For these reasons, we strongly recommend you read and contemplate no more than one chapter at a time.

May God bless you with purity of His truth as you seek it through His Word and the Holy Spirit.

Chapter 1

Bible Versions and Reading the Bible

Misleading Christian sound bite: All Bibles teach the same thing. A scriptural verse in isolation may be understood without additional context.

All Bibles are not the same. Different Bibles often have many small differences, and in some cases these differences can lead to a significant change in meaning. This has the potential to mislead God's people, especially when our doctrine is based on sound bites. Many readers of God's Word may not recognize how the Bibles were created, who created them, and the differences in techniques used to translate them.

It is true that some are being saved with many different versions of the Bible, and as such we are not going to speak specifically for or against any one version of scripture. A true faith would seem to result from reading many of them. Often, those who accept Christ do so with a profound sense of gratitude for what God has done for them. After understanding their need for salvation, they accept Christ through the faith that God has provided them. Thank God for that. However, that does not mean that all Bible versions teach the exact same thing.

Nevertheless, there are versions of the Bible that tend to be either more or less accurate representations of the underlying language.

Bible Versions

The problem is that as we study God's Word, we can easily be misled about the truth of God's Word. Consider for a moment some of the changes in the various versions of the Bible. Some new versions remove various verses or parts of verses, and some versions add words. Some change the meaning.

	KJV **(Textus Receptus)**	**New Versions**
Matthew 18:11	"For the Son of man is come to save that which was lost."	NIV, NAS, NWT: verse removed
John 14:16	"And I will pray the Father, and he shall give you another Comforter, that he may abide with you for ever."	NIV: "And I will ask the Father, and he will give you another advocate to help you and be with you forever."
Acts 8:37	"And Philip said, If thou believest with all thine heart, thou mayest. And he answered and said, I believe that Jesus Christ is the Son of God."	NIV, NAS, NWT, RSV: verse removed
Romans 8:1	"There is therefore now no condemnation to them which are in Christ Jesus, who walk not after the flesh, but after the Spirit."	NIV: "Therefore, there is now no condemnation for those who are in Christ Jesus."

2 Corinthians 2:17	"For we are not as many, which corrupt the word of God: but as of sincerity, but as of God, in the sight of God speak we in Christ."	NIV: "Unlike so many, we do not peddle the word of God for profit. On the contrary, in Christ we speak before God with sincerity, like men sent from God."

Consider John 14:16 for just a minute and compare the two versions. One version says the Holy Spirit "may abide with you forever" and the other says that the Holy Spirit will "be with you forever." That is quite a difference. One version promises potential but the other promises assurance.

However if we go back to the Textus Receptus and Codex Sinaiticus we find the same thing in both. The idea of abiding or being with you is rendered in the subjunctive mood. What is the subjunctive mood? The subjunctive mood indicates possibility, not certainty. The action referenced (in this case abiding with) may or may not occur, depending upon circumstances. Hence the KJV renders the verse more accurately. We can see how even small changes in interpretation may have critical impact on doctrine. Clearly there are more and less accurate versions of scripture. This is probably why the early church did not believe all of the things that we now believe today.

The comparisons above do not even include versions that stretch the meaning of scripture even further. Consider The Message Bible, which has some radical changes. Just look at the verse in Matthew 5:5, which communicates a completely different idea than most bibles. The Message version might easily be interpreted to say that we are blessed (a reference to the saved) when we are living in sin.

	KJV (Textus Receptus)	The Message
Matthew 5:5	"Blessed are the meek, for they shall inherit the earth."	"You are truly blessed when you are content with just who you are – no more, no less."

Romans 8:1	"There is therefore now no condemnation to them which are in Christ Jesus, who walk not after the flesh, but after the Spirit."	"With the arrival of Jesus, the Messiah, that fateful dilemma is resolved. Those who enter into Christ's being-here-for-us no longer have to live under a continuous, low-lying black cloud. A new power is in operation. The Spirit of life in Christ, like a strong wind, has magnificently cleared the air, freeing you from a fated lifetime of brutal tyranny at the hands of sin and death." (Actually Romans 8:1–2)
Romans 8:35	"Who shall separate us from the love of Christ? Shall tribulation, or distress, or persecution, or famine, or nakedness, or peril, or sword?"	"Do you think anyone is going to be able to drive a wedge between us and Christ's love for us? There is no way! Not trouble, not hard times, not hatred, not hunger, not homelessness, not bullying threats, not backstabbing, not even the worst sins listed in scripture."

1 Corinthians 6:9–11	"Know ye not that the unrighteous shall not inherit the kingdom of God? Be not deceived: neither fornicators, nor idolaters, nor adulterers, nor effeminate, nor abusers of themselves with mankind, Nor thieves, nor covetous, nor drunkards, nor revilers, nor extortioners, shall inherit the kingdom of God. And such were some of you: but ye are washed, but ye are sanctified, but ye are justified in the name of the Lord Jesus, and by the Spirit of our God."	"Don't you realize that this is not the way to live? Unjust people who don't care about God will not be joining in his kingdom. Those who use and abuse each other, use and abuse sex, use and abuse the earth and everything in it, don't qualify as citizens in God's kingdom. A number of you know from experience what I'm talking about, for not so long ago you were on that list. Since then, you've been cleaned up and given a fresh start by Jesus, our Master, our Messiah, and by our God present in us, the Spirit."

There are also perverted versions of the Bible. For example, the Queen James Bible (certainly not God's Word) has been changed to eliminate references to homosexual behaviors.

However, it is not the purpose of this book to contrast all of the differences between different versions of the Bible or their historical lineages. We have the opportunity to find information about this online. Generally, the closer we get to source manuscripts (the original Greek and Hebrew manuscripts), the better.

Often when we facilitate studies, we use a three-step process. The first step is to use a given version, such as the NASB; the second step is to see how that contrasts with an authorized version of the King James Bible, and the third step is to review the context of the underlying language (Hebrew, Greek, or Aramaic), especially for key concepts (that is, those that are doctrinal in nature), words, verb tenses, and moods. There are tools online that allow us to conduct such an examination.

In today's churches, sometimes individuals create messages based on different Bibles. We cannot speak to what may motivate individuals to quote from multiple Bibles in a single lesson, but there is no need for it. There may be a desire to create the message they want to deliver (which may be somewhat different from what God was actually communicating), and different versions may help them do that, or there may be honest naiveté about what the individual versions say and their differences. We are not here to assess motives behind such an approach or to say this is necessarily wrong, but every Christian should always examine what is said from the pulpit, and this takes more than just a cursory reading of a single passage. Each message must be tested.

Remember that those Bibles created through dynamic or paraphrasing translation techniques may be less accurate than versions that are closer to a word-for-word translation, since they rely on assumptions around *intended* meaning generated from the perspective of the paraphrasing persons. They are translated by people, and in some cases they are the same people who embrace and espouse differing doctrines. We cannot see the hearts of individuals, and so it can be challenging to automatically trust that all versions of the Bible were faithfully translated.

When the evil one wants to lead us away from God, rarely does he do it directly. He is smarter than that. He knows we can recognize obvious forgeries. Instead, he changes a few small things over time. He mixes truth with falsehood, making it much harder to discern the changes, especially for Christians who do not regularly spend time in the Word.

Consider the words of the serpent in Genesis: "And the serpent said unto the woman, Ye shall not surely die: For God doth know that in the day ye eat thereof, then your eyes shall be opened, and ye shall be as gods, knowing good and evil" (**Genesis 3:4–5**). We see that Satan mixes truth ("know good and evil") with a lie ("shall not surely die"). However, over time, we end up at the same place which is a spoken gospel that is different from the one that God preserved. We know that Paul warned about that.

Problems in Trying to Understand the Bible through Sound bites

Many Christians have fallen into a dangerous trap. They read parts of the Bible and then quote specific snippets of scripture without examining the supportive context. Often, they do not take the time to try to resolve apparently conflicting passages but instead camp out on selective sound bites regardless of what the larger context of scripture says. Scripture is often quoted without the context needed to provide insight into how to interpret a given passage.

If we opened a book and read every tenth sentence, we could quote what the seventieth sentence said, but we would have missed the larger context into which that seventieth sentence belonged. This is where Christians get into trouble. We all know that scripture interprets scripture. Some passages require consideration of a larger context of scripture to determine the actual meaning—and this is especially the case when there appear to be conflicts. There are both vertical (above and below a passage) context and horizontal (across books) context. Both are important to accurate interpretation.

Suppose we open a book and read just one sentence: "So Bill killed Jim." As it turns out, we may make a judgment based on that sentence, thinking Bill was a murderer or Bill was evil. But suppose the prior sentence was "Bill had been doing everything he could to protect his family from Jim and his array of weapons" or "Jim was shooting at Bill's house." Does this change the context of the first sentence we read? Do we have a different judgment about Bill? What if the sentence were in another place in the book? What if there were a history of all that Bill had done to avoid Jim and his murderous heart? Comprehensive context is critical to understanding scripture as it is for any work.

God's Word is meant to be read in its entirety, not just in single sentences upon which we build doctrine. Hence, just quoting scriptural sound bites can be dangerous. Sound bites, while not necessarily false, often do not encapsulate the larger truth of scripture. It is the reason we have so many divisions over errant doctrine. Sound bites are too simplistic to grant true understanding in many cases.

But we must be different. This is part of what seeking God is all about; part of what being called out is all about. We need to spend time in His word to understand the full truth of a given matter using the breadth of scripture. When we read the Bible over and over, it helps us to understand His Word in a way that simply cannot be done with "sound bites" or only the reading of selective passages.

There are many different examples in the Bible which can cause problems if quoted in isolation. Examples include:

- "If any man come to me, and hate not his father, and mother, and wife, and children, and brethren, and sisters, yea, and his own life also, he cannot be my disciple" (**Luke 14:26**).
    - Commentary: Are we really to hate our father and mother? The underlying word for hate (Greek *miseo*) means exactly that: to hate or detest. No, we are taught, "Honour thy father and thy mother: that thy days may be long upon the land which the Lord thy God giveth thee" (**Exodus 20:12**).
- "All things are lawful for me, but all things are not expedient: all things are lawful for me, but all things edify not" (**1 Corinthians 10:23**).
    - Commentary: Are all things really lawful for Paul? Is it lawful for Paul to murder or steal? Clearly not, for even if the old written law has been fulfilled, these are in direct violation of the law of the spirit and the commandments which we are told to keep in the New Testament.
- "Let your women keep silence in the churches: for it is not permitted unto them to speak; but they are commanded to be under obedience, as also saith the law" (**1 Corinthians 14:34**).
    - Commentary: Are women supposed to be completely silent and not speak at all?

Each of these passages does not teach what the single sound bite (just the passage read in isolation) seems to teach. Yet this approach is often used in quoting other "truths." In order to properly interpret these passages, other scripture is required. In some cases the context is right beside the sound bite, and in others the context is in other places throughout scripture. But taking the time to read scripture over and over, relying on the Holy Spirit's help will put us in a position to understand the truth of God's Word more effectively.

Many see "apparent" conflicts within the New Testament. But it is not that God's Word that contradicts itself. Instead it indicates that Bible passages quoted in isolation, may not offer the truth of a given matter. We say "apparent" because we are convicted that all scripture, properly understood, is true. When we struggle with the truth of scripture it is often because we do not have sufficient context to understand the sound bite or because we neglect to investigate the perceived discrepancies.

There are also words which, at face value, can lead us into trouble because of the way in which they are translated. Below are several verses that could cause a problem depending on the version of the Bible we use.

- (KJV) "Thou art of purer eyes than to behold evil, and canst not look on iniquity: wherefore lookest thou upon them that deal treacherously, and holdest thy tongue when the wicked devoureth the man that is more righteous than he" (**Habakkuk 1:13**).
- (KJV) "I form the light, and create darkness: I make peace, and create evil: I the Lord do all these things" (**Isaiah 45:7**).

Both of these passages could be considered to problematic. For example, the passage in Habakkuk 1 says that God cannot look on evil, yet we know that He sees the evil of men every day. He directly testifies to it throughout the Old Testament (Jonah 1). We have to consider the breath of scripture to understand the point being made.

Now consider Isaiah 45:7. If we look more carefully at the underlying word for evil (Hebrew *rah*), we see that it means calamity and disaster which are punishments, but not the creation of evil itself. Some newer versions render Isaiah 45:7 (ex. NIV, Holman) more accurately but this can also be discerned by going back to the original language. These are examples of reading something which should cause us to do a deeper investigation for we know that the Lord is not the author of evil, yet does see evil (Proverbs 15:3, Hebrews 4:13, and Job 28:24).

It is of note that many atheists whom I [Gregg] debate will quote this passage to show me that God is the Creator of evil and if He really does exist (which they don't believe) that He does not merit worship. Even those who name Jesus Christ as Lord sometimes claim the same thing; that is God creates evil. Not so.

Many Modern Church leaders concentrate their sermons and lessons on the New Testament, especially Paul's epistles. Because we spend so much time in the New Testament, we often interpret scriptures in the New Testament without really understanding who God is. Consequently, the Modern Church does not do a good job of presenting who God truly is.

Some of these understandings of who God is based solely on the New Testament are made the basis of doctrine but are inconsistent with the nature of God as revealed in the Old Testament. God revealed much of Himself, His nature, and His expectations in the Old Testament. Since we know that the nature of God does not change, we need to read the Old Testament to fully understand the nature of our God. It is an aid to understanding New Testament teachings.

We can look at the other examples and understand how the larger picture of scripture must be used to understand what a particular verse in scripture refers to and/or how the language is being used. When we come upon a verse that gives us pause, either because it seems to conflict with other scripture or seems inconsistent with the nature of God, we must stop to do the investigation. We must care enough to do that investigation ourselves. If the investigation does not address the issue, pray intently about it. In this manner, we will be able to get to the truth of the matter.

Try not to run to commentary of other men, at least not until you have evaluated the passage in the light of other scriptural passages on the point, and perhaps looked at the words, tenses, and moods used in the original language. This does not mean that men will always mislead us, but they may, often unintentionally. There are conflictive commentaries. We cannot discern the hearts of those writing various commentaries, regardless of the period during which they lived. Some of those who participated in interpreting scripture had their own doctrinal biases.

Even those who apparently had (that is externally viewed) great hearts were from time to time mistaken. There are no "perfects" among men. For this reason, we are to build our foundation on Christ and His Word, not other men. God taught, through the Apostle John: "These things have I written unto you concerning them that seduce you. *But the anointing which ye have received of him abideth in you, and ye need not that any man teach you: but as the same anointing teacheth you of all things, and is truth, and is no lie*, and even as it hath taught you, ye shall abide in him" (**1 John 2:26–27**). Some of the most influential "Christian" men in history have lead people away from Christ.

Key Thoughts

It is important for all who truly desire to seek what the Lord is telling us to try to stick with versions of the Bible which have not been radically changed (paraphrased or "amplified") by men. We should also try to consistently do research when we are in question about specific passages which may seem to contradict the rest of scripture or the nature of God. Yet the only way we can get to a place of understanding "apparent" conflicts is to read scripture often.

When there is doubt, we should seek to confirm what is said in a given version by looking at earlier versions of God's Word and the underlying language; that is Hebrew, Greek, or Aramaic. Consider the words, tenses and moods of the verbs being used. There are a number of Internet resources which can be used to assist in this search for the truth.

We must be careful about building doctrine or quoting scripture purely on scriptural sound bites. The only way to be able to effectively understand what a passage says is to read the breadth of scripture over and over. This will aid us in understanding how the various parts of scripture relate to each other, to understand the nature of our God, and to understand His priorities.

When we read passages that give us pause or result in an apparent conflict, let's take the time to try to understand what God is teaching us through investigation *and prayer*. God clearly teaches us that the Holy Spirit will lead us into truth when we are *earnestly seeking* it. God desires for us to know the truth, but it is He to whom we must go.

Chapter 2

The Nature of God

Misleading Christian sound bite(s): Our God is love only. God will forgive every Christian no matter what they do. No one should fear God. God is our friend.

We have all heard the lessons on the nature of God whether delivered as comprehensive lessons or sound bites on individual attributes. Yet, how much time do people really spend discussing the true nature of God? Doesn't it seem like all the time is spent on discussing God's more beneficial attributes without presentation of His fearsome attributes? In today's church, we often see the nature of God presented incompletely.

Modern sermons are woefully disconnected from the sermons of yesteryear. Indeed, the Bible itself tells us "The fear of the Lord is the beginning of knowledge: but fools despise wisdom and instruction" (**Proverbs 1:7**). Yet in the Modern Church we often spend too much time declawing God. In the Modern Church He is often portrayed as closer to a teddy bear than a consuming fire. We know there is a purpose to the fear of the Lord because the Bible tells us so: "The fear of the Lord tendeth to life: and he that hath it shall abide satisfied; he shall not be visited with evil (**Proverbs 19:23**).

An Unbalanced View of God

Misunderstanding the nature of God is one of the causes of errant doctrine in the Modern Church. Many churches spend their time describing an all loving, all forgiving God, who just wants nothing more than to be our friend. We focus far too much on our position as adopted sons and daughters, refusing to examine the larger picture of scripture. In secular circles we often hear that "God became a Christian in the New Testament." Heresy.

The nature of our God is revealed more in the Old Testament than the New Testament largely because of His longer interaction with man. Before Jesus' ministry here on earth, God dealt with man directly and through prophets for the preceding thousands of years (with notable absences). But Christians spend so much time in the New Testament and specifically the epistles (or letters) of Paul, they forget part of the purpose of the Old Testament and even the teachings of Jesus Christ in the New Testament. Through the Old Testament we get an important perspective of who God is. Consider the following.

God killed everyone in the world except eight (8) people when he saved Noah and his family (Genesis Chapters 6–9). He killed Uzzah for steadying the ark when the oxen stumbled (2 Samuel 6:6–7). He killed David and Bathsheba's son, a product of their illicit union (2 Samuel 12:14). He rejected Saul as king over Israel for not killing the cattle of the Amalekites as commanded (1 Samuel 15:10–26). He destroyed those wandering in the desert after freeing them from Egypt because of their lack of faith and disobedience (Numbers 14:20–23). He killed a man of God for listening to another man who claimed to be a prophet instead of obeying God (1 Kings 11:13–19). He refused to let Moses enter the Promised Land because he disobeyed and struck the rock instead of talking to it (Numbers 27:12–14). He killed the sons of Aaron for offering unauthorized fire (Leviticus 10:1–2). He killed 250 and 14,700 Israelites for grumbling and rebellion (Numbers 16). God killed Ananias and Sapphira for lying to the Holy Spirit (Acts 5:1–11). God said he would kill the children of Jezebel to punish her (Revelation 2:23).

Most of these killed or punished were punished for failing to obey God. Consider Uzzah. The death of Uzzah appears to have resulted from a relatively minor transgression (Uzzah's steadying of the Ark). We might conjecture why God struck Uzzah dead for what appeared to be a good deed, but scripture tells us that Uzzah should have not touched the Ark under any circumstance; this is what was commanded. Clearly Uzzah did not need to steady the Ark; God could have done this. Uzzah did not have the faith to obey.

Even David, a man after God's own heart, who also sinned, was afraid of the Lord that very day. "And David was afraid of the Lord that day, and said, How shall the ark of the Lord come to me?" (**2 Samuel 6:9**). David probably assumed that the Lord would forgive Uzzah, but was reminded of how our Lord hates disobedience.

The Bible is equally filled with demonstrations of God's love, God's mercy, and God's grace. Indeed, where would we be without these? We would also be destroyed. He did not punish Abraham for lying, He took away David's sin for killing Uriah the Hittite, He rescued Israel time and time again after punishing them for their unfaithfulness, He sent His Son to die for our sins, and He gives us the Holy Spirit. Clearly God does have the attributes that are spoken of almost exclusively in our churches today so the error is not there.

But where is the balance? The problem with the Modern Church is it focuses just on the beneficial attributes of God but refuses to acknowledge the more fearsome side of God. We have lost our fear of God. This has caused us in many cases to ignore His will. Biblically, fear of the Lord saves from death. The God of the Old Testament, which is the same God we worship today, does have a fearful side to Him. He is more than a God of love, mercy, and forgiveness. We read, "The fear of the Lord is a fountain of life, To depart from the snares of death" (**Proverbs 14:27**). Through our lack of fear however, we often trivialize sin.

Our God does not change; the God of the New Testament is the same God as the God of the Old Testament. Indeed, we are blessed with a consistent and trustworthy God, for otherwise there would be nothing in which we can trust. "Every good gift and every perfect gift is from above, and cometh down from the Father of lights, with whom is no variableness, neither shadow of turning" (**James 1:17**). "Jesus Christ the same yesterday, and today, and forever" (**Hebrews 13:8**).

"For I am the Lord, I change not; therefore ye sons of Jacob are not consumed" (**Malachi 3:6**). God himself tells us that He does not change. That does not mean that he does not change His mind or what He will do. "God is not a man, that he should lie; neither the son of man, that he should repent: hath he said, and shall he not do it? or hath he spoken, and shall he not make it good?" (**Numbers 23:19**).

This scripture in Numbers suggests God does not change His mind but this is not what it actually says. We see in scripture that God has appeared to change His mind on several occasions (*e.g.,* the Israelites, the Ninevites, Hezekiah's Death). God specifically sent Isaiah to tell Hezekiah to put his affairs in order for Hezekiah was going to die (Isaiah 38:1). But after Hezekiah sought the Lord's mercy through tearful prayers, Hezekiah was given another 15 years of life.

So we must look for a deeper meaning. The word "repent" (Hebrew *nacham*) means to be sorry or regretful, not to "turn around or change one's mind" as "repent" (Greek *metanoeō*) means in the New Testament. There are also plenty of times that God has done exactly as He said He would, and has not changed His mind. But it is the essence of our God that does not change. He hates sin. He expects respect and worship. He loves us greatly, but that love does not extend to unlimited tolerance for sin or rebellion. God treats everyone in a just manner. He is equitable, moral, and holy. However, with God there is balance.

As many have testified, our God is loving and merciful. There are many examples throughout the Old and New Testament of our God's love and mercy, including the sacrifice of His Son Jesus Christ, on the cross. But there are also many examples of God's wrath being poured out on those who disobey. The sacrifice of Jesus Christ does not protect us from God's wrath if we are committed to disobedience. Far too many people who claim to be Christians are in exactly this place. They claim to believe, but are committed to disobedience. Yet the Modern Church, through the doctrine it presents, seems to say this is unimportant.

God's Patience is not Unlimited

We seem to think (and some teach) God has an unlimited tolerance for sin and rebellion. In some churches, it is taught that no amount of sin or rebellion has an eternal impact on the "believer" with the potential exception of the degree of rewards, and can never result in loss of salvation. The Modern Church, for the most part, has completely misunderstood and erroneously taught how God reacts to willful and regular disobedience.

Yes, our God is patient; but that patience is not unlimited. Our

God does not reward *or welcome into His kingdom* those committed to disobeying or rebelling against Him. Not only is this against His nature as revealed in scripture, it is stated directly: "For thou art not a God that hath pleasure in wickedness: *neither shall evil dwell with thee.* The foolish *shall not stand in thy sight*: thou hatest all workers of iniquity" (**Psalm 5:4–5**).

God reinforces this to the Galatian church when he says, "Be not deceived; God is not mocked: for whatsoever a man soweth, that shall he also reap. *For he that soweth to his flesh shall of the flesh reap corruption; but he that soweth to the Spirit shall of the Spirit reap life everlasting*" (**Galatians 6:7–8**). We know that because of the contrast between "life everlasting" and "corruption," this is directly addressing salvation. Corruption (Greek *phthora*) means "destruction, perishing" and is spiritual death.

God even tells us that His patience is limited: "Thou hast forsaken me, saith the Lord, thou art gone backward: therefore will I stretch out my hand against thee, and destroy thee; *I am weary with repenting*" (**Jeremiah 15:6**). Even the nearly infinite mercy of God had been tested to the point where He would no longer accept any more repenting and was going to destroy the sinners. God weighs the heart. He knows if our repentance is sincere, or whether we are simply going through the motions.

A similar teaching exists in the parable of the unfruitful tree: "He spake also this parable; A certain man had a fig tree planted in his vineyard; and he came and sought fruit thereon, and found none. Then said he unto the dresser of his vineyard, Behold, these three years I come seeking fruit on this fig tree, and find none: cut it down; why cumbereth it the ground? And he answering said unto him, Lord, let it alone this year also, till I shall dig about it, and dung it: *And if it bear fruit, well: and if not, then after that thou shalt cut it down*" (**Luke 13:6–9**). God is the "certain man" who owned the vineyard, and even though God relented in cutting down the fruitless tree for another year (an act of mercy), God's patience with the tree not bearing fruit was waning thin and would not go on forever.

What did God say to Ezekiel about those who sin against Him by being unfaithful (ex. disobeying)?

> "Son of man, if a country sins against me by being unfaithful and I stretch out my hand against it to cut off its food supply and send famine upon it and kill its people

and their animals, even if these three men—Noah, Daniel and Job—were in it, they could save only themselves by their righteousness, declares the Sovereign Lord. *"Or if I send wild beasts through that country and they leave it childless and it becomes desolate so that no one can pass through it because of the beasts, as surely as I live, declares the Sovereign Lord, even if these three men were in it, they could not save their own sons or daughters. They alone would be saved, but the land would be desolate"* (**Ezekiel 14:13–16**).

Noah, Daniel and Job could not even save their own sons or daughters. Wow.

God does not reward sinners. God does discipline us to be more righteous; that is a scriptural teaching. However, we exercise our free will in how we respond to God's discipline. When we say free will, we mean the practical free will God allows us in choosing as He has specifically presented to us in scripture. God's discipline does not always result in our returning to Him. This is what much of scripture teaches. Consider the following two examples.

In the first example, we are told to watch for the Lord's return. The warning accompanying it is that those who are not ready for His return will be lost. Jesus talked about a servant whose actions went from being consistent with his faith to being inconsistent with it:

> "Watch therefore: for ye know not what hour your Lord doth come. But know this, that if the goodman of the house had known in what watch the thief would come, he would have watched, and would not have suffered his house to be broken up. Therefore be ye also ready: for in such an hour as ye think not the Son of man cometh. Who then is a faithful and wise servant, whom his lord hath made ruler over his household, to give them meat in due season? Blessed is that servant, whom his lord when he cometh shall find so doing. Verily I say unto you, That he shall make him ruler over all his goods. But and if *that evil servant* shall say in his heart, My lord delayeth his coming;

And shall begin to smite his fellowservants, and to eat and drink with the drunken; The lord of that servant shall come in a day when he looketh not for him, and in an hour that he is not aware of, *And shall cut him asunder, and appoint him his portion with the hypocrites: there shall be weeping and gnashing of teeth"* (**Matthew 24:42–51**).

If the Lord's discipline was sufficient and certain to ensure that the servant returned to Him, there would be no need to worry about the servant not being ready. There would be no need for Jesus to warn His listeners to "watch." This is the central message of the parable. Again, we see the warning to us to use our free will to act faithfully until our Lord's return. We see the evidence of this same servant, who was initially faithful, slowly becoming unfaithful because of his emerging thinking that his master was staying away. Once the servant decides that his master is staying away he then begins to act in an evil manner after having previously acted faithfully. Upon the master's return, the Lord does not discipline him and bring him back. In fact, the opposite occurs. The servant is condemned to hell. We must be watchful because we do not know when our Lord will return or when we will die. But be aware there are clear warnings to believers who are not acting faithfully at the Lord's return, whether He comes to us or we die and appear before Him.

God does try to disciple us, but we retain our free will. Consider the Israelites of the Northern kingdom. God specifically sends Amos (Amos 4, v6–11), to confront the Israelites of their wickedness and reminding them of God's repeated attempts, through increasing levels of discipline, to get them to return to Him. Yet in each case, the result was the same: "ye have not returned to me." Now God is threatening to destroy them for their unwillingness to "return to Him." In His mercy, He is giving them one more chance, yet they reject this final opportunity and are killed and a remnant captured by the Assyrians. This type of attempt to get His people's attention through prophets happened multiple times in the Old Testament. It is one of the greatest witnesses that God is not manipulating men to bring them to Himself, but rather leading them.

We find a second example in Paul's first epistle to the Corinthians, where he confronts them about a Christian living in sin, commanding them to expel the immoral brother (something that few in the Modern Church take seriously):

> "It is reported commonly that there is fornication among you, and such fornication as is not so much as named among the Gentiles, that one should have his father's wife. And ye are puffed up, and have not rather mourned, that he that hath done this deed might be taken away from among you. For I verily, as absent in body, but present in spirit, have judged already, as though I were present, concerning him that hath so done this deed, In the name of our Lord Jesus Christ, when ye are gathered together, and my spirit, with the power of our Lord Jesus Christ, To deliver such an one unto Satan for the destruction of the flesh, that the spirit *may* be saved in the day of the Lord Jesus" (**1 Corinthian 5:1–5**).

Look carefully at the wording. While Paul does command to turn the sinning brother over to Satan to in effect be disciplined, Paul does not end the rationale with the phrase "that the spirit *will* be saved in the day of the Lord Jesus" but rather "that the spirit *may* be saved in the day of the Lord Jesus." This is written in the subjunctive mood again indicating there is the possibility that the spirit of the man may be saved and he will not experience spiritual death. Paul recognizes that the discipline may be sufficient to bring the brother back to his senses and repentance, but it also may not be sufficient. This is consistent with the Old Testament since we see many times that the discipline of the Lord was not sufficient to bring those back to Him.

But one of the most challenging teachings heard, which disregards the nature of God, is if a person *sins enough,* God will discipline them, up to and including, killing them. Yet those same people believe that those disciplined by God by punishment of death will go to heaven. While there are scriptures that teach the Lord's discipline, it is often misunderstood in light of other scripture. It is also inconsistent with the nature of a just God.

Think about this for a minute. In effect, some in the Modern Church teach God will reward sin. That is, the more we sin, the sooner we go to be with the Lord. Let us say again what some in the Modern Church believe: the more we sin, the sooner we go to be with the Lord. Let this sink in. Some Modern Church leaders teach this nonsense because of the adherence to the belief that a believer can never lose his salvation, and the need to reconcile that preconception with scripture that teaches God's discipline sometimes results in death. The Modern Church has created a doctrine which teaches that those, like Ananias and Sapphira, who are killed by God for sin, especially in His anger, still go to heaven.

Certainly some have died because of the Lord's discipline and yet are with the Lord today. There is no question about that. Moses is such an example. But the issue was, and always will be, the heart. Moses had a heart to obey God and even though he failed occasionally, such failures were not spiritually fatal. But there is spiritual fatality reaped from ongoing apathy, outright rebellion, or trivialization of sin. None of these are within the will of the Father. We trivialize the sacrifice of our Lord and are committed to grieving the Holy Spirit when we don't care enough to work hard at avoiding sin.

Think about the specific teachings in the New Testament about those who continue in sin. We are taught these believers, specifically referenced as such, were warned by Paul: "I have also told you in time past, that they which do such things shall not inherit the kingdom of God" (**Galatians 5:21b**). We know that on-going sin, which is refusing to submit to and be led by the Holy Spirit, is spiritually fatal for this is what is taught in scripture.

What would we say about the Israelites who continued to test the Lord over and over and of whom God said "they shall never enter my rest?" Do you really believe they are in heaven, given that God killed them in His anger? They exhibited a pattern of disobedience. God is able to discern the heart and whether it is inclined to obey or disobey; whether it is inclined to seek His will or its own will. God tries to lead us to be righteous. But there are plenty of "believers" who claim Christ, whose church leaders insist they are saved, and yet are committed to disobedience. They have developed hard hearts over time; sin is no big deal to them.

Consider again Ananias and Sapphira. They were likely church members whom God killed (in Acts 5) for lying to the Holy Spirit. Some teach they are with the Lord now (although none of us know for sure). So let's examine this. The last verse describing this event is recorded as, *"Great fear seized the whole church* and all who heard about these events" (**Acts 5:11**). Why? If the church believed then, as much of the Modern Church does now, that God had simply taken them to heaven in-spite of their grievous sin, why would there be fear instead of rejoicing for the mercy of God? No, they understood that these two people were probably doomed to hell, hence the "great fear."

Death is not to be feared. It has been swallowed up. What is to be feared is a life lived without knowing our Lord and what He has done for us. We all die physically; even those in the church at the time that Ananias and Sapphira lived. The Modern Church struggles with the difference between temporal (earthly) and eternal punishment. But this life is not what is most important.

We must remember that the next life is better than this life for those that truly know Christ. Paul made this point quite eloquently when he wrote, "For I am in a strait betwixt two, having a desire to depart, and *to be with Christ; which is far better"* (**Philippians 1:23**). Any doctrine we develop which prioritizes this life over eternal life is inconsistent with the larger picture of scripture. We act in this life to take hold of eternal life, the true life. So when God kills someone for regular and intentional sin, we have two possible conclusions we can draw. Either God is rewarding sin by bringing committed sinners into His presence sooner (because it is a better place to be) or those killed for their sin have to deal with eternal repercussions.

Why does God discipline His children? "For they verily for a few days chastened us after their own pleasure; but he [God] for our profit, *that we might be partakers of his holiness"* (**Hebrews 12:10**). Our holiness does not come exclusively from God alone otherwise there would be no reason to discipline us to share in His holiness. If God kills us, we have lost the ability to follow His command: "Be ye holy; for I am holy" (**1 Peter 1:16**). Consider why God would not disciple Ananias and Sapphira rather than kill them.

The Modern Church's teachings suggesting that those killed by God's discipline automatically spend eternity in heaven are compromised because they are based on doctrinal ideas rooted in the priority of this life over the next, which is antithetical to what scripture teaches: "Ye adulterers and adulteresses, *know ye not that the friendship of the world is enmity with God?* Whosoever therefore will be a friend of the world is the enemy of God" (**James 4:4**). Our worldly perspective leads us to want to believe that a God who killed rebellious people in anger, will, in the next moment, turn around and welcome those same rebellious people into His kingdom.

Why are we addressed as adulterers and adulteresses here? It is because often our first love is the world and the things of the world. This is idolatry; the same sin for which Israel was regularly punished and the same sin of many in the Modern Church. God views this as spiritual adultery - see the book of Hosea. But the Modern Church feeds this love of the world in too many ways. When our first focus is not God, we are involved in some type of idolatry. The Modern Church can be so focused on the benefits of this life that even some espoused doctrine now prioritizes this life over the next. This is in complete opposition to those now giving their lives to do the Lord's work. These people doing the Lord's work are looking ahead to their reward as Paul did in Philippians 3:8–12.

God often killed the Israelites for their unfaithfulness, but always spared a faithful remnant. We tend to think in earthly terms, even when reading scripture, but we are to have a heavenly focus; that is the perspective the Holy Spirit leads us to have. Even though we live in this world, we are not *to be* of this world. We are strangers and pilgrims on this earth. To this end, we must be careful to avoid building doctrine on earthly perspectives or desires.

Rather, we are to be citizens of heaven: "For our conversation is in heaven; from whence also we look for the Saviour, the Lord Jesus Christ" (**Philippians 3:20**). Conversation (Greek *politeuma*) means "government or administration" so our government is in heaven, not here on earth, where we remain strangers and pilgrims as long as we are here. We are not citizens here but strangers. We are citizens of heaven if our focus is where it should be.

God's Desires and our Relationship with Him

God desires our worship and the building of a true relationship with Him. When we seek the kind of relationship He desires, we spend time with Him. We seek to learn His ways. We seek to understand what pleases Him and what angers Him. We think about Him. This is what pleases God. Think about our own children. What pleases us about our relationship with them? The model is very similar (except that our Father in heaven is the perfect parent).

Jesus also pointed out to His disciples that He was our Master and Lord: "Ye call me Master and Lord: and ye say well; for so I am" (**John 13:13**). This is who our Lord is. Not some friend that we have the flexibility to ignore. We are not sons or daughters who can blithely go about disobeying or rebelling against our Father. We are to obey our Father. Jesus called out the hypocrisy of calling Jesus our Lord and then not doing what He says: "Not every one that saith unto me, Lord, Lord, shall enter into the kingdom of heaven; but he that doeth the will of my Father which is in heaven" (**Matthew 7:21**).

But who can call Jesus Lord? "Wherefore I give you to understand, that no man speaking by the Spirit of God calleth Jesus accursed: and that no man can say that Jesus is the Lord, *but by the Holy Ghost*" (**1 Corinthians 12:2**). Therefore those who sincerely call Jesus Lord are led to do so by the Holy Spirit.

But even this verse must be understood in context. This does not mean that no one can physically say that "Jesus is Lord" for, "Not every one that saith unto me, Lord, Lord, shall enter into the kingdom of heaven; but he that doeth the will of my Father which is in heaven" (**Matthew 7:21**). There will be plenty of people who call Jesus Lord, but only by submitting to the Holy Spirit can they really mean it. Many will call Jesus Lord without really submitting to Him.

Paul also acknowledged himself a bondservant in Romans 1:1. Remember that we were bought at a price, "*For ye are bought with a price: therefore glorify God in your body, and in your spirit, which are God's*" (**1 Corinthians 6:20**). Who are bought? Slaves. As much as this may offend our American sensibilities, this too is part of the relationship with our God; indeed it is the key part.

Now, Jesus does call us friends: "Henceforth I call you not servants; for the servant knoweth not what his lord doeth: but I have called you friends; for all things that I have heard of my Father I have made known unto you" (**John 15:15**). Jesus stated this for relational purposes, drawing out the differences of knowing and not knowing what comes from the Father. However, we must understand the nature of such friendship. It does not make us equals as a friendship of the world might.

True believers also adopted into God's family: "Wherefore thou art no more a servant, but a son; and if a son, then an heir of God through Christ" (**Galatians 4:7**). Note that even though we do hold position as a member of God's family, we are *adopted* members of the family.

We have been grafted into Christ:

> "And if some of the branches be broken off, and thou, being a wild olive tree, wert grafted in among them, and with them partakest of the root and fatness of the olive tree; Boast not against the branches. But if thou boast, thou bearest not the root, but the root thee. Thou wilt say then, The branches were broken off, that I might be grafted in. Well; because of unbelief they were broken off, and thou standest by faith. Be not highminded, but fear: *For if God spared not the natural branches, take heed lest he also spare not thee. Behold therefore the goodness and severity of God: on them which fell, severity; but toward thee, goodness, if thou continue in his goodness: otherwise thou also shalt be cut off*" (**Romans 11:17–22**).

We Gentiles, by nature, are not native-born members of God's family. The Jewish people are. But the unbelieving Jewish people have been "broken off" so that believing Gentiles might be grafted in, *as long as they continue in their faith*. So the relationship of believers with our God is not just as sons or daughters, or just as friends, or just as slaves. These are all different facets of our relationship with God.

However, we must be very careful not to use the concept of our relationship as sons, daughters, or friends to translate to some concept of equality with God, where we are free to dictate the terms of the relationship. Indeed, God tells us who His true sons are in Romans 8:14; it is those believers who are led by the Spirit. We must never take for granted that our relationship grants us the right to either ignore the Spirit or disobey God, or that we are somehow equals in determining what is right and wrong.

Indeed, a true love for God should motivate us to spend more and more time with Him, not less and less. While this will grow our love for Him, it should also deepen our respect for Him, and keep us in awe of

His great power. Jesus told His twelve disciples, "And fear not them which kill the body, but are not able to kill the soul: but rather fear him which is able to destroy both soul and body in hell" (**Matthew 10:28**). We must understand that we were bought at a price, and regardless of these multiple facets of our relationship with God, we are His bondservants, created to serve Him here (Ephesians 2:10) and in eternity (Revelation 22:3,9).

God Knows our Heart

We must guard our hearts. We are deceived if we believe that our actions and motives can be hidden from God. The Bible is full of warnings to man about God knowing the heart. We may think that we can fool God or take for granted that He cannot see our hearts, but both of these are untrue. God tells us regarding the Word, "For the word of God is quick, and powerful, and sharper than any two-edged sword, piercing even to the dividing asunder of soul and spirit, and of the joints and marrow, and is a *discerner of the thoughts and intents of the heart*" (**Hebrews 4:12**). God also warns us with the following words, "Every way of a man is right in his own eyes: but the Lord pondereth the hearts" (**Proverbs 21:2**).

This ability to discern the heart applies to all things. When we confess our sin, God knows if we are truly sorry. When we repent, God knows if we mean it. When we help others, God knows if it's a heart to help or a heart to receive praise. When we judge other's sinful actions, God knows if it's a heart to help or a heart to condemn. God knows if we think more of others or less of others. When we give, God knows if we are doing it cheerfully. In short, God knows all things about our hearts. Let us never make the mistake that we think we can fool Him. We must guard our hearts.

Because there is so much deceit in this world, we can unintentionally fool ourselves. We know that other people cannot see our hearts, and so without carefully thinking this through, we may reach the same conclusion about God. But our God knows. People who are committed to sin, even while perhaps doing good things, do not fool God. Church leaders who trivialize sin or obedience do not fool God. This is critically important because many do not fully understand or teach the implication of God's knowledge of the heart. Indeed, some of the doctrines embraced by the Modern Church do not seem to even consider God's knowledge of the heart.

Jesus said the first and greatest commandment was, "Thou shalt love the Lord thy God with all thy heart, and with all thy soul, and with all thy mind" (**Matthew 22:38**). It takes precedence even over loving our neighbor which is the second commandment. How do we love God? We love God by obeying Him. Scripture teaches us, "For this is the love of God, that we keep his commandments: and his commandments are not grievous" (**1 John 5:3**). John 14:15 echoes the same.

We must remember that God understands us in a way that we cannot understand other human beings, and that at times, we cannot even understand ourselves. We cannot hide any selfish motive, selfish act, or anything else from our God. We must work to train ourselves, even though we live in this world, to constantly keep in mind who we serve and His capabilities. We must train ourselves, through His help, to guard our own hearts and minds. It is the reason that the apostle Paul wrote that we should be "Casting down imaginations, and every high thing that exalteth itself against the knowledge of God, and *bringing into captivity every thought to the obedience of Christ*" (**1 Corinthians 10:5**).

We must always remember that God has been, and continues to be, angry with His people when they rebel against Him. The Old Testament is full of examples where God's people have spiritually prostituted themselves before Him. They turned to other gods. They acted unjustly. They disobeyed. They were unfaithful. They ignored Him or were apathetic towards Him and His commands. Since we know that God does not change, we can expect that He is upset with many who call Him Lord act in this day and age.

Key Thoughts

While our God has great love, he is also a just God. He is worthy of our love, respect and worship. This is His world and He owns everything in it. He created everything. He is our Lord and master. He does not change like shifting shadows. We are to fear God, who literally holds the power over physical and spiritual life and death (Matthew 10:28). We should be forever thankful that He is a God of love, who paid the ultimate price to redeem us and gives us the Holy Spirit who, if we let Him, will guide us to make decisions that honor Him.

We must look at the nature of God in the Old Testament to understand scripture in the New Testament. We must be careful to consider the entire counsel of God, and not simply that which describes the New Covenant. The New Covenant has not in any way changed the nature of our God.

Our relationship with God is complex; we are "sons of God," "friends of God," "heirs of God," "disciples," and "bondservants." Focusing too heavily on any one relational construct to the detriment of the others can lead us to some misunderstandings. We must be especially careful to avoid thinking our position as friends is similar to a worldly friendship. Paul recognized first and foremost, he was a bondservant of Jesus Christ and so should we.

We must also recognize that nothing is hidden from God. He understands our hearts and knows what motivates us. We should always keep this in mind as we live our lives. To focus on honoring Him is the purest of motives. To share His gospel makes us a faithful messenger. To love Him above everyone and everything else, and to love others more than our selves, is of great value to God.

Chapter 3

Listening to Man and Not God, False Prophets

Misleading Christian sound bite(s): As iron sharpens iron, so one man educates another. We need not worry about false teachers since our salvation is totally secure no matter what we believe or who we follow. We should follow other men's teachings if they are successful, for God is blessing them.

As of the writing of this book, there are thousands of different Christian denominations with many different doctrines. This very fact is inconsistent with the idea that scripture is truth. Listening only to men can be fraught with danger, yet it is something that Christians are doing more and more. Yet we as Christians are not to be lazy with our salvation; we are to contend for the faith.

Too many of us do not have the passion to be in God's Word, which would be the natural outcome if we were being led by the Holy Spirit. In failing to be in God's Word, we have effectively outsourced our salvation to church leaders and/or other people. While there are diligent church leaders, there are also those who struggle with presenting the truth of scripture. Lessons and sermons often originate from the Internet rather than scripture. In Jeremiah 23, God condemns leaders who destroy and scatter the sheep of His pasture.

When we love and cherish our intimate and growing relationship with Christ based in His Word, we know that some of the things that our church leaders tell us expose a heart apart from God. Even though all men occasionally err, if we don't consistently see the heart for God in Sunday sermons and lessons, we have a problem. Jesus said, "for of the abundance of the heart his mouth speaketh" (**Luke 6:45**). Even though we cannot fully know a person's heart, we have some insight into a person's heart by what they say and what they do. Our heart before God should reflect our love of Him, not our love of one another's teachings.

The evidence of listening to men alone, apart from scripture, is all around us. We see clearly enough, using evidence provided in the introduction and what is happening in our culture that what men alone are leading us toward often is wrong. Emerging doctrine is increasingly an enabler of sin. We see this by the fruits of what is produced. Just because God is allowing this to occur, we should never assume that God is okay with what is being taught and the way we are behaving. Remember God suffered the Israelites for long periods of time before punishing them.

Evolving Doctrine and Its Causes

If we look at the historical church, its leaders have been all over the place in terms of their views on scripture. Many people today refer to the leaders of the Reformation and their views, but many of the beliefs and doctrines of the Reformers were not shared by those believers living closer to the time when scripture was actually written. Believers in the early church also had many doctrinal differences with the later orthodoxy of the early Catholic Church. This means that the so-called truth of God, when placed in men's hands, has historically changed, and is changing even to this very day. Yet that is inconsistent with the absolute truth of scripture inspired by a God that can see across time.

If we simply look back at the history of the Christian church, it becomes very easy to see how men have led people away from God. The doctrines of false religions are constantly changing. True Christianity is based on God and His Word, which do not change. Man does. The fastest way for Christians to put themselves in eternal danger is to listen to men only. We are called to get our truth from God and His Word, not other men. This is not new. Every writer of a New Testament epistle warns Christians against false teachers.

The Israelites, when they had God as king, were not satisfied with God as their king and wanted a human leader like the nations around them, and so they got Saul. We know how that turned out. We are the same today. We listen to our pastors and Sunday school teachers, but we don't spend time reading scripture with the aid of the Holy Spirit. We spend so much time quoting and referencing other men that we forget to rely on scripture. When we do quote scripture, often we do so in sound bites which do not in and of themselves adequately reflect the entire truth of scripture. Because we tend to be lazy with our salvation, we tend to take the easy road, letting other men do the "hard work" and relying primarily on them for truth. This approach is filled with danger.

Many of the teachings of the Modern Church expose a heart apart from God. Our doctrine is evolving, but not in a good way. Indeed, the evidence of errant doctrine is all around us. Men are following other men just as they do in Judaism, Islam and Mormonism. Yet this was never God's intention for the church. Men who were seeking the truth were to go to scripture and be guided by the Holy Spirit. When we are told things by other men, we are to confirm what we were told in scripture (Acts 17:11).

While we thank God for those who are faithful shepherds, we must realize that in the end, we are responsible before God. We don't want to follow in other religions' footsteps where we, by default, create a "priest class" who are the only ones who know the "secrets of the faith." We are commanded to seek the truth in scripture (2 Timothy 2:15) while being led by the Spirit: "But when he, the Spirit of truth, comes, he will guide you into all the truth" (**John 16:13a**).

So what has happened? We have created doctrinal "truths" which don't accurately reflect what the Bible teaches. For example, a lack of understanding of just one aspect of the nature of God *(e.g.,* a God who does not change), can lead to doctrinal error in the New Testament. Too often we present the gospel in a manner that does not offend, in order to protect our human edifices (by keeping the pews and coffers full) even though, "Howbeit the most High dwelleth not in temples made with hands; as saith the prophet" (**Acts 7:48**). But the gospel is designed to offend and to create division. Not division within the body of Christ, which is to be unified in truth, but divided from the world. Instead we are doing the opposite. *We are dividing the body and unifying with the world.*

God set the expectation for His true followers: "Yea, and all that will live godly in Christ Jesus shall suffer persecution" (**2 Timothy 3:12**) and "Suppose ye that I am come to give peace on earth? I tell you, Nay; but rather division" (**Luke 12:51**). Yet the number of people that truly follow Christ is much smaller than many would suppose. The Bible is full of examples of God using remnants of His people because there were few that actually did His will.

Christ tells us to be baptized. Some Modern Church leaders say we don't have to be. Christ tells us to obey. Many Modern Church leaders preach that obedience plays no part in our salvation, and/or that obedience is legalism, claiming that obedience is "works." Many Christians trivialize sin. Christ paid a high price to free us from sin and commanded us to go to extremes to avoid sin. Christ spoke of hell. Some professing Christians and even church leaders tell us there is no such place. In short, so many pastors and televangelists seem to be convinced that leading people to Christ is about themselves and the "truths" they embrace, that they actually lead people away from a solid relationship with Jesus Christ.

Some church leaders see themselves in a tough spot. If they speak the full truth, they may well lose followers. Yet this is exactly what they are called to do. They, like all believers, are commanded to faithfully teach the gospel, no matter where it leads. If they water down the gospel, treat as unholy the blood of Christ, or misrepresent scripture, they are putting members of their congregations at risk, and are risking their condemnation as false teachers.

Beginning fairly early in church history, church leaders have focused on building these expansive earthly churches which require significant amounts of funding to remain viable. It is a short step to compromise the Gospel to keep people engaged so that the church does not go bankrupt. We can imagine that in many cases, compromise is considered justifiable through a "greater good" concept. Yet this is a temporal (worldly) perspective, not a spiritual one. It is interesting to note that in the Philippines often the nicest buildings in the poorest areas are the churches. Would we have been wiser to invest the resources God provides in helping to bring people to Christ rather than building these large structures which will be destroyed anyway? Are we focusing on the right things?

We must be wary of anyone using scripture to suggest either that sinning is trivial or routine, or that it has no effect on our salvation. We must be on the alert for those who teach that being committed to engaging the flesh is irrelevant to the issue of salvation, whether taught directly or indirectly. Scripture expressly warns about the possibility of disobedience (continual or habitual sin) resulting in the loss of salvation. We must understand that God hated sin enough to send His Son to die an agonizing death for our sin. It is therefore only natural for the true believer who is indwelt and led by the Holy Spirit, to also hate sin and to try his best to avoid it. Let us offer a key thought: Any doctrine of man which results in increased sin is not a true doctrine of God, but of the evil one.

> Any doctrine of man which results in increased sin is not a true doctrine of God, but of the evil one.

Many Denominations, One Spirit, One Truth

Within many of the emergent and ecumenical movements (to bring all "Christians" under one movement), we often see doctrine downplayed, with the explanation that no one can arrive at the true doctrine, or that correct doctrine is not critical. In other cases, compromises of key scriptural concepts occur. Scriptural truths often take a back seat to what people want to believe. We see people using the culture to change the true meaning of scripture. We see integration of incompatible "truths," as if truth was not paramount.

Part of this disunity is the result of improper individual motivations. Part of this disunity is the result of lack of understanding of scripture. While we may be able to conclude that different people, in good conscience, may come to a different understanding of doctrine, we cannot conclude that the Holy Spirit is leading people into different doctrinal truths. *Hence, where conflicting doctrines are espoused, at most one doctrine can be correct, but perhaps none are.* There is one Holy Spirit, and He will lead those who submit to Him "into all truth" (**John 16:13**). God is not divided, and neither is His truth. Thus, no matter how well-intentioned a person may be, there is a chance he is lacking a correct understanding of doctrine.

We have developed much of our orthodoxy because we fail to see the true harmony of God's Word as revealed by the Holy Spirit. There are many places in scripture where there appear to be conflicts. However, it is our conviction and experience that almost all apparent scriptural conflicts can be resolved through further scripture study and prayer. Understanding is to be sought from, and granted by, the Holy Spirit. Knowing the nature of our God is also critical to scriptural understanding. But if we operate just in sound bites, without seeking God's counsel and a wider perspective of scripture, we often do not get to the full truth that the Bible teaches.

We are responsible to prayerfully work through apparent scriptural conflicts, not simply listen to men who may ignore inconvenient or apparently conflicting scripture. We cannot see other men's hearts, but the Holy Spirit can. He will reveal the same doctrinal truths to all people who earnestly seek them. God is not a respecter of persons; He wants all men to know the truth (1 Timothy 2:4). And His truth is absolute; like God Himself, it does not change. This is part of the evidence that the Modern Church has problems. We are pursuing different doctrinal truths, when scripturally, there is only one.

Paul had to reason from scripture to convince people of specific things, such as proving that Jesus was the Christ (Messiah). We are no different. We should never take a few scriptural passages from which we declare a doctrine, especially when there are other scriptures which seem to clearly refute that doctrine. This "cherry picking" approach to scripture, like "cafeteria Christianity," is incompatible with truly seeking God's truth. Scripture is harmonious, but the shallowness of our pursuit of the truth leads us to take shortcuts, which often lead to doctrinal error. This happens in too many (but thankfully not all) churches.

It is true that Christ has established His church on earth but we must remember that "a church" is not necessarily "the church." Christ's church is not the four walls of a building, nor is it the Modern Church movement, nor a given Christian church, nor even a given denomination. Christ's church is the men and women on this earth who have been called by God and have answered God's calling through the faith God gave them. It is those, who once they have been called, try to live a faithful life walking with the Holy Spirit and enduring to the end.

We know that the Christ's church is not led exclusively by godly men. If the Holy Spirit were truly leading all of the Modern Church in the truth, Christianity would not have different doctrines and be divided as much as it is. God is not divided *and there is only one truth.* The Holy Spirit does not lead us into different doctrinal truths. Nor is being in the majority safe; scriptural history testifies to the fact that few actually find the truth.

Different doctrines are a red flag indicating that errors have crept into the Modern Church. When we focus on listening to other men, and refuse to earnestly contend for the faith through study of the scripture and being guided by the Holy Spirit (as scripture commands), we can easily be misled. It is not challenging to understand how we end up in with so many different denominations. But this is not of God. It is of men. Think about just a few of the errant doctrines espoused by "Christian" writers, pastors, teachers and seminaries today:

- Homosexual lifestyle and acts okay?
- Abortion okay?
- No such thing as Hell?
- God wants us to live in luxury?
- Multiple paths to God?
- Obedience not important to salvation?
- Once Saved, Always Saved?
- Christians sinning all the time?
- Living in sin expected by God?
- Living in sin rewarded by God?
- No need to be baptized?
- Marriages annulled?
- Pre-marital sex okay?
- God of the Bible the same as the God of the Quran?
- Christians accepting the mark of the beast still saved?
- God always controls humans?

Does any of this sound consistent with the larger context of scripture? Following men leads to division. Paul warned the church in Corinth about division created by following men and chastised them for doing so:

> "And I, brethren, could not speak unto you as unto spiritual, but as unto carnal, even as unto babes in Christ. I have fed you with milk, and not with meat: for hitherto ye were not able to bear it, neither yet now are ye able. For

ye are yet carnal: for whereas there is among you envying, and strife, and divisions, are ye not carnal, and walk as men? *For while one saith, I am of Paul; and another, I am of Apollos; are ye not carnal?* Who then is Paul, and who is Apollos, but ministers by whom ye believed, even as the Lord gave to every man?" (**1 Corinthians 3:1–5**).

The Modern Church is divided on many doctrinal issues, but scripture indicates God wants unity in the body of Christ: "Is Christ divided? was Paul crucified for you? or were ye baptized in the name of Paul" (**1 Corinthians 1:13**)? We are to have the same mind and the same judgment (1 Corinthians 1:10) in God's church (not the building, but the body of Christ). This is where the Holy Spirit leads. There are many efforts to minimize this division under concept of "keep focused on the most important aspects of Christianity," yet even there we see division.

Certainly there are different perspectives over non-doctrinal issues that God does reveal to people. The leading of the Holy Spirit can guide us to either take or not take some action. There is division that occurs over non-doctrinal issues. Division occurs over priorities, over personalities, over approaches to seeking the lost, etc. But these are not the divisions that are most detrimental.

The divisions which do the most damage are those that embrace different doctrinal truths. The Holy Spirit may guide us toward different scriptural perspectives on non-doctrinal issues, but never towards doctrinal differences. This might be stated slightly differently. God does not lead people to form different religions (or denominations) based on diverse and conflicting truths. Indeed, the single greatest charge levied by the secular community against Christianity is the charge of hypocrisy. The foundation of the scriptures is unified. When we divide based on doctrine, we do not honor God, but rather honor other men instead of God. Scripture makes it clear that the calling is to be unified over correct doctrine (the truth).

As such, the lack of unity in Christendom is the result of man's efforts. It has nothing to do with God. Jesus desired and prayed for unity for believers, but He prayed

> One of the main reasons the church has fractionalized is because men study other men instead of just God's Word.

for that unity to be *based on the truth:* "Sanctify them through thy truth: thy word is truth" (**John 17:17**). One of the main reasons the church has fractionalized is because men study other men instead of just God's Word. Either we lack the faith to believe God when He tells us that the Holy Spirit will lead us into all truth, or we too lazy or too uncommitted to God to seek His truth in scripture and prayer. Relying on the words of men is the exact same thing that those in other religions do. There are many men who believe they are led by the Holy Spirit, but are not. Many refuse to persist in spending time in God's Word, yet the only way to get to the truth of God's Word is through persistence in reading and striving to understand what God's Word says, along with seeking the guidance and insight of the Holy Spirit.

There are church leaders claiming that their church is Christ's church while preaching "soft rebellion" against the Lord. We define "soft rebellion" as any teaching which downplays the commands of scripture, or even attempts to use other scripture to invalidate the commands of our Lord. Examples of this include statements such as "you cannot lose your salvation after you have accepted Christ," "your past, present and future sins are forgiven when you come to Christ," "one need not be baptized to be saved," "our obedience adds nothing to what Christ did on the cross," "we sin all the time," "you are anything that God is," "we no longer sin because of Christ's sacrifice," "confession of our sins is not needed," "obedience after coming to Christ is 'works-based' salvation," and similar types of statements. God warns about such men when He says plainly, "Woe be unto the pastors that destroy and scatter the sheep of my pasture saith the Lord" (**Jeremiah 23:1**).

These types of statements lead people to act in a manner inconsistent with what our Lord teaches. They trivialize the price Christ paid. Only we can discern, through scripture and the Holy Spirit, whether a given church leader and congregation are led by the Lord. While some parts of the Modern Church earnestly follow the gospel, many follow other men's interpretations of the gospel. *This is not trusting in God, but rather men.* It is not relying on the Holy Spirit for truth, but instead relying on men for the truth. We must be concerned about those who are committed to trusting in men. Probably the majority of today's Christians trust the doctrines of men because they refuse to prioritize the earnest study of God's Word. They compartmentalize their spiritual life into Sunday morning, and leave it there to survive or die on its own. Others trust in other men simply because their teaching appeals to the flesh; it is much easier to be a Christian using doctrine watered down by men.

Many churches that compromise the gospel, like the Laodicean Church described in Revelation 3, grow quickly. That is because men, not having learned to crucify their sinful nature, have always wanted to eat their cake and have it too (the best in this life and the best in the next life). Yet this is in opposition to Jesus' teaching that, "For whosoever will save his life shall lose it: and whosoever will lose his life for my sake shall find it" (**Matthew 16:25**). In short, we need to be careful of all sorts of movements that seem on the surface to be of God, but may in fact not be of God.

Think for a moment about the condemnation of the Lord to lying prophets: "I have seen also in the prophets of Jerusalem an horrible thing: they commit [spiritual] adultery, and walk in lies: they strengthen also the hands of evildoers, that none doth return from his wickedness: they are all of them unto me as Sodom, and the inhabitants thereof as Gomorrah" (**Jeremiah 23:14**). What are Modern Church leaders doing when they proclaim that no matter how much sin one is practicing, he remains saved? Aren't we giving false hope to evildoers, who consequently don't repent?

Many have developed tests in their own minds and then quote these tests to other people to declare where God is working. For example if we see a "Christian" church growing rapidly, we may assume that God is working there, but we see Islam and other religions growing at even faster rates than Christianity. The same claims which church leaders in the Modern Church make about the growth of their own churches being of the Lord are being repeated in those religions and in churches which are also growing fast, but are divorced of truth. Muslim Imams are claiming the growth of their mosque is of God (Allah). Mormon Bishops are claiming growth in their temples and wards is of God. The list goes on and on.

Should we then assume that because these religions are growing faster that God is blessing them even more? No. Many will find the broad road to destruction (Matthew 7:13). Just because a church is growing rapidly does not mean its growth is of God. While Christian churches do grow because of God, people often fail to consider that those leading people away from God are often even more successful because they appeal to the flesh and the world.

Worse yet, if the truth is not being preached from the pulpit, their congregations may also be headed down the broad road to destruction. Popularity and rapid growth should raise red flags, not automatically create confidence in God's blessing. This is exactly the false teaching that scripture prophesizes. *The only true measure of an effective ministry is its alignment with the Word of God.* Filled seats and souls claiming acceptance of Christ without submitting to the Holy Spirit count for nothing.

True Disciples

Supposedly the focus of the Modern Church has been on bringing people to Christ. While that goal is laudable, the Bible is very clear: not all that name Christ as Lord will be saved. Again we remind you of the words of Jesus: *"Not every one that saith unto me, Lord, Lord, shall enter into the kingdom of heaven; but he that doeth the will of my Father which is in heaven. Many will say to me in that day, Lord, Lord, have we not prophesied in thy name? and in thy name have cast out devils? and in thy name done many wonderful works?"* (**Matthew 7:21–22**). Jesus answered those who would claim to be His followers, but were not, with the condemnation, "And then will I profess unto them, I never knew you: depart from me, ye that work iniquity" (**Matthew 7:23**).

Note that Jesus did not say "you never knew me," but rather "I never knew you." There are many that believe in Jesus Christ whom He does not know as His sheep because they refuse to do the will of the Father as led by the Holy Spirit. This can apply even to those doing miracles. Those Jesus confronted were doing miracles; they knew that God was real, but refused to submit to the will of the Father. This is the reason that in the Great Commission Jesus commanded His faithful eleven disciples not only to make disciples, but also follow up on the initial conversion and baptism by *"Teaching them to observe all things* whatsoever I have commanded you" (**Matthew 28:20**). Our claims of knowing Jesus Christ do not necessarily equate to Him knowing us. He wants a commitment and a relationship, not just an acknowledgement.

A personal relationship with Jesus Christ involves much more than just intellectually acknowledging Christ as Lord and Savior, yet this is often the shallow focus of the Modern Church. Most in the Modern Church would say that after accepting Christ, we need not do the Father's will to be saved. Others might speculate that the Father has only one will, based on one verse: "And this is the will of him that sent me, that every one which seeth the Son, and believeth on him, may have everlasting life: and I will raise him up at the last day" (**John 6:40**).

Yet we see scripturally there is more to the Father's will. Let us review the words of Jesus: "Not every one that saith unto me, Lord, Lord, shall enter into the kingdom of heaven; *but he that doeth the will of my Father* which is in heaven" (**Matthew 7:21**). Remember, the condemnation of Jesus is to those that acknowledge Him as Lord yet refuse to do the will of the Father. If the only and singular will of the Father was to accept Jesus as Lord, then His words would not make sense or would be false but this is not possible because God is truth (John 14:6). There are other passages of scripture where we are taught what the Father's will is. One example is "For this is the will of God, even your sanctification, that ye should abstain from fornication" (**1 Thessalonians 4:3**). Jesus specifically confronts those that call Him "Lord, but do not follow through with obedience to the Father's will.

The difference between correct and incorrect doctrine is often a salvation-determining issue. God inspired Paul to warn Timothy: "Take heed unto thyself, and unto the doctrine; continue in them: *for in doing this thou shalt both save thyself, and them that hear thee*" (**1 Timothy 4:16**). Think about Paul's warning to those preaching a different gospel in church in Galatia (Galatians 5:7–12). We have developed much of our errant orthodoxy because we fail to see the true harmony of God's Word.

Being in a church which teaches some doctrinal truths does not necessarily qualify one for being in the body of Christ. In Revelation, Jesus condemns specific communities of believers in certain cities for their lack of deeds, false doctrine, tolerance of sin, and/or lukewarm attitude towards our great God. These condemnations in some cases imply loss of salvation based on their actions. In others, Jesus gives specific guidance which, if heeded, will get them back on the narrow way that leads to life.

Consider what Jesus said to the church in Sardis:

> "And unto the angel of the church in Sardis write; These things saith he that hath the seven Spirits of God, and the seven stars; *I know thy works, that thou hast a name*

that thou livest, and art dead. Be watchful, and strengthen the things which remain, that are ready to die: for I have not found thy works perfect before God. Remember therefore how thou hast received and heard, and hold fast, and repent. If therefore thou shalt not watch, I will come on thee as a thief, and thou shalt not know what hour I will come upon thee. *Thou hast a few names even in Sardis which have not defiled their garments;* and they shall walk with me in white: for they are worthy. *He that overcometh, the same shall be clothed in white raiment; and I will not blot out his name out of the book of life,* but I will confess his name before my Father, and before his angels. He that hath an ear, let him hear what the Spirit saith unto the churches" (**Revelation 3:1–6**)

Jesus condemned most of those in the church as "dead." They were going to church, listening to sermons, and even had a reputation of being spiritually alive because of their works, but they were not. Yet Jesus told them that there are few that had not "defiled their garments." What is the implication of "walk with me in white"? Consider Revelation 7:14, Revelation 19:7–8, and Revelation 19:14. Jesus finished with the promise and warning that for those that overcome, He will not "blot out his name out of the book of life."

The church in Sardis had leaders just as we do, yet Jesus condemned the people in the church congregation, underscoring our responsibility before God. Jesus even condemned those that had a reputation for being alive. In the eyes of men, this church seemed like it was doing the will of God, perhaps even growing in numbers, but it was not spiritually alive. For another church, Jesus threatened to take away their lamp stand which we know gives light. There is no reason for God to threaten to take away their lamp stand if He knew the churches were building true disciples and those in them would return to Him. These are to be examples for us to consider.

Scripture shows clearly that we have the ability to be led away from God. We must hold church leaders accountable for deviating from the truth we find from reading the Word of God. Far too often church leaders preach what we want to hear, not what we need to hear. When we hear something from the pulpit that contradicts scripture, we often accept it because it is something we want to hear, because it is something we lack the knowledge to challenge, or because we are apathetic. God condemns all of these failures in scripture.

We do not desire to follow a religion. We desire to follow Christ. We don't seek a relationship with a church or church leader. We seek a relationship with our God first and foremost. We should be about obeying His commands with the right heart. The apostle James wrote, "Pure religion and undefiled before God and the Father is this, To visit the fatherless and widows in their affliction, and to keep himself unspotted from the world" (**James 1:27**).

We must be very careful about being religious and following religious leaders, for if history is any guide, men will continue to mess up spiritual truths. Just consider a common theme in most churches: one need not obey (or even try to obey) God after coming to Christ to be saved. Can we see how far we have fallen?

Following God has never been about being in the majority; indeed, biblically, those truly seeking God are almost always in the minority (the narrow way of Matthew 7:14). Being in the mainstream of Christianity can be dangerous. God delivered and started over with faithful remnants in Israel many times. Think about the time (1 Kings 19) that God told Elijah that there were 7,000 in Israel which had not bent their knee to Baal. But that is 7000 out of how many? This was after David conducted his ill-advised census of the fighting men in Israel and Judah counting more than 1,500,000 fighting men (7000/1,500,000 = less than ½ of 1%), and that excluded the Levites, Benjamites, women and boys below fighting age. Stick to the narrow road of scripture and prayer.

Jesus said "Enter ye in at the strait gate: for wide is the gate, and broad is the way, that leadeth to destruction, and many there be which go in thereat: Because strait is the gate, and narrow is the way, which leadeth unto life, *and few there be that find it*" (**Matthew 7:13–14**). God himself said that few find it - *few*. But those headed for destruction? Many.

Some might conjecture that this verse in Matthew 7 was written to the entire world's population. However, we know "all scripture is God breathed" (**2 Timothy 3:16a**) and that God inspired Matthew to include this teaching of Jesus (and there are many more teachings not included as per John 21:25) to the Jews to whom Matthew was writing. Even if it is written to the general population of the world, professing Christians are said to make up almost 30% of the world's population – far more than "few."

What is a few? Well, numerically this is hard to pin down. In modern terms it usually means 3%-5% although this can vary somewhat, but it is not 25%-30% of the world's population or even close to it. Yet the reading of the text is unmistakable. There will be many fewer people saved than those the Modern Church recognizes as saved based on their proclamations from the pulpit that all that profess faith in Christ will be saved. Finally, there is little reason to tell non-Christians, who largely don't read the Bible, that only a few will be saved. No, this teaching is designed to educate and warn Christians and professing Christians.

But look at the context of what follows shortly thereafter. Jesus then told His disciples "Not everyone that saith unto me, Lord, Lord, shall enter into the kingdom of heaven; but he that *doeth the will of my Father* which is in heaven" (**Matthew 7:21**). In these two passages in Matthew 7 we see that many who think they are right with God are not, even though they acknowledge Jesus as Lord. Is the Modern Church helping to create true Christians, or is it, through hollow philosophies and errant doctrine, creating false, yet professing, believers with dead faith?

Some might be reassured by the vast number of saints in heaven described in the book of Revelation. But we must remember the context. There do appear to be many who will be saved: "After this I beheld, and, lo, a great multitude, which no man could number, of all nations, and kindreds, and people, and tongues, stood before the throne, and before the Lamb, clothed with white robes, and palms in their hands" (**Revelation 7:9**).

These are the saved, but they are the saved over all of human history. Yet we see the same thing in Luke 12 where we are told, "In the mean time, when there were gathered together an *innumerable multitude of people*, insomuch that they trode one upon another, he began to say unto his disciples first of all, Beware ye of the leaven of the Pharisees, which is hypocrisy" (**Luke 12:1**). We must be careful of making assumptions as to what an innumerable of people is.

Finally, though we believe that we are in the end times, we do not actually know when Christ may return. There may be many, many more generations of human beings, some of whom will come to truly know Jesus Christ in great numbers. As such, any attempt to quantitatively define the multitude in Revelation 7 cannot be linguistically supported. We as human beings want to believe that all will be saved. In our Bible studies, one of the single greatest things we must deal with is the concept that only through Christ will people be saved. You would be surprised at how many people want to believe that those who never knew Christ will also be saved. To even maintain this simple truth can cause people to abandon a Bible study.

We have entered a time where people will not endure sound doctrine as referred to in scripture: "For the time will come when they will not endure sound doctrine; but after their own lusts shall they heap to themselves teachers, having itching ears" (**2 Timothy 4:3**). While there is little doubt that some people are being saved through the Modern Church, the concern is for the larger population of the Modern Church which may have escalating numbers of unsaved being lulled into a false sense of security.

Listening to Men

Most deception throughout the world comes from men. It is the reason we have as many different religions as we do. Almost all religions, save the one with supernatural evidence of its origin (the Bible), have a foundation of men's teachings. Men want to follow other men rather than the one true God. This is true in other religions, but it is also true in Christianity.

It is clear that God uses the church, but are church leaders doing what God commands? In many cases, we see church leaders teaching lessons that are more based on human desire or "philosophy and vain deceit" (**Colossians 2:8a**) than scripture. If we look at the first century church, we see leaders committed to public reading of scripture. This is most closely aligned with expository teaching in the Modern Church. Even the exhortation to Timothy by Paul, "Preach the word; be instant in season, out of season; reprove, rebuke, exhort with all longsuffering and doctrine" (**2 Timothy 4:2**), commands the idea to *present* scripture, not interpret it through preconceptions formed from the doctrines of men. Christ said we only have one teacher (Himself). Christ teaches us through the Holy Spirit.

But in some cases, we have taken creative license with that concept and now not only read scripture, but state individual interpretation as well.

This is one of the ways we end up at divided doctrine, for not all church leaders preach the same messages. The right heart before God does not rely on men for truth, but on the Holy Spirit. The right heart before God does not try to lead people *away* from what God commands, but *towards* what God commands.

Consider carefully the words of Jesus in condemning the Pharisees: "But woe unto you, scribes and Pharisees, hypocrites! for ye shut up the kingdom of heaven against men: for ye neither go in yourselves, neither suffer ye them that are entering to go in" (**Matthew 23:13**) and, "Woe unto you, scribes and Pharisees, hypocrites! for ye compass sea and land to make one proselyte, and when he is made, ye make him twofold more the child of hell than yourselves (**Matthew 23:15**).

Jesus condemned the Pharisees for slamming the door to the kingdom of heaven in other men's faces. The Pharisees themselves would not enter, and they were preventing others from doing so. God teaches that men prevent other men from entering the kingdom (*e.g.*, Matthew 24:24). Furthermore, once they had travelled over long a distance to make a proselyte, having proclaimed the one true God to him, Jesus condemns them for turning him into a son of hell (in fact, a two-fold son of hell). If we follow them, men have the capability to mislead us terribly, even to the loss of our salvation.

We even need to be careful of passages that seem to suggest we should listen to other men alone; that is, apart from, or instead of, scripture. For example, here is a commonly misunderstood passage: "Iron sharpeneth iron; so a man sharpeneth the countenance of his friend" (**Proverbs 27:17**). It is often used in Christian circles today, because of paraphrases, to mean that one man explains the gospel to another or one man reveals truth to another, but that is not the essence of the underlying Hebrew. Countenance (Hebrew *paniym*) means "face." There is nothing in the passage concerning knowledge. It is more akin to encouragement. Yet this is another sound bite that can get us into trouble because we use it to mean that one man instructs another. This does not mean we are not to obey Christ's Great Commission; it does mean we are to teach the gospel and obedience to Christ's commands *through scripture.*

Consider all of the apocalyptic prophecies originating from Christians. Many have tried to state the date and time of Christ's return. Yet God tells us clearly, "But of that day and hour knoweth no man, no, not the angels of heaven, but my Father only" (**Matthew 24:36**). Each and every attempt has failed, yet many keep trying to pin down that day. These false prophets are, in direct opposition to what God says, leading men astray. In recent times, those stating the arrival of Christ on a specific date have led their followers to take all sorts of self-destructive actions. Why? It is because men listen to other men instead of reading scripture. Christ wants us always to "watch" and "be ready," by leading the life of obedience He commanded (e.g., Matthew 24:42–51).

Consider for a moment the teaching in scripture where we have a man of God who was specifically instructed by God (just as we are by God's Word) not to go to a place and eat or drink:

> "Now there dwelt an old prophet in Bethel; and his sons came and told him all the works that the man of God had done that day in Bethel: the words which he had spoken unto the king, them they told also to their father. And their father said unto them, What way went he? For his sons had seen what way the man of God went, which came from Judah. And he said unto his sons, Saddle me the ass. So they saddled him the ass: and he rode thereon, And went after the man of God, and found him sitting under an oak: and he said unto him, Art thou the man of God that camest from Judah? And he said, I am. Then he said unto him, Come home with me, and eat bread. And he said, I may not return with thee, nor go in with thee: neither will I eat bread nor drink water with thee in this place: For it was said to me by the word of the Lord, Thou shalt eat no bread nor drink water there, nor turn again to go by the way that thou camest. He said unto him, I am a prophet also as thou art; and an angel spake unto me by the word of the Lord, saying, Bring him back with thee into thine house, that he may eat bread and drink water. But he lied unto him. So he went back with him, and did eat bread in his house, and drank water" (**1 Kings 13:11–19**).

Here we see another man, claiming to be a prophet of God, telling the true prophet (the man of God who had received direct instruction from God), that the true man of God was to do what God had personally told him not to do. Sound familiar? It sounds like the Modern Church's teaching on baptism, or the lack of need for obedience after coming to Christ; God commands both. Many in the Modern Church say one or both are unnecessary. What happened to the true prophet who did not listen to God, but rather listened to the man who claimed he was a prophet? He was killed by God.

The moral of the story is clear. Listen to God and not to men, especially when they tell us things conflicting with what God tells us. How do we know what conflicts? Through examining scripture and listening to the Holy Spirit. We must not make the assumption that men know more than God does. If the Holy Spirit is in us, don't we trust God to lead us into the truth?

While it is perfectly acceptable to listen to those in the Modern Church deliver messages, they must not be automatically trusted, for they are human with their own motivations. It is we who must verify what they say using the breadth of God's Word and the Holy Spirit (Acts 17:11). We see in scripture that men can lead other men to lose their salvation if they are blindly trust and follow false teachers (Matthew 24:11, Matthew 24:24, Acts 20:29–31, 2 Corinthians 11:13–15, Colossians 2:8, and 2 Peter 2:1, to name just a few). This is the reason for all the warnings to Christians about false prophets, and the reason that Paul cried over a span of three years over his spiritual children (Acts 20:29–31), fearing their salvation would be jeopardized by false teaching.

We must be faithful to examine what is said from the pulpit. There have always been church leaders and false teachers who do not have pure motives. We are responsible for working out our salvation; *the idea that we can simply take on faith what a church leader says is exactly what the evil one desires – our trust in other men instead of in God.* Do we care enough to ensure that we are following our heavenly Father and not just men? Or is it more important to insure your house than your eternal destiny?

Consider for a moment the social gospel. The social gospel focuses on scriptural teachings to focus on the problems of other people – a good idea right? The problem is the social gospel too often ignores foundational priorities set by God. What did Jesus say the most important commandment was?

> "But when the Pharisees had heard that he had put the Sadducees to silence, they were gathered together. Then one of them, which was a lawyer, asked him a question, tempting him, and saying, Master, which is the great commandment in the law? Jesus said unto him, Thou shalt love the Lord thy God with all thy heart, and with all thy soul, and with all thy mind. This is the first and great commandment. And the second is like unto it, Thou shalt love thy neighbour as thyself. On these two commandments hang all the law and the prophets" (**Matthew 23:34–40**).

The social gospel often focuses on the needs of others while downplaying or ignoring the first and greatest commandment to love God above all else. We also see the lack of focus on obedience in much of the Modern Church, in spite of the fact that Jesus drew a specific relationship between love of God and obedience. No obedience, no love: "Jesus answered and said unto him, If a man love me, he will keep my words: and my Father will love him, and we will come unto him, and make our abode with him" (**John 14:23**). Jesus said the same thing in John 14:15 and John 15:10. Indeed, obedience is God's test of our love. So if we claim we love God, but are committed to disobeying Him, we are liars. God reinforced this with, *"He that saith, I know him, and keepeth not his commandments, is a liar,"* and the truth is not in him" (**1 John 2:4**).

We have lots of secular organizations in the world helping other people, some without a clue about who God really is. Let us give them full credit for trying to help others – may God bless them with knowledge of the truth. But the difference between a Christian and a non-Christian is not how much they help others. It is how much they love God; that is the first and greatest commandment. From God's perspective, every good thing comes out of a supreme love for Him.

The difference is that the Christian obeys the first and greatest commandment, while the non-Christian does not. That is the true differentiator. The loving and helping of others is a natural outcome of the Holy Spirit's leading: knowing and loving our God, what He did for us, and how much he loves us. So the social gospel puts the cart before the horse. Once we get our relationship with God right, all else comes into focus.

False Teachers

The Bible is full of warnings about false teachers, which should convince the faithful that men can mislead them. An example is found in Paul's warning to the elders of the church in Ephesus: "For I know this, that after my departing shall grievous wolves enter in among you, not sparing the flock. Also of your own selves shall men arise, speaking perverse things, to draw away disciples after them. *Therefore watch, and remember, that by the space of three years I ceased not to warn every one night and day with tears*" (**Acts 20:29–31**). Paul also told the brothers in Galatians 4:11, that he fears his labor might have been "in vain." Paul was worried that false teachers would lead them away from the true faith.

Paul's tears were because he feared some he led to Jesus Christ would be lost, not that they might just lose out on some reward. Because of his love, he was genuinely concerned for the salvation of those he taught. Paul's reaction, a man full of tears, is that of a man that fears for his spiritual children – that those he loved would be separated from Christ. He did not fear for their physical deaths, knowing that we all die and the faithful who die "in Christ" will go to be with the Lord.

Paul clearly knew that there was the potential that false teachers could lead "his [spiritual] children" away from God and away from salvation. Yet even false teachers cannot separate us from God *unless we let them* by making the choice to embrace their lies. Only if we know scripture can we accurately discern the difference between truthful and errant teachings.

The reason that so many do not worry about false doctrine or false teachers, even though God warns us repeatedly in scripture, is because they believe that no matter what they believe or do, they cannot be lost. This is in stark contrast to what scripture teaches. There are many places where scripture teaches about false teachers and their impact on the faithful, but because so many people believe that a person cannot be lost after accepting Jesus Christ, there is no real reason to worry about false teachers and false prophets. Remember that Paul's warning in Acts 20 is to those who have accepted

> The reason that so many do not worry about false doctrine or false teachers, even though God warns us repeatedly in scripture, is because they believe that no matter what they believe or do, they cannot be lost.

Jesus Christ (the church elders at Ephesus). There is simply no reason for Paul to have this reaction if a believer cannot lose his salvation.

Paul warned Timothy to "Take heed unto thyself, and unto the doctrine; continue in them: for in doing this thou shalt both save thyself, and them that hear thee" (**1 Timothy 4:16**). The word saved (Greek *sozo*) here is the same word used in other passages that describe salvation, including, "And they said, Believe on the Lord Jesus Christ, and thou shalt be saved, and thy house" (**Acts 16:31**) and, "That if thou shalt confess with thy mouth the Lord Jesus, and shalt believe in thine heart that God hath raised him from the dead, thou shalt be saved" (**Romans 10:9**).

Correct doctrine clearly is a salvation-determining issue. Paul warned the Galatians about a different gospel. We know there is a single truth and we know that the Holy Spirit leads us to that single, consistent truth, so what can we conclude about all these doctrinal variations? The only conclusion we can reach is that the divisions in Christ's church, too often caused by false teaching, are not of God but of the evil one in his attempt to draw us away from God and devour us.

Consider what God teaches us about false prophets and their doctrine:

- "Then the Lord said unto me, The prophets prophesy lies in my name: I sent them not, neither have I commanded them, neither spake unto them: they prophesy unto you a false vision and divination, and a thing of nought, and the deceit of their heart" (**Jeremiah 14:14**).
  - Commentary: Shows that people can be misled. Only time with God and His Word can prevent us from being misled. Remember the purpose of prophets in the Old Testament. They didn't just foretell the future, they communicated God's message to the people of Israel (and others). We have His Word and the Holy Spirit to do the same thing.
- "My people are destroyed for lack of knowledge: because thou hast rejected knowledge, I will also reject thee, that thou shalt be no priest to me: seeing thou hast forgotten the law of thy God, I will also forget thy children" (**Hosea 4:6**).
  - Commentary: Reveals that lack of knowledge can destroy God's people. The text indicates that the destruction is

eternal. Our best defense against errant doctrine is an intimate knowledge of God and His Word. It is a natural thing to strive for if we truly do love God first and foremost.
- "Beware of false prophets, which come to you in sheep's clothing, but inwardly they are ravening wolves. Ye shall know them by their fruits. Do men gather grapes of thorns, or figs of thistles? Even so every good tree bringeth forth good fruit; but a corrupt tree bringeth forth evil fruit. A good tree cannot bring forth evil fruit, neither can a corrupt tree bring forth good fruit. Every tree that bringeth not forth good fruit is hewn down, and cast into the fire. Wherefore by their fruits ye shall know them" (**Matthew 7:15–20**).
  - Commentary: Warns of the existence false prophets and indicates how we may be able to recognize them. Perhaps more importantly, what happens to the tree that does not produce good fruit?
- "And many false prophets shall rise, and shall deceive many" (**Matthew 24:11**).
  - Commentary: During the end times, many will be deceived. Why the warning from God if there were no eternal impact? Our salvation is by far the most important thing; it is what Jesus Christ died for.
- "Now I beseech you, brethren, mark them which cause divisions and offences contrary to the doctrine which ye have learned; *and avoid them*" (**Romans 16:17**).
  - Commentary: Warning to avoid those that cause divisions and offenses, which are departures from *true doctrine* which is given to us through the Holy Spirit. It is never unwise to separate over incorrect doctrine, especially if those who are espousing it are unwilling to earnestly contend for the faith themselves.
- "Beware lest any man spoil you through philosophy and vain deceit, *after the tradition of men*, after the rudiments of the world, and not after Christ" (**Colossians 2:8**).
  - Commentary: Warns Christians against following men rooted in tradition and philosophy based on the world.

The word "spoil" indicates potential eternal consequences. Tradition and philosophy plays a central role in many of the world's religions (including some Christian religions). *But we are called to a relationship, not a religion, not tradition, and not worldly philosophies.*

- "Now the *Spirit speaketh expressly, that in the latter times some shall depart from the faith*, giving heed to seducing spirits, and doctrines of devils; Speaking lies in hypocrisy; having their conscience seared with a hot iron" (**1 Timothy 4:1–2**).
  - Commentary: A clear warning that people can be led away from true faith and lose their salvation. What do demons want to do? They want to tear us away from the truth of scripture, the foundation of our faith and our salvation.
- "But evil men and seducers shall wax worse and worse, deceiving, and being deceived" (**2 Timothy 3:13**).
  - Commentary: Note that the evil deceivers become more deceitful, while their followers become more susceptible to being deceived. Mark the fact that God allows people to be deceived largely because they do not love the knowledge of the truth.
- "For the *time will come when they will not endure sound doctrine*; but after their own lusts shall they heap to themselves teachers, having itching ears" (**2 Timothy 4:3**).
  - Commentary: Doesn't this sound a lot like many of today's churches? Preachers proclaim from the pulpits what the congregation wants to hear, instead of the scriptural truths they need. Why? Probably because of fear many in the congregation will leave if given the hard truths of scripture.
- "But there were false prophets also among the people, even as there shall be false teachers among you, who privily shall bring in damnable heresies, even denying the Lord that bought them, and bring upon themselves swift destruction. And many shall follow their pernicious ways; by reason of whom the way of truth shall be evil spoken of. And through covetousness shall they with feigned words make merchandise of you: whose judgment now

of a long time lingereth not, and their damnation slumbereth not" (**2 Peter 2:1–3**).

- ◦ Commentary: This prophecy warns of false prophets who will enter the church and lead many down the broad road to destruction. Both the false prophets and those who follow them are damned.

Unity in the Truth

We have, however, arrived at a time where many would claim that unity is more important than doctrine; that being unified with other men is more important than taking a stand for God. The first century church chose truth over unification. Paul confronted Peter about his errant actions. Scripture tells us explicitly that doctrine is important to maintaining our salvation.

If we start believing untrue things in order to achieve unity, are we really remaining in the faith? Scripture would seem to indicate otherwise. Why the dire warnings about false teachers and their "not sparing the flock?" A foundational question is: can we arrive at the correct doctrine? We can, but it takes prayer, the a close examination of the Word of God, and the leading of the Holy Spirit, not simply listening to other men and automatically accepting what they say. If we have to make a choice between following the truth of God and following men, there is no question where our loyalties should lie.

Many evangelical church leaders refuse to unify with other denominations because of their errant doctrine. This is generally a good thing. Combining churches with differing doctrines results in even greater doctrinal conflicts. Yet those same church leaders often insist upon their congregations being unified in acceptance of their teachings, regardless of how errant their teachings are. I [Gregg] have been in churches where church leaders have claimed that failure to unify is a sin, while scripture warns us to separate from false teachers. Church leaders make the errant (and arrogant) assumption that everything that comes from them is a faithful representation of the Word of God. Not always true. The division in Christianity testifies to this, and so does the state of much of the Modern Church.

What is the problem? These church leaders are talking about unifying to them and their teachings, not to the truth as Jesus commanded. They are not talking about unifying with other brothers and sisters, but only with those they shepherd. They are talking about unifying to their own churches, not necessarily Christ's church. Anytime a church leader tries to convince us that not unifying with his church is a sin, we should consider it a warning sign. This is more typical of a church leader building a cult than of the church leader helping to cultivate a relationship between a believer and God.

If there were a single set of doctrines that all embraced, unity would be easier to achieve. In reality there is a single set of correct doctrines; it's just that all men don't know those doctrines and hence the divisions. We must acknowledge that as men, we have our sinful nature to contend with. But we each will be held accountable to the Word of God. To this end it should motivate us to spend the time with God and His Word. If correct doctrine is the foundation of unity, most other things take care of themselves.

Even attempts to unify believers under the philosophy of "major in the majors" and "minor in the minors" are dangerous. It is simply a way of saying that all that God has to say is not equally important. It is one of the ways in which we get differing doctrines. Yet even some of the most basic of scriptural foundations are under attack by the Modern Church. We as men have trouble even determining what the majors and the minors really are. For example the doctrine of Once Saved, Always Saved (because of the frequent number of references, we will hereafter refer to the doctrine as **OSAS**) is often considered a minor issue, yet the doctrine is at the heart of a person's salvation.

We understand the idea of unity and the disappointment when there are those that leave a body of believers because we have both led Bible studies for many years. We are always disappointed when someone leaves the study, yet we try very hard to remember our purpose. It is to help the people in the study know God better and get closer to Him, without us being in the way. We don't ask that people remain in our studies, knowing that in reality that the study is there for God's glory and for them, and ultimately they still have free will. God may lead people to the study or may lead them away from it. Or their flesh may lead them away. Either way, we try to make an honest effort not to make it about us, but Him. We don't want their loyalty; we only seek to strengthen their loyalty to God. *The same should be true of any faithful church leader.* They are not there for us to follow them; they are to be there to help us get closer to God.

Sometimes men want to follow other men because the teachings of these other men make it easy to be a Christian. For example, we never see Christ trivialize sin; in fact we see the opposite. However, this is exactly what some in the Modern Church do. It is always easier to appease men's consciences than tell them the truth. It keeps them coming back. If they were told the truth, many may simply leave the congregation. It is easier to attract and keep people in a church when human doctrines are used (either purposefully or inadvertently) to mislead people in order to appease their consciences, even though the truth of scripture is only partially represented.

This is the same problem the Israelites had. They wanted a king like every other nation. They wanted to follow a man instead of God. So they asked God for a king but this did not work out well from that point forward. I [Gregg] asked a Rabbi friend of mine whether Israel as a country acknowledges that it was a mistake to ask God for a human king. A resounding "yes" was the answer. They can now look back and see what the insistence on leaning on men, in this case Saul, produced.

We as human beings must escape the trap of blindly following other men. We cannot truly discern the hearts of other men; only our God can. We may see evidence that a person is a true follower of God, but we have seen over and over again that those that seem to be following Christ have committed horrible acts. We may have some evidence of the condition of their hearts, but their hearts, like ours, can be desperately wicked. Our best defense against errant doctrine is to know the Word of God as led by the Holy Spirit.

This is not designed to be a condemnation of all in the Modern Church – far from it. Jesus developed His church here on earth and He established the structure and roles. As such, God does use men and women to do His will, and part of that will is shepherding others. Indeed, there are some great men and women who have served our Lord over the years. In fact, the entire Bible is full of God using men and women. This is not in question.

But here is the critical observation. Just because a person carries a title or role in a church does not mean they are led of God. We cannot assume that because an individual carries a title or leads a church, he is being faithful or even truthful. Sometimes church leaders will tell us that God put them there. Did God put the Imams in place? Did God put the false teachers in place? Our God allows many men throughout the world to rise to power and deceive many to destruction. It happens outside of Christianity and it happens inside of Christianity. We are responsible for our own salvation, and God has told us how to avoid them.

We are warned about false prophets. Church leaders are subject to the same weakness of the flesh we all are. They may or may not be diligent and they may or may not have an upright heart. Just as we see in Revelation 2 and 3, the fact that a church claims to be part of Christ's church does not mean that they act like it. The human ego can submit to the devil faster than any other part of our being. We see it in our churches and in our society.

Look at all the evil Israelite kings in scripture and how often God called out a faithful remnant because most of the Israelites had abandoned Him or done evil in His sight. People were being led into evil. We are also reminded of the time in Israel when there was no king and God assessed what was happening in Israel: "In those days there was no king in Israel, but every man did that which was right in his own eyes" (**Judges 17:6**). This happens when we take our focus off our God; it happens today.

Remember that Jesus confronted the Pharisees (the religious leaders of the day) when He told them "Woe unto you, scribes and Pharisees, hypocrites! *for ye compass sea and land to make one proselyte, and when he is made, ye make him twofold more the child of hell than yourselves*" (**Matthew 23:15**). Jesus said they were literally creating children of hell. In today's day and age, we hear church leaders claiming that their leadership is confirmed by God, all the while teaching inaccurate doctrine.

Therefore, it can be a critical mistake to blindly outsource our salvation to a church leader. Even those in the Modern Church who seem like they may have the right heart, may not. The only true test for a church leader is his alignment with the Word of God.

The Source of Truth

Many Christians today neither read the Word of God regularly nor spend time validating what is taught from the pulpit. Our sinful nature can be so insidious. When we read what other men write and say, we can be led to believe the untrue. Why? Because half-truths spoken or written may allow us to engage our flesh; we want to have heaven and everything in this world as well. This is especially true in America where our culture routinely intersects or conflicts with our relationship with God. We are surrounded by such incredible prosperity that we tend to read scripture and interpret it through the lens of our culture. How dangerous!

Following other men makes it easier to be a Christian, because instead of reading the Bible, we outsource our pursuit of the truth to other people. But we don't see the heart of these other people. More importantly, it means we avoid doing the things that draw us closer to God. Through sheer laziness or a failure to prioritize their relationship with Him, most American Christians do not study scripture or spend time with God, in direct disobedience to His command to seek the truth through the Word of God and the Holy Spirit.

I [Gregg] read an interesting exchange on a website where an agnostic's question about Mark 16:16 was answered by a Christian organization. How did it answer? It started by quoting F.W. Farrar, a canon of the Anglican Church, in giving the answer. The answer used human references to minimize what scripture actually says.

This is a common problem in today's Modern Church. Do we believe that scripture is insufficient? Do we believe God, who told us that the Holy Spirit will lead us into truth? What did God tell us about boasting about human leaders? "So then, no more boasting about human leaders!" (**1 Corinthians 3:21**). We must follow God, not men. We cannot be lazy with our salvation, that is, our eternity, and listening only to men without validating what they say by confirming it in scripture is the epitome of laziness, and has the potential to put our eternity in jeopardy.

If men would spend time earnestly seeking the truth through God's Word and praying for understanding, the Holy Spirit would lead all committed believers seeking the truth into a single truth. The Holy Spirit does not lead some men into one truth and other men into a different truth on the same topic. There is one truth about a given doctrinal matter. Period. Our God is not a God of division, disorder or confusion. So when we look at the historical figures of the Reformation and other periods, we can come to only one conclusion: some were not led by the Holy Spirit in the doctrine they taught, for not all agreed on a single truth, even on some very basic doctrinal issues.

Even worse, many of our leaders, under the banner of grace, think that it is okay that men believe in all sorts of different doctrines. Some of the discussions with church leaders would scare most sincere Christians. They willingly accept the concept of differing and diverse truths. But it should not be so. Truth is of critical importance in what we teach to others. Accepting different and diverse truths only leads to confusion. It reinforces errant doctrine, which causes men to stumble. Finally, it is the foundation of accepting all other lies; once a person starts to accept multiple truths, it is a very short step to no truth.

Some of the most radical and ungodly doctrines have arisen out of the work and words of men, and yet men continue to study other men rather than the Word of God. Is God divided? No! God is unified and His Word stands. While the wisdom of God is manifold, it does not reveal itself in conflicting truths, especially on matters of doctrine.

Who did David, the man after God's heart go to for truth? The Levites? No, he went to God. As Jesus said, "But the hour cometh, and now is, when the true worshippers shall worship the Father in spirit and in truth: for the Father seeketh such to worship him. God is a Spirit: and they that worship him must worship him in spirit and in truth" (**John 4:23–24**). When we are committed to the truth, through frequent study of His Word and prayer, He will be faithful and reveal the truth to us.

One of the saddest things that we often see in the offices of church leaders is a library of books written by various theological experts," often containing conflicting information. In short, we are so obsessed with listening to other men (and women) that we forget to go to the real source of the truth. If we really believe Jesus Christ when He said, *"Howbeit when he, the Spirit of truth, is come, he will guide you into all truth: for he shall not speak of himself; but whatsoever he shall hear, that shall he speak: and he will shew you things to come"* (**John 16:13**), why would we not go to the Spirit as the source of truth? Do we believe God? Do we believe that God will show us the things that are important through the Holy Spirit? It is the reason (although this is just another book) that we see the need for Christians to go to God's Word regularly, and to consider it the final authority on all spiritual truth.

"But the anointing [of the Holy Spirit] which ye have received of him abideth in you, and ye need not that any man teach you: but as the same anointing [the Holy Spirit] teacheth you of all things, and is truth, and is no lie, and even as it hath taught you, ye shall abide in him" (**1 John 2:27**). A

similar teaching exists in John 16:13. This is the same reason that Jesus himself taught us, "But be not ye called Rabbi: for one is your Master, even Christ; and all ye are brethren" (**Matthew 23:8**). For those with a genuine faith, we have the Holy Spirit which will convict us of the truth as we read scripture.

Elihu, in his discourse with Job, understood that true understanding comes from God. He told Job: "But it is the spirit in a person, the breath of the Almighty, that gives them understanding" (**Job 32:8**). Who did David look to for truth? We see David ask God to "Lead me in thy truth, and teach me: for thou art the God of my salvation; on thee do I wait all the day" (**Psalm 25:5**). The theme is repeated over and over; God (through His Spirit) is the source of our understanding. It is the reason we are so often warned about false teachers in the Old and New Testament (Jeremiah 23:16, 2 Timothy 4:3–4 and Matthew 7:15–20).

In fact, this issue calls into question the whole Modern Church model. If we spent the time to investigate everything said from the pulpit, that would be fine, but the problem is we usually don't. We are not focusing enough on the true source of truth, which is God. But this is our responsibility (2 Timothy 2:15). It is the reason that the men of the past put their hope for understanding in God and not in men.

In churches we have attended, we often hear things from the pulpit that came from other men and not scripture. This happens routinely. When Bible studies are conducted where is the first place that men often go? To the Bible? Not always. Often they go to a Bible Study Guide. Is this wrong? Not necessarily, but it places a further burden on the reader to verify from scripture if what is written is true.

Some of the Bible Study Guides we have seen which cover certain books of the Bible do exactly what the Catholic Church tends to do. They eliminate pieces of scripture which may either cause confusion, are divisive, or which do not support a doctrinal position they hold. This approach to studying scripture is highly indicative of a religion, not a relationship. Some religious leaders have determined that nominal Christians are unable to figure out what God is trying to teach them, even though they have the Holy Spirit available to them.

Doctrinal orthodoxy at times appears to be built on biblical sound bites or on ideas people want to be true, rather than the full truth of scripture. These approaches of arriving at "the truth" are doomed to fail because they are based on human ideas, concepts and reasoning (Proverbs 3:5), rather than on the full counsel of God. All scripture is true; not just the parts that we want to be true to support a given orthodoxy. All scripture is true, even if we cannot discern all concepts initially.

While there can be value in having additional knowledge available when reading the Bible (*e.g.*, Study Bible footnotes), God will give us all the understanding we need to love and serve Him. He will convict us of the truths and the lies. Our primary need is a relationship with Christ, not just a relationship with a church. This is a great failing. We have seen some significant evils come out of a relationship with the church or a church leader instead of a relationship with Christ. A true relationship with Christ naturally results in wanting to spend time with Christ, and the best ways to spend time with Christ are in studying God's Word and in prayer. Both of these will lead us to truth.

The Most Important Step We Can Take
If there is only one thing to take from this entire book, please let it be this.

> Please spend increasing amounts of time with God in His Word and in prayer, asking for wisdom and understanding of His Word. Seek to earnestly listen to the Holy Spirit. Nothing will bring you closer to God and give you a better understanding of the truth.
>
> This should be your primary source of truth, for God will NOT mislead those earnestly seeking the truth, whereas men may.

This is natural for those who prioritize God in their life. Spend the time to really get to know the Lord through study of scripture. This is the only way that a person can discern the truth of what is preached. We should all be willing to take the time to reconcile apparent scriptural conflicts through prayer.

Remember that God will send a powerful delusion to those not committed to the truth:

> "And with all deceivableness of unrighteousness in them that perish; *because they received not the love of the truth*, that they might be saved. And for this cause God shall send them strong delusion, that they should believe a lie: That they all might be damned who believed not the truth, but had pleasure in unrighteousness" **(Thessalonians 2:10–12)**.

While written about unbelievers, this would also apply to those who claim to believe but live a lifestyle opposed to God. They are hypocrites and their destiny is the same as unbelievers. Not all who name Christ as Lord will be saved as demonstrated in Matthew 7:21.

Christians sometimes talk about the fact they cannot understand scripture. But God has promised that His Holy Spirit will reveal the truth to His followers (John 16:13, quoted above). If we are committed to His truth and will put in the time with Him in His Word and in prayer, He will give us insight, He will give us understanding, He will give us truth. This is part of what trusting in God looks like. We should trust Him, rather than trust in other men or our own understanding.

When we have challenges in understanding, we must remember that it is the Holy Spirit that leads us into all truth; not ourselves, not other men, but God: *"But the Comforter, which is the Holy Ghost, whom the Father will send in my name, he shall teach you all things, and bring all things to your remembrance, whatsoever I have said unto you"* **(John 14:26)**. Believe this. Believers are all commanded to read scripture (2 Timothy 2:15) and earnestly pray to God for understanding His truth (John 16:13), wherever it may lead (putting aside our preconceptions), and then wait on God for that understanding.

The Bereans were called "noble" because they examined scriptures to see if what Paul and Silas said was true: "And the brethren immediately sent away Paul and Silas by night unto Berea: who coming thither went into the synagogue of the Jews. These were more noble than those in Thessalonica, in that they received the word with all readiness of mind, and searched the scriptures daily, whether those things were so" (**Acts 17:10–11**).

We are to do the same – earnestly test everything said from the pulpit against scripture. Make time to do this. We must not outsource out salvation to other individuals by default, no matter how much we trust them and their theology. Even the most committed preacher or teacher can have a mistaken view of a passage of scripture, or say something in a way that can be misunderstood. Furthermore, with the world full of false teachers, and that number likely to grow as we get closer to our Lord's coming, we must be especially vigilant.

A final word on false teachers is in order. False teachers have no ability themselves to separate us from Christ *unless we decide to follow their false teachings*. To follow their false teachings without testing what they say against scripture can only put us at risk. But false teachers and prophets, *if we allow them*, have the ability to lead us away from God. False prophets are misled by the evil one, whether they recognize it or not. God has devoted a number of verses in His Word to warn us about such people. Remember, God holds us all responsible for studying His Word to ascertain His truth. (2 Timothy 2:15).

Let us all spend more time in scripture daily, putting aside our preconceptions and praying to the Holy Spirit for guidance and understanding. It is amazing what God has revealed to us (Gregg and Ed) when we spend time in His word. There is little doubt that if believers will stop listening *exclusively* to church leaders and spend more time in God's Word, He will, through His Holy Spirit, reveal the truth of scripture to all who earnestly seek it. If you put aside your preconceptions and honestly, prayerfully seek the truth, you will find that, over time, your understanding of scripture will conflict with some of your previous doctrinal beliefs and some of the doctrines being taught by many of the Modern Church leaders.

Key Thoughts

It is clear that God warns us to be watchful because many false prophets will arise and mislead many (Matthew 24:11). Some of these are in churches and some are on radio and television, in books and other places. Believers need to be both aware of and avoid false prophets and false teachers. All preaching and teaching should be tested against the Word of God. If we are committed to truth and seek His truth, God will reveal the truth to us through His Spirit. Men are not guaranteed to be a credible source of authority that should be automatically trusted. When we follow men and not Christ, we are committing the cardinal sin – placing our faith in other men instead of God.

Jesus specifically identified who leads us into truth – the Holy Spirit (John 16:13). We cannot blindly trust the leaders in our local church (or anyone else) to tell us the truth; we must rely on God. No church leader will be able to save us or pay for our sins. It is God that leads us in all righteousness. Furthermore, God is not a respecter of persons; biblical truth that He will reveal to us, He will reveal to you, and biblical truth He will reveal to you, He will reveal to us. That is if we are committed to the truth and we earnestly seek it. For God desires us to have the wisdom to recognize errant doctrine from true doctrine, and to be unified in the truth.

Remember what the Lord God told the Israelites.

> "Hear, O Israel: The Lord our God is one Lord: And thou shalt love the Lord thy God with all thine heart, and with all thy soul, and with all thy might. And these words, which I command thee this day, shall be in thine heart: And thou shalt teach them diligently unto thy children, and shalt talk of them when thou sittest in thine house, and when thou walkest by the way, and when thou liest down, and when thou risest up. And thou shalt bind them for a sign upon thine hand, and they shall be as frontlets between thine eyes. And thou shalt write them upon the posts of thy house, and on thy gates" (**Deuteronomy 6: 4–9**).

Knowing what God says is the primary defense against misguided men and against errant, new age, and evolving doctrine. Remember that divided and conflicting doctrine has been evolving over hundreds of years.

The Holy Spirit is all we need and He will lead us into the truth if we are committed to the truth and spend the time with God seeking His truth.

Once again, the single greatest piece of advice we can give any true follower of Jesus Christ:

> Please spend increasing amounts of time with God in His Word and in prayer, asking for wisdom and understanding of His Word. Seek to earnestly listen to the Holy Spirit. Nothing will bring you closer to God and give you a better understanding of the truth.
>
> This should be your primary source of truth, for God will NOT mislead those earnestly seeking the truth, whereas men may.

Chapter 4

The Law

Misleading Christian sound bite(s): We are not under the law.

You have probably heard it said from the pulpit that we are not under the law. While this is stated explicitly, "For sin shall not have dominion over you: for ye are not under the law, but under grace" (**Romans 6:14**), we need look at the full teaching of God's Word to understand what this really means.

We don't interpret this to mean that it is okay to murder or steal because we are not under the law. We don't believe that abortions are okay, whether we are undergoing the procedure or supporting those that embrace such sin. Few in the Modern Church would teach such. These violate the 10 original commandments as given as well as the two greatest commandments given by Jesus which summarize the law and the prophets.

What is the Law?

There are multiple parts to the law. In total there are 613 mitzvah which have been extracted from the Old Testament. There are 365 positive mitzvah (think "thou shalt") and 248 negative mitzvah (think "thou shalt not"). There are the ceremonial (*hukkim* or *chuqqah*), moral (*mishpatim*), and civil parts to the law. Christ's coming has freed us from the ceremonial law which Christ fulfilled for all time.

We are also freed from the civil parts of the law which have been set aside as a part of the Old Covenant. No longer do we perform sacrifices to pay for sin. We have a perfect sacrifice that is there for all time. We also have systems of government which serve to address the civil part of the law. There are often earthly punishments in man's law associated with violating many of the commandments. We are now to submit ourselves to the authorities. When we violate the law we may receive the punishment from the authorities who act as God's servants (Romans 13).

The moral part of the law, however, remains in effect because the Holy Spirit leads us to keep the moral law. God inspired Paul to tell the Galatians, *"But if ye be led of the Spirit, ye are not under the law"* (**Galatians 5:18**). This is a conditional statement (note the "if"). Led means we are following where the Holy Spirit leads us. But this is not a dismissal of the law; indeed the Holy Spirit sets an even higher standard. We are now under the law of the spirit.

The Holy Spirit however, does not lead us to sin. So when we are sinning, we are refusing to be led by the Holy Spirit. This does not mean that we are necessarily under judgment of the law. It does mean we are to keep the law of the spirit. The Holy Spirit, if we are indwelt, does not lead us to ignore or violate the moral law for that either offends God or hurts our fellow man. The apostle Paul wrote, *"Do we then make void the law through faith? God forbid: yea, we establish the law"* (**Romans 3:31**). This is the faith which manifests itself in aligned actions. It says *we* establish the law.

Christ did come to fulfill the law. He, unlike the rest of us, kept the law perfectly and so was able to fulfill it. However, just because Christ fulfilled the law and became for us the perfect sacrifice, this does not in any way mean that we are not still led by the Holy Spirit to keep the moral elements of the law.

God never expected us to discard the moral law which helps us fulfill the two greatest commandments. Jesus taught us, when a teacher of the Law came to him and asked "Master, which is the great commandment in the law? Jesus said unto him, Thou shalt love the Lord thy God with all thy heart, and with all thy soul, and with all thy mind. This is the first and great commandment. And the second is like unto it, Thou shalt love thy neighbour as thyself. On these two commandments hang all the law and the prophets" (**Matthew 22:36–39**).

Although we may not be under judgment of the law, we are to follow the moral law which embraces the Ten Commandments and other moral commands. Each of the 10 commandments, save the one to Honor the Sabbath (and this is disputable since the disciples in Acts did keep the Sabbath) are reiterated in the New Testament. Many times we are taught to keep God's commandments. God inspired John to write, "For this is the love of God, that we keep his commandments: and his commandments are not grievous" (**1 John 5:3**).

Walking with the Spirit and the Law

But there is more to the story than the law. The Holy Spirit leads us to fulfill not just the letter of the law, but also the spirit of the law. The spirit of the law in which the Holy Spirit leads us is a much higher standard than the written law. As such, we should in no way believe that we are immune from the moral law or that it does not apply to us. When we yield to the Holy Spirit, we keep the law. Failing to keep this part of the law is equivalent to rejecting or grieving the Holy Spirit. Our freedom in Christ is not freedom to violate the moral law. Paul made this very clear in Romans 6. Consider the following verses of that chapter:

> The Holy Spirit leads us to fulfill not just the letter of the law but also the spirit of the law.

> "What shall we say then? Shall we continue in sin, that grace may abound? God forbid. How shall we, that are dead to sin, live any longer therein?" [**v1–2**], "For sin shall not have dominion over you: for ye are not under the law, but under grace. What then? shall we sin, because we are not under the law, but under grace? God forbid. Know ye not, that to whom ye yield yourselves servants to obey, his servants ye are to whom ye obey; whether of sin unto death, or of obedience unto righteousness?" [**v14–16**], "Being then made free from sin, ye became the servants of righteousness." [**v18**], and "But now being made free from sin, and become servants to God, ye have your fruit unto holiness, and the end everlasting life." [**v22**]

We are never to trivialize or minimize sin, especially willful sin: "Keep back thy servant also from presumptuous sins; let them not have dominion over me: then shall I be upright, and I shall be innocent from the great transgression" (**Psalm 19:13**). There are those who would say that rejecting the Holy Spirit and where He leads is the unforgivable sin.

When Jesus taught his disciples, He emphasized the law of the spirit (analogous to the spirit of the Law) which is an expansion of the written law. He did not in any way minimize or abrogate the written law, but in fact emphasized the necessity of obeying the (inward) spirit of the law, and not just the (outward) letter of the law. "Ye have heard that it was said by them of old time, Thou shalt not commit adultery: But I say unto you, That whosoever looketh on a woman to lust after her hath committed adultery with her already in his heart" (**Matthew 5:27–28**). Jesus started by stating the originally given commandment, and then expanded the letter of the law covering adultery to the spirit of the law covering adultery. This is the standard that the Holy Spirit sets for us.

In the first three chapters of Paul's epistle to the Galatians, Paul condemned those who were starting to depart from the gospel Paul preached (through the incorporation of works as a part of salvation), yet later in the same letter he specifically stated that if they did not reject the deeds of the flesh, they would not inherit the kingdom of heaven (Galatians 5:21). So wouldn't these seem to be in conflict? Not necessarily.

The discriminating issue is how they were led. *We have no fear if we are led by the Holy Spirit.* Also according to Galatians 5:18, we are not under the written law if we are led by (that is following) the Holy Spirit. Why? Because the Holy Spirit leads us to keep the moral law, so those submitting to His will and being led by Him are in no danger of violating the written law as long as their will is submitted to His will.

This is what scripture teaches. The Holy Spirit leads us to keep the moral law because keeping the moral law fulfills the two greatest commandments. Keeping the moral law is also consistent with doing the Father's will (in unity with the leading of the Holy Spirit). We must understand, however, that being *indwelt* by the Holy Spirit is not necessarily being *led* by the Holy Spirit; more on that point later.

Obedience to the Spirit (which includes Obedience to parts of the Law)

Jesus also taught in the great commission to "Go ye therefore, and teach all nations, baptizing them in the name of the Father, and of the Son, and of the Holy Ghost: *Teaching them to observe all things* whatsoever I have commanded you: and, lo, I am with you always, even unto the end of the world. Amen" (**Matthew 28:19–20**). Jesus told His faithful eleven disciples (and by extension, us) to teach others to obey everything that he had commanded them, which included both the moral law and His specific commandments. Jesus himself stated both the letter and the spirit of the law.

A similar teaching is found in Paul's epistle to the church in Rome, "But now we are delivered from the law, that being dead wherein we were held; that we should serve in newness of spirit, and not in the oldness of the letter" (**Romans 7:6**). This passage specifically tells us to serve in the spirit of the law, not the letter of the law. Again the spirit of the law is an expansion of the letter of the law. Jesus affirmed this in Matthew 5 in His well-known Sermon on the Mount.

The right heart before God seeks to do what is right, not just keep the letter of the law. Trying to keep the letter of the law is what the Pharisees were condemned for. Jesus confronted the Pharisees, telling them, "Woe unto you, scribes and Pharisees, hypocrites! for ye pay tithe of mint and anise and cummin, and have omitted the weightier matters of the law, judgment, mercy, and faith: these ought ye to have done, and not to leave the other undone" (**Matthew 23:23**). Jesus was confronting the Pharisees for being guilty of violating the spirit of the law and adhering only to the letter of the law. Even though the commandments do not directly address judgment, mercy and faith, these come through the law of the spirit.

No one can be saved through the law because none of us can fully keep it: "For whosoever shall keep the whole law, and yet offend in one point, he is guilty of all" (**James 2:10**). However, we are to try our best to keep the law of the Spirit. We do this by yielding our will to the Holy Spirit, who leads us to keep that law which embraces the commands of God at both the letter and spiritual level.

So while we are not technically under the written law (and thank God that our salvation does not depend on keeping all the law), we are under the law of the Spirit, which leads us to keep both the letter of the moral law and the spirit of the moral law. By following the Holy Spirit and yielding to His calling, we automatically keep the letter and spirit of the moral law. This is the calling of Jesus, yet we must be careful, because the concept offered in isolation that we are "not under the law" can create confusion.

Hence the moral law remains in place, and if we follow the first and greatest commandment and the second commandment (Matthew 22:36–39) by submitting to the Holy Spirit, we automatically fulfill the moral law, because the moral law addresses our dealings with God and others. There is consistency between where the Holy Spirit leads us and the moral law. Many misinterpret the concept "we are not under law but grace." We are not under the law *if we submit to the Holy Spirit* (Romans 8:1,4–6), who helps us keep the law. Elements of the moral law are restated in the New Testament to Christians with the warning that those who live in rejection of the moral law and thus the Holy Spirit will not enter the kingdom of God (*e.g.,* Romans 6:16 and Galatians 5:18–21).

Obedience

We must realize that the Holy Spirit does not lead us to disobey. When we do disobey we are not walking with the Holy Spirit. In multiple places we are told that those who walk by the Holy Spirit have nothing to fear. Paul, in his letter to the Romans, writes, "There is therefore now no condemnation to them which are in Christ Jesus, who walk not after the flesh, but after the Spirit" (**Romans 8:1**).

This claim of *condemnation-free living applies only to those who are walking according to the Spirit* (which, by the way, is not replicated in some versions of the Bible but a similar teaching exists in Romans 8:4 in almost all versions). Condemnation-free living does not apply to those willfully refusing to walk with the Holy Spirit. It is because the Holy Spirit leads us to do what is right in God's sight. *We* must submit to the Holy Spirit.

Freedom in Christ was never designed to result in our violation of God's moral laws or living in rebellion to the law of the spirit. The freedom granted us in Christ was designed to remove the condemnation all mankind is under before coming to Christ, since no one (except Christ) can keep all the law, and therefore stand condemned before God as slaves to sin (Romans 3:23; 6:14, 16, 18, 23). Additionally, that freedom removed the burden of the other parts of the law such as sacrifices and ceremonies.

But the freedom in Christ was never designed to be an enabler of evil. However, when we are presented with the sound bite "we are not under the law," this can easily be misconstrued to mean that we are free to ignore what God teaches us in the 10 commandments or the other commands of Jesus Christ. Not so. Anyone who believes this is rejecting the leading of the Holy Spirit.

Paul continued his letter to the saints at Rome (Romans 1:7), inspired of God, with this warning, "For if ye live after the flesh, ye shall die: but if ye through the Spirit do mortify the deeds of the body, ye shall live" (**Romans 8:13**). Other warnings in Romans 6 are quoted in the preceding section. Similarly, Paul wrote to the Christians in Galatia, "For he that soweth to his flesh shall of the flesh reap corruption; but he that soweth to the Spirit shall of the Spirit reap life everlasting" (**Galatians 6:8**). *The theme is repeated; walk by the Holy Spirit and we are not under the letter of the law* (Galatians 5:18), *and the reason is clear. The Holy Spirit leads us to keep the moral law and not just the letter of the moral law but the spirit of the moral law as well.*

But woe to those who rationalize that they are allowed to sin because they are not under the law and that somehow freedom in Christ "frees" them to violate the moral law, with no eternal consequences. They are skating on the thin ice of Galatians 5:21 and are rejecting the leading of the Holy Spirit. We should always strive to walk with the Holy Spirit and not grieve the Holy Spirit. Paul draws the distinction between those who have the indwelling of the Holy Spirit and those who walk in the Holy Spirit: "If we live in the Spirit, let us also walk in the Spirit" (**Galatians 5:25**). It is clear from scripture that, just because we may have the indwelling Holy Spirit, it does not mean that we will be led by the Holy Spirit. This is something that many people miss. Scripture tells us that those who are committed to walk in the flesh are at risk.

Walking in the Flesh

So what is walking according to the flesh? There are some indications in Galatians 5:19–21, but it goes far beyond that list. We walk in the flesh any time we disobey God or refuse the Holy Spirit's leading. When we seek our will above God's will (see Matthew 26:39, 42), we are not living in faith; we are trusting in our own reasoning and desires. Walking in the flesh is to prioritize the world and ourselves rather than God. Walking in the flesh is minimizing, justifying and excusing sinful behavior. Walking in the flesh is ignoring the needs of others. Walking in the flesh is idolizing things of this world by placing them ahead of God.

We American Christians are far too often committed to living in the flesh. We all too often ignore the Holy Spirit. Why do we do this? It is because many of us want to eat our cake and have it too. That is, we want to be with God for eternity (and avoid the lake of fire), but we also want to have the worldly pleasures here as well. But what does scripture say? "Ye adulterers and adulteresses, know ye not that the friendship of the world is enmity with God? *whosoever therefore will be a friend of the world is the enemy of God"* (**James 4:4**). We would do well to heed James' admonition.

Key Thoughts

While perhaps semantic in nature, we remain under the moral law of God. The Holy Spirit leads us to live a life following both the letter and spirit of the moral law. However, we are no longer under the civil or ceremonial parts of the law. Those who would claim that one need no longer follow the moral law do not understand where the Holy Spirit leads and risk leading others to oppose the Holy Spirit.

Remember the two greatest commandments Jesus spoke of embody the law and the prophets. But loving the Lord God is first, and throughout the Bible God clearly equates loving him with obeying him. Most of the 10 commandments have, through direct quote or command, have been re-affirmed in the New Testament, most by our Lord Himself. The reaffirmation of our Lord addresses not only the letter of the law, but the spirit of the law. This is what the Holy Spirit leads us to keep and it is this reason that we also keep the law (because the Holy Spirit leads us to). Our focus as followers of Christ must be to listen to the Holy Spirit and follow His law (the law of the Spirit).

However, when we refuse to follow the moral law, we are not walking in the Holy Spirit, but rather grieving the Holy Spirit and searing our conscience. Rejecting or resisting the Holy Spirit on a regular basis after we have accepted Jesus Christ demonstrates a false or compromised faith before the Lord. Those who are not led by the Holy Spirit and are refusing to follow where He leads, are at risk, for they are not doing the

Father's will (Matthew 7:21). Remember that in one of the last books written in the New Testament (long after Jesus' departure) we are taught, "He that saith, I know him, and keepeth not his commandments, is a liar, and the truth is not in him" (**1 John 2:3**). The Holy Spirit leads us to keep the commandments.

While following the moral law as led we are by the Holy Spirit, we demonstrate love and respect for God and His commands as well as exercising love for our fellow man. Those who are walking with the Holy Spirit and are listening to His guidance will know that, and will seek to obey both the letter and spirit of the moral law. Those who are being truly led by the Holy Spirit are doing the Father's will and have no fear of the future.

Chapter 5

Salvation and Eternal Life

Misleading Christian sound bite(s): We are saved when we accept Christ

From the pulpit, we often hear salvation defined as a point in time event that occurs when we accept Jesus Christ. There are a few scriptures that seem to reaffirm this idea, but the overall message of the New Testament is that salvation is a process and the resultant eternal life is something we realize in the future. It is inconsistent with the breadth of scripture to assume that we achieved eternal life at the moment we first received Christ, regardless of what we may have been taught.

When are we Really Saved?
There is no doubt that the process of salvation starts when we accept Jesus Christ by faith, and can start no other way (John 14:6), but scripture tells us that is not the end of the story. This is the reason that the Bible speaks of salvation in different tenses.

There are five key parts to salvation. These are faith, justification, regeneration, sanctification, and glorification. Justification and sanctification are both based on our faith (given by God) in Jesus Christ and what He did for us. Based on the tenses and moods used in scripture, we know that faith is a continuing action: belief (faith) and eternal life are inextricably linked. Like the old song about the horse and carriage, you can't have one without the other.

Saving faith = Salvation   No Saving Faith = No Salvation

Receiving the promises of God is based on the continuing action of faith. There are almost no examples of the aorist tense (that is factual and timeless) being used to describe faith (or belief). Instead, faith is spoken of in the present tense (continuous or ongoing). John 3:16, the best-known salvation verse in the Bible, illustrate the point. The word "believeth" (Greek *pisteuō*) is rendered in the present tense, not the aorist tense. The idea that faith must be ongoing is also anchored by many straightforward passages in English that tell us our faith must endure. Several of those passages are discussed below.

This indicates a problem in Modern Church teaching. God's Word in both Greek tenses and plain language (English) teach us that faith must endure to be effective and that enduring faith produces eternal life, *in the future*. Most will acknowledge that we have free will after we accept Jesus Christ. Although some in the Modern Church acknowledge a person has the free will to give up his faith, many church leaders still teach that even abandoning faith in Christ cannot result in loss of salvation. This directly contradicts what scripture teaches: loss of faith results in loss of the hope of salvation (*e.g.*, 1 Corinthians 15:1–2, Matthew 10:22, Hebrews 6:4–6, and Hebrews 10:38–39, etc.).

But there are significant problems with considering justification as a one-time event with permanency. Remember what justification means; it means being declared righteous. God himself tells us "Little children, let no man deceive you: he that doeth righteousness is righteous, even as he is righteous" (**1 John 3:7**). But we have come to a time where we invalidate this very teaching because we believe that we have no responsibility before God.

There are many straightforward passages which tie justification to the faith God gave us (e.g., Romans 3:28 and Romans 5:1). For example, in Romans 3:28, the verb tense is the present tense. This means that justification is continuous, based on our continuing faith. It is not a one-time event. The problem is English Bible versions often render it in the past tense. We must decide what to do with our faith, not assume it is God's responsibility to maintain it as most Calvinists claim (see Chapter 13, "Calvinism and its Impact on the Modern Church").

We are commanded to "be strong" and "stand fast in the faith." (1 Corinthians 16:13). If God were in total control of our faith, there would be no reason for this command. There are similar commands throughout the New Testament. There are also straightforward passages telling Christians not to sin and warning of the eternal consequences of willful or continual sin. Finally, there are passages that tell us our actions affect our justification. Again this is not because actions save us, but it is because our faith leads us to act. There is a clear relationship scripturally: faith results in works which results in justification. This is what scripture teaches. Hence any teaching which suggests that once we accept Christ we are forever justified, no matter what we do, cannot be scripturally supported.

Scripturally, initial justification does not seem to equal realized salvation. Justification is a requirement for salvation but it does not guarantee salvation. Faith (a true and living faith) is the basis or the foundation of being justified and being justified is a requirement for salvation, but faith may fail. When faith permanently fails, as scripture says it can, so does our justification. So we cannot say that our justification upon first coming to Christ equates to final, permanent salvation.

Remember Jesus prayed in the garden for Peter's faith not to fail even though it did (Luke 22:32) and Peter had to be restored (John 21:15–17). Being justified at one moment in time does not guarantee one's justification will remain intact unto salvation. We, through our God-given free will, can rebel against God and refuse to live faithfully. There are too many descriptions of failed faith in scripture to believe that once one has faith, it is preserved to eternity.

We also read about our works playing a part in justifying us, "But wilt thou know, O vain man, that faith without works is dead? *Was not Abraham our father justified by works*, when he had offered Isaac his son upon the altar? Seest thou how faith wrought with his works, and by works was faith made perfect? And the scripture was fulfilled which saith, Abraham believed God, and it was imputed unto him for righteousness: and he was called the Friend of God. Ye see then how that by *works a man is justified, and not by faith only*" (**James 2:20–24**). The passage clearly teaches that part of the way in which we maintain our justification is through exercising our faith to act in obedience to God's commands, as Abraham did. This also implies that justification cannot be singularly permanent at the acceptance of Christ. Keep in mind that works are *evidence* of our faith; *the basis of salvation remains faith.*

If the commonly adopted definition of justification were correct (justification at one moment in time equals permanent salvation), the full array of scriptural warnings to Christians throughout the New Testament about the eternal consequences of our actions would not be valid. It is one of the biggest mistakes the Modern Church makes. Interpreting all scriptures which plainly define the eternal consequences of not being faithful as being unrelated to salvation is simply not being faithful to God's Word.

How we choose to live our life is as important to God as is our belief in Jesus Christ, because it testifies to the genuineness of our faith. Our justification is primarily by faith but evidentially by works. True faith begets works. What we do with the choices God gives us is critically important. Again, God sees our faith in Jesus Christ not as something done once, but rather a continued belief over a life time (as confirmed by the repeated use of the word belief in the Greek present tense).

To God, the true believer not only believes, but puts that belief into action as led by the Holy Spirit. Do we remain justified if we live in rebellion to God or refuse to act in a manner consistent with our faith? Much of the Modern Church would say "yes." Scripture says otherwise. This occurs because Calvinistic tendencies have crept into their belief system where they see God as responsible for everything. Yet scripture after scripture teaches of man's responsibility, both in the Old and New Testament. Once again, this does not mean man earns his salvation.

If the Modern Church's teaching of "point in time salvation" is correct, many of the teachings of Jesus and the warnings to the churches in the epistles and in the book of Revelation are either lies or deceptions. We know this is inconsistent with the nature of our God and His Word. Indeed, some of the Modern Church doctrines have made God and His Word out to be untruthful.

What does the Bible teach us about willful sinning after accepting Jesus Christ?

> "For if we sin wilfully *after* that we have received the knowledge of the truth, there remaineth no more sacrifice for sins, But a certain fearful looking for of judgment and

fiery indignation, which shall devour the adversaries. He that despised Moses' law died without mercy under two or three witnesses: Of how much sorer punishment, suppose ye, shall he be thought worthy, who hath trodden under foot the Son of God, and hath counted the blood of the covenant, *wherewith he was sanctified*, an unholy thing, and hath done despite unto the Spirit of grace? For we know him that hath said, Vengeance belongeth unto me, I will recompense, saith the Lord. And again, The Lord shall judge his people. It is a fearful thing to fall into the hands of the living God" (**Hebrews 10:26–31**).

The passage itself clearly speaks about a believer: "*he was sanctified.*" Unbelievers are not sanctified. The passage talks specifically about God *judging His people*. If we were fully justified forever at the acceptance of Christ regardless of what we do after that moment, this scripture and others would be untrue. We are reminded that many Christians today are in exactly this place. They accept and embrace all sorts of ungodly beliefs and live in rebellion against God.

This passage warns us that those who willfully sin after accepting Christ are no longer covered by Christ's sacrifice. They are no longer considered righteous (that is, justified). In short, the idea that all future sins have been forgiven at the moment we accept Christ, and hence at that moment we are permanently justified (permanently declared righteous) is clearly refuted in scripture.

Each time we confess our sins and seek forgiveness we maintain our justification because we are living *faithfully*. This is the trustworthy interpretation of 1 John 1:9. Remember we are justified at a point in time when we accept Jesus Christ because *all previous sins* have been forgiven; we have been declared righteous *at that point*. This is consistent with the Greek tenses used in salvation passages and what we find in many other passages as well. The error comes in assuming that the justification is permanent. Our justification stands or falls based on our faith. We know from scripture however faith is not necessarily permanent. For more on this point, see Chapter 11, "Once Saved, Always Saved (OSAS)."

Regeneration occurs when we accept Jesus Christ and we receive the

Holy Spirit, in effect being born spiritually, or "born again" (John 3:3). God gives us the faith to "receive Him" (John 1:12), but He does not force us to receive Christ. He gave us the free will to apply or reject the faith He gave us. Similarly, the Holy Spirit indwells us and will lead us to do His will if we use our free will, to submit to His leading. Alternatively, we can reject His leading and live in rebellion against God.

While the concepts of justification, regeneration, and glorification are pretty well defined, the Modern Church teaches the concept of two types of sanctification: positional and progressive sanctification. This may be because the Greek word translated "sanctification" (being made holy; set apart for God) and the associated Greek verbs are generally stated using the aorist tense (indicating a timeless event). However, there are a couple of cases where the present tense (ongoing action) verb is used. Thus the ideas of two types of sanctification are part of a man made concept; not necessarily scriptural.

The idea presented from many Modern Church pulpits is that we are sanctified in Christ regardless of what we do, based on an act of faith in accepting Christ (positional sanctification). The Modern Church teaches there is also progressive sanctification (growing toward spiritual maturity) in which we play a part. By dividing sanctification into these two forms, the Modern Church can justify its position on OSAS, teaching believers they can reject progressive sanctification and remain saved, because they are permanently sanctified in position only.

Yet the critical issue is this: both justification and sanctification stand on the foundation of our faith in Jesus Christ. Many New Testament passages warn us that our faith is subject to change, and is something we have a part in maintaining. Our faith does come from God, but what we do with it is within our free will. Otherwise there would be no "shipwrecked faith" (1 Timothy 1:19 and 2 Timothy 1:20) for God is not the author of corruption. Shipwreck is destruction. Only something that exists can be destroyed. Many in the Modern Church espouse the concept of being finally justified and finally sanctified at the moment of first belief. However, scripture tells us both are based on our true and living faith which must endure over our lifetime.

God knows who will take the faith He has given them, will accept Jesus Christ and will remain faithful throughout their lives. He knows the future. God can consider these people already justified and sanctified at any point in the past, even "from the foundation of the world" (Revelation 13:8). These are the believers God knows will "endure" and enter the kingdom.

To Him, their salvation can appear as a "done deal." From His perspective, the sanctification of His faithful servants can appear as a one-time event in what we consider the past but which God can state as simply a timeless event. Hence the use of the aorist tense in some verses to refer to sanctification. However, from the human perspective, we are creatures of time, and scripture makes it clear that what the Modern Church calls "progressive sanctification" is a necessary part of the salvation process. To this end, we end up trying to resolve a timeless event (aorist tenses) with an event with ongoing result (perfect tense). Our creation of two types of sanctification is an effort to resolve this verb discrepancy. But it does not necessarily follow that the two are separate logically.

Peter commanded us to be holy through our behavior in 1 Peter 1:14-16; hence we have a part in being holy (sanctified). Paul addresses this as well. Continued obedience to God results in holiness (sanctification), finally producing "everlasting life," but continuing in sin would produce spiritual death:

> "I speak after the manner of men because of the infirmity of your flesh: for as ye have yielded your members servants to uncleanness and to iniquity unto iniquity; even so now yield your members servants to righteousness unto holiness. For when ye were the servants of sin, ye were free from righteousness. What fruit had ye then in those things whereof ye are now ashamed? *for the end of those things is death*. But now being made free from sin, and become servants to God, ye have your fruit unto holiness, *and the end* everlasting life" (**Romans 6:19–22**).

Paul's warning is clear; do not expect to enter the kingdom if you continue to live in disobedience to God (sin). We have been made free from sin. We are further commanded to "Follow peace with all men, and holiness [sanctification], without which no man shall see the Lord" (**Hebrews 12:14**). These are clear warnings. The scriptures are clear: sanctification is a requirement for one to receive eternal life. Therefore, it is not possible for a person to actually have permanent, eternal life at the moment he first comes to Christ. He has entered through the narrow gate; he has the *hope* of eternal life. If, like the thief on the cross, he dies shortly thereafter, and continues to believe in Jesus Christ, he then receives it at death.

Paul wrote of himself, "That I may know him, and the power of his resurrection, and the fellowship of his sufferings, being made conformable unto his death; *If by any means I might attain unto the resurrection of the dead. Not as though I had already attained,* either were already perfect: but I follow after, if that I may apprehend [lay hold of] that for which also I am apprehended of Christ Jesus. Brethren, I count not myself to have apprehended [laid hold of]: but this one thing I do, forgetting those things which are behind, and reaching forth unto those things which are before" (**Philippians 3:10–14**).

Paul knew that when he wrote this, that he had not attained the salvation which the Modern Church often tells us we already have. The Modern Church presents salvation as something fully accomplished. Paul knew he had to continue "reaching forth" for what is ahead. Paul understood that the life we lead is critical to maintaining the faith God has given us, and, at the same time, our faith is demonstrated in the life we lead. We are to keep our focus on the eternal future because it will guide our steps now. Our journey towards eternal life begins on this earth, but is not complete while we are still on this earth; it is what lies ahead.

Here are some other verses indicating that we have not yet received eternal life:

- "And ye shall be hated of all men for my name's sake: but he that endureth to the end shall be saved" (**Matthew 10:22**).
    - Commentary: Note that salvation is future ("shall be") and, consistent with many scriptures, that we must endure to the end to be saved.
- "That if thou shalt confess with thy mouth the Lord Jesus, and shalt believe in thine heart that God hath raised him from the dead, thou shalt be saved. For with the heart man believeth unto righteousness; and with the mouth confession is made unto salvation" (**Romans 10:9–10**).

- Commentary: At first glance, suggests that one is saved once one believes. In reality, this passage addresses the vitally necessary starting point of salvation (entering in through the narrow gate - Matthew 7:13–14) but does not describe the whole process (the narrow way). The verbs "believing" and "confessing" in verse 10 are present tense forms, indicating a continuing action of believing and confessing. They denote a "process of faith" which continues to justify us.
- "And that, knowing the time, that now it is high time to awake out of sleep: for now is our salvation nearer than when we believed" (**Romans 13:11**).
    - Commentary: Paul, writing to believers states our salvation is nearer (indicating it is not already received) and contrasts it with the time we (first) believed, further indicating that our initial belief and our receiving salvation do *not* occur at the same time.
- "For the preaching of the cross is to them that perish foolishness; but unto us which are saved it is the power of God" (**1 Corinthians 1:18**).
    - Commentary: Commentary: This passage in the KJV suggests that those discussed are already saved, but the tense in the Greek here more accurately reflects "being saved," demonstrating a process. More modern versions with paraphrases render this as "being saved" and "are perishing," both referring to an ongoing process.
- "To deliver such an one unto Satan for the destruction of the flesh, that the spirit may be saved in the day of the Lord Jesus" (**1 Corinthians 5:5**).
    - Commentary: Since the day of the Lord Jesus is in the future (as we understand time being linear), the saving of the sinner, if it happens, will occur in the future. Notice also the context; that is the spirit *may* be saved. No guarantee. It is Paul's hope, but with no guarantee, that this person would suffer and return to God.

- "*By which also ye are saved, if ye keep in memory what I preached unto you, unless ye have believed in vain*" (**1 Corinthians 15:2**).
  - Commentary: Suggests that we are saved conditionally because of the word "*if*" which could not be the case if salvation were immediate and irrevocable upon accepting Jesus Christ. This verse tells us that salvation comes later.
- "But let us, who are of the day, be sober, putting on the breastplate of faith and love; and for an helmet, the *hope of salvation*" (**1 Thessalonians 5:8**).
  - Commentary: The *hope* of salvation. Hope is repeatedly spoken of throughout the New Testament. We hope in what is to come; not what we already possess.
- "So Christ was once offered to bear the sins of many; and *unto them that look for him* shall he appear the second time without sin unto salvation" (**Hebrews 9:28**).
  - Commentary: Teaches that Christ will appear a second time and bring salvation *to those looking for Him*. Those looking for Him are those who truly believe at the time He appears. Otherwise, they would no longer be looking. This also shows that salvation is in the future.
- "For ye have need of patience, that, after ye have done the will of God, ye might receive the promise. For yet a little while, and he that shall come will come, and will not tarry. Now the just shall live by faith: but if any man draw back, my soul shall have no pleasure in him. But we are not of them *who draw back unto perdition*; but of them that believe to the saving of the soul" (**Hebrews 10:36–39**).
  - Commentary: Teaches that we will receive the promise by patience and doing the will of God. Patience is required because *we have not already received salvation*. Even though there is a closing encouragement to those who live by faith, but to those who draw back (abandon their faith), we see the result: perdition.

Some of these passages indicate a verb which describes an ongoing event or duration while others speak of a future tense verb. Since we know that God's Word does not contradict itself, we must conclude that salvation is a process with the lynchpin and starting point of our individual salvation being the acceptance of Jesus Christ as Lord and Savior. *Only after God's work, and our lives lived before the Lord is complete, may we consider salvation eternal and irrevocable.* Any attempt to do so before that time is inconsistent with scripture. Only in this manner can all seemingly present and future references to eternal life be reconciled.

When Does Eternal Life Begin?

Many people view eternal life to be given to us when we accept Jesus Christ, and there are some scriptures suggesting that. However, the comprehensive biblical picture suggests that acceptance of Jesus Christ is but the beginning of a process leading to eternal life. Eternal life has a present component and a future component. People hold the view of immediate eternal life even though some passages suggest salvation is a continuing process.

Salvation is a process that produces sanctification through a true and living faith; sanctification results in eternal life: "But now being made free from sin, and become servants to God, ye have your fruit unto holiness, and the end everlasting life" (**Romans 6:22**). Since we, like Paul, have not yet attained eternal life ("the resurrection of the dead" in **Philippians 3:11**), we must also "press toward the mark for the prize" (**Philippians 3:14**).

If even the apostle Paul did not think he had yet attained eternal life, why do Modern Church leaders tell their congregations they already have it and can never lose it? Is this some of the false teaching condemned in scripture? Scripturally, we then can lose our hold on future salvation since we have not yet fully attained it. We stand only by a true faith. We can probably all agree that once we are with Jesus Christ, we are permanently saved. But until we reach that event we have the power, through our God-given free will, to interrupt the process.

Paul underscores this point:

> "And not only they, but ourselves also, which have the firstfruits of the Spirit, even we ourselves groan within ourselves, waiting for the adoption, to wit, the redemption of our body. For we are saved by hope: but hope that is

seen is not hope: for what a man seeth, why doth he yet hope for? But if we hope for that we see not, then do we with patience wait for it" (**Romans 8:23–25**).

Our body has not been redeemed; we wait for it. As with all types of hope, we do not hope in what we already have (as some teach it), but rather we hope in that which is to come. Yet the Modern Church often discounts the scriptural idea of hope and replaces it with certainty and the idea of future salvation and replaces it with past salvation.

Consider the verse, "For by grace are ye saved through faith; and that not of yourselves: it is the gift of God: Not of works, lest any man should boast" (**Ephesians 2:8–9**). Many would say this affirms that we are saved when we accept Jesus Christ. But the tense of the verb "saved" is the present tense in the Greek indicating a continuing action. The takeaway from this verse, when properly understood ("we are being saved"), is that salvation is not yet completed.

Similarly, the Greek tenses in other passages stating the conditions for final salvation always (except one case: Mark 16:16) omit the aorist tense (single timeless act) and instead use the present tense (continuing action). But the one exception, the Mark 16:16 verse, does not even appear in some Bibles, because Bible scholars generally agree that Mark 16:9–20 was not in the earlier, more reliable manuscripts (as late as the fourth century, according to Eusebius and Jerome), but was added later. These passages all indicate that our salvation is a process that is not yet completed.

So when does eternal life really begin? The passages that affirm the giving of the Holy Spirit state that He is given as a deposit or earnest: "Who hath also sealed us, and given the earnest of the Spirit in our hearts" (**2 Corinthians 1:22**). The word earnest (Greek *arrabōn*) means down payment, a pledge of future performance. In most real estate purchases, for example, the buyer and seller both sign a contract in which the buyer promises to buy and the seller promises to sell a certain piece of real estate owned by the seller. Since it takes time for the paperwork to be done (preparation of the deed, etc.), the buyer deposits something of value (usually money) with either the seller or a third party to show he is "in earnest" about his agreement to purchase. This deposit is called "earnest money." It is a pledge given to ensure that he will do what he said he would.

In the same way, Paul wrote, our receipt of the Holy Spirit was an "earnest" (pledge or deposit) to assure us that God would fulfill His promise of eternal life to those who were faithful in keeping their part of the promise.

There is no need for a deposit for something we have already received. It is a down payment on something *we are to receive* (future tense), which is eternal life. God's deposit is an indication of His truthfulness and faithfulness, yet we still have conditions we must meet to receive what He promised. This is true for the direct teachings about eternal life and even those passages which reference transactional semantics: words like "earnest" and "deposit." So the teaching of scripture is that we have not yet received eternal life, but that we have the hope of eternal life. If we are truly faithful we will be receive the promised eternal life in the future.

In the synoptic gospels and the Pauline letters, eternal life is sometimes referred to as a future event and sometimes as a past event and there are many distinctions between this life and eternal life. It would be misleading to refer to eternal life as in the future if we had it permanently from the moment we accepted Christ. Some of these scriptures indicating we receive eternal life in the future include:

- "But he shall receive an hundredfold now in this time, houses, and brethren, and sisters, and mothers, and children, and lands, with persecutions; and in the world to come eternal life" (**Mark 10:30**).
  - Commentary: Note that eternal life is not received until we are "in the world to come."
- "Wherefore if thy hand or thy foot offend thee, cut them off, and cast them from thee: it is better for thee to *enter into life* halt or maimed, rather than having two hands or two feet to be cast into everlasting fire. And if thine eye offend thee, pluck it out, and cast it from thee: it is better for thee to enter into life with one eye, rather than having two eyes to be cast into hell fire" (**Matthew 18:8–9**).
  - Commentary: Entering [eternal] life is a *future activity*. Note that it is contrasted with being thrown into fire which is also a *future event* which only happens after physical death.
- "Who will render to every man according to his deeds: To them *who by patient continuance in well* doing seek for glory and honour

and immortality, *eternal life*: But unto them that are contentious, and do not obey the truth, but obey unrighteousness, indignation and wrath" (**Romans 2:6–8**).
  - Commentary: Eternal life or wrath is rendered to a person *later* on based on their choices (demonstrated faith or continued sin).
- "And not only they, but ourselves also, which have the firstfruits of the Spirit, even we ourselves groan within ourselves, *waiting* for the adoption, to wit, *the redemption of our body*. For we are saved by hope: but hope that is seen is not hope: *for what a man seeth, why doth he yet hope for*? But if we hope for that we see not, then do *we with patience wait for it*" (**Romans 8:23–25**).
  - Commentary: As discussed above, we only *hope* in what we have not yet received.
- "That I may know him, and the power of his resurrection, and the fellowship of his sufferings, being made conformable unto his death; If by any means I might attain unto the resurrection of the dead. *Not as though I had already attained*, either were already perfect: but I follow after, if that I may apprehend that for which also I am apprehended of Christ Jesus." (**Philippians 3:10–12**).
  - Commentary: Paul recognizes that he has not attained that which is ahead (resurrection of the dead - salvation). Indeed, he understands that he is following a path (the narrow way of Matthew 7:14).
- "For bodily exercise profiteth little: but godliness is profitable unto all things, having promise of the life that now is, and *of that which is to come*" (**1 Timothy 4:9**).
  - Commentary: States outright that eternal life is to come. We don't have it yet.
- "Charge them that are rich in this world, that they be not highminded, nor trust in uncertain riches, but in the living God, who giveth us richly all things to enjoy; That they do good, that they be rich in good works, ready to distribute, willing to communicate; Laying up in store for themselves a good foundation against the time to come, that they may lay hold on eternal life" (**1 Timothy 6:17–19**).

- ○ Commentary: Why would they need to "lay hold on eternal life" if they already had it? Note the need for "good works" as a "foundation of the *time to come*."
- "For if Jesus had given them rest, then would he not afterward have spoken of another day. There remaineth therefore a rest to the people of God. For he that is entered into his rest, he also hath ceased from his own works, as God did from his. Let us labour therefore to enter into that rest, lest any man fall after the same example of unbelief" (**Hebrews 4:8–11**).
  - ○ Commentary: Believers are to labor to enter into the rest God promised, but notice that unbelief (not total unbelief in Christ but insufficient belief to obey God's commandments) can prevent a believer from entering God's rest. Entering into "that rest," (eternal life) is clearly described as a *future* event.
- "In hope of eternal life, which God, that cannot lie, promised before the world began" (**Titus 1:2**).
  - ○ Commentary: As seen in 1 Thessalonians 5:8, we see that we have *the hope of salvation*, of eternal life in the future. We do not hope for what we already have.

There are other biblical passages that suggest that the life we currently live is not eternal life. We all take for granted that there is nothing eternal about our current bodies, and we will eventually have glorified bodies. Indeed, we live in a world of decay and destruction. Paul tells those in the Galatian church, *"For he that soweth to his flesh shall of the flesh reap corruption; but he that soweth to the Spirit shall of the Spirit reap life everlasting"* (**Galatians 6:8**).

This clearly demonstrates that those decisions we make here, namely whether to sow to the Spirit or to sow to the flesh, determine what *we will reap* in the future (future tense). Eternal life is to be reaped in the future. The very metaphor of sowing and reaping suggest a difference in time between the work of planting and harvesting. If our decisions here and now make no difference, then why is this passage here?

Paul, speaking of God, wrote, *"Who will render to every man according to his deeds: To them who by patient continuance in well doing seek for glory and honour and immortality, eternal life: But unto them that are contentious, and do not obey the truth, but obey unrighteousness, indignation and wrath*" (**Romans 2:6–8**). Again, we see eternal life as being received at a future time, and further making the point that patient continuance is required. This is yet another passage proclaiming that our decisions after coming to Christ affect our eternal destiny, which will be determined in the future.

All of these passages suggest that eternal life is a future event. However, there are other passages, mostly in the writings of John, which seem to indicate that the nature of eternal life begins when we accept Jesus Christ. Such passages include, "And this is life eternal, that they might know thee the only true God, and Jesus Christ, whom thou hast sent" (**John 17:3**) and, "Verily, verily, I say unto you, He that heareth my word, and believeth on him that sent me, hath everlasting life, and shall not come into condemnation; but is passed from death unto life" (**John 5:24**). Once again, "believeth" is the translation of a Greek word in the present tense, indicating a continuing action, which could be translated "continues believing."

The use of the Greek present tense (continuing action) tell us that the references in John suggest that for those who remain faithful, true saving faith leads to eternal life. The key phrase, as in so many of such passages is belief (or faith). If we truly believe then we will live a life that will result in our goal of eternal life, as more fully discussed in Chapter 16, "Saving Faith." The point here is that eternal life is the result of *continued* faith, which is not complete until our life here is finished. Just because a person comes faithfully to Jesus Christ and is justified and saved does not mean they will remain saved.

Those who accept Jesus Christ and live a life consistent with the claimed faith, doing the Father's will, have indeed taken hold of eternal life now which will be fully manifest at a later time. *However, those who accept Jesus Christ and then are committed to live a life inconsistent with that faith will not continue on the path to eternal life and will not receive the promise of eternal life because they did not keep the promise with a true and saving faith.* However, it appears to the authors that the overwhelming weight of scripture indicates eternal life is something we receive in the future, at the end of this life.

Enduring in the Faith

We are responsible for enduring in the faith as long as we are in this life (Matthew 10:22 and Philippians 3:7–14). If we submit our will to the Holy Spirit, He will guide us "into all truth," which will keep us in the faith and doing His will (John 14:6 and Matthew 7:21). However, our God-granted free will allows us to interrupt sanctification by refusing to be led by the Holy Spirit. There are many passages written to Christians commanding *us* to do or not do something. Many are written with specifically stated salvation-based implications. But even when there are no specifically stated conditions, there are often unstated conditions, as the Israelites found out the hard way.

Many today teach that *God* is solely responsible for us enduring, citing passages like Philippians 1:6. Yet a major theme of the Bible, if not *the* major theme, is God guiding (through His Word and the Holy Spirit) man to live a life that is pleasing to God. How many times has God, throughout the Bible, lifted men up for their righteous decisions (obedience to God's commands) and punished them for their unrighteous decisions (disobedience and sin)? We must endure: "Let us hold fast the profession of our faith without wavering; (for he is faithful that promised)" (**Hebrews 11:23**). "Cast not away therefore your confidence, which hath great recompence of reward. For *ye have need of patience*, that, *after ye have done the will of God*, ye might receive the promise (**Hebrews 10:35–36**). This clearly states that after "*ye* have done the will of God" that "*ye* might receive the promise." We must submit to the Holy Spirit, as we are called to do. Only then can we do the will of God (John 15:5).

Make no mistake however, God is there to help. He helped Peter and he will help us. That is the reason for the Holy Spirit who "teaches us all things" and assists us in living holy lives until the coming of our Lord. We must never minimize the significance of God's part in our salvation. He loves us and desires us to be united with Him, but it is also erroneous to believe we have no part in our own salvation. This does not mean we save ourselves. Many theologians

> We must never minimize the significance of God's part in our salvation. He loves us and wants us to be united with Him, but it is also erroneous to believe we have no part in our salvation. This does not mean we save ourselves.

can only see the binary here – that we either save ourselves or God saves us. This is a false dichotomy.

But the truth is more subtle. It can be literally damning that people are taught they have no part in their own salvation. It is not consistent with scripture, nor does it lead to good outcomes, because we still retain our sinful nature and worldly focus. We may be given a gift, but God has allowed us to choose what to do with that gift. We still have our free will, which we can use to obey God or to rebel against Him. We must remain faithful and endure in the faith, following the leading of the Holy Spirit.

When we are faithful, *we allow God to do His work through us* (John 15:5). *We do this by submitting our will to His will.* That is the part we play in our salvation. This is the natural outcome of having a true faith instead of a shallow, intellectual faith. Once we submit our will to the Holy Spirit's lead, God does His work through us. The only part we play in our salvation is submitting to His call by receiving Christ (John 1:12), and thereafter doing His will by submitting to the Holy Spirit, who will do God's will *through us*. He does the work, if we submit in obedience to His lead. But God will not force us; He wants us to choose Him and demonstrate that faith with obedience (John 15:10).

God is the initiator; we are the respondents. This is true before we know Christ and after we accept Christ. God calls us, giving the faith to accept Jesus Christ, but we must respond. Once we have accepted Jesus Christ, we must then submit to the Holy Spirit. These are who God calls the true sons (Romans 8:13). God will lead us, but through our free will, we may either submit to the Holy Spirit or reject the Holy Spirit. If we try our best to walk the path marked out for us, yielding to the Holy Spirit, we have no fear of what the future holds. This is the meaning of the good conscience towards God which Paul talked about: "And herein do I exercise myself, to have always a conscience void of offence toward God, and toward men" (**Acts 24:16**).

Key Thoughts

Salvation is not simply a point in time event which in fully achieved with our acceptance of Jesus Christ. That moment is, however, the beginning of the process. Salvation is a journey in which we have the ultimate guide (God), but we must make the journey which Jesus described as, "narrow is the way" (**Matthew 7:14**). It is a process in which we must be a willing participant. This does not mean that we save ourselves. We could do nothing without Christ (John 15:5). God will bear fruit through us if we let Him.

However, we must continue to remain faithful (endure) to the one who has called us, and seek to follow Him, walking with and being led by the Holy Spirit. We have it within our free will, as granted by God, to lose our justification and sanctification by losing our faith (or living in sin). Both of these stand on the foundation of our faith. We see places in the Bible where the faith of believers is compromised, dead, placed on other things, lost, and shipwrecked.

Eternal life does not begin in this life according to scripture. Whether we receive eternal life is partially dependent on our decisions in this life, most notably to endure and to walk with the Holy Spirit, because He leads us to do the Father's will. We know from scripture that Paul did not consider himself to have achieved his objective and so he strived (acted faithfully) to attain that which was in front of him. Although Christ gives us eternal life, that life is a future event, not simply a *fait accompli*, something already achieved when we accept Christ.

Understanding the nature of eternal life and its timing also helps us to understand other doctrines which we will discuss in future chapters.

Chapter 6

Faith and Works

Misleading Christian sound bite(s): Salvation is by faith alone, through God's grace. What we do or say (or fail to do or say) after coming to Christ is irrelevant. Works are irrelevant to salvation.

This is one of the most challenging and misunderstood of all modern teachings. Over-simplification of the doctrine of salvation by grace can cause misunderstandings and inadvertent rebellion against God. While there is no question that salvation is by grace through faith, we in the Modern Church have incorrectly developed the notion that it is possible to believe in something and then live in contradiction of that stated belief, with no eternal consequences. The Bible does not teach this.

True Faith

True Christians make an attempt to maintain and live their faith. Not once, but every day. Does this mean they are perfect? No, however their goal is to please their master and not rebel against, disobey, or ignore His teachings. This is the single most important factor we use when determining if an individual has a heart for God. For example, if a church leader spends a lot of time telling people they need not obey God, need not to deny themselves, and need not put God first, we immediately suspect that the church leader may be more about his church, garnering followers, and pleasing men than about pleasing God.

The sound bite "by faith alone" gets us in trouble. Men have taken the scriptural concept to an extreme where it was never meant to go, and in doing so created all sorts of other scriptural conflicts. This was probably an overreaction to earlier (pre-reformation) church teachings which focused on works, *but both deny the balance of scripture.* The Modern Church largely preaches an intellectual faith. This is a faith often devoid of demonstration through obedience. As a result, we have all sorts of people with dead or compromised faith in our midst. Scripture teaches the opposite; that demonstrated faith is true and saving faith.

The theme of the need for demonstrated faith repeats itself over and over in scripture. We Christians are warned directly about the adverse eternal consequences of what the Modern Church teaches: "Not every one that saith unto me, Lord, Lord, shall enter into the kingdom of heaven; but he that doeth the will of my Father which is in heaven [will enter]" (**Matthew 7:21**) and "And why call ye me, Lord, Lord, and do not the things which I say?" (**Luke 6:46**).

In a related passage, Jesus told His faithful eleven disciples, "I am the true vine, and my Father is the husbandman. Every *branch in me* that beareth not fruit he taketh away: and every branch that beareth fruit, he purgeth it, that it may bring forth more fruit" (**John 15:1–2**). Notice that the branches that do not bear fruit are first attached to the vine, representing Christ as stated. They are believers, part of the body of Christ, represented by the complete plant. But the non-bearing branches are removed from the vine. A few verses later, we learn that these branches are the ones who refuse to abide in Christ, and are cast into the fire and burned (John 15:6). Do not forget that Jesus is giving this warning to His eleven most faithful followers, and all true believers: "Abide in Me or suffer eternal damnation." There is no way to reconcile His warning with the Modern Church's current teaching on salvation. True and saving faith produces evidence of that faith.

This metaphor of the vine and branches is also used by Paul in Romans 11, again with the warning that we can be removed from the vine, which represents Christ [v22], if we do not demonstrate true faith. Notice in Jesus' analogy, true faith is demonstrated by bearing fruit, which we can only do by abiding in Him (John 15:5). This is not to say we are saved by works; we are saved by faith. But it is a false claim to say that we can live any way we want and be continuing on the narrow way to salvation. Both are extremes that are untrue. We are to do the will of the Father, which includes abiding in Christ, and being led by the Spirit, who will do God's work through us *if we let Him.*

If the Modern Church is correct in believing that one need not seek to do the will of the Father after accepting Jesus Christ, many, many passages of scripture are rendered untrue. Indeed, even the judgments determining who will enter the kingdom of God focus not on faith, but evidence of that faith demonstrated through works (*e.g.*, Matthew 25:32–46). If some leaders in the Modern Church do believe that one needs to seek to do the will of the Father (and this is where the Holy Spirit leads), then they have embraced what scripture teaches, but exactly what the sound bite denies. Yet because the Modern Church too often operates in sound bites, the correct explanation of the sound bite is often missing, and many in the evangelical churches are misled.

Acting faithfully and bearing fruit, which is something more than professed faith alone, is a necessary component of a true and saving faith. It is faith which manifests itself in seeking to do the Father's will as led by the Holy Spirit (and we know that only those led by the Holy Spirit are the true sons of God (Romans 8:14). Take note: to be led by the Holy Spirit, one must be following the Holy Spirit. We discuss more about saving faith in Chapter 16, "Saving Faith."

Furthermore, if the Modern Church believes that the only will the Father has for our lives is belief in Jesus, then again it denies the truth of many other scriptures. With this sound bite, the Modern Church embraces the concept that one may "believe" and then live any way he wants and expect to spend eternity with God. Church leaders using this sound bite have totally dissociated faith and action, misleading millions into a false sense of "*unconditional*" eternal security." But true and saving faith is not dissociated from action (except in the most extreme cases, such as a deathbed confession). Faith comes first, but true and saving faith produces demonstrable results, because those having it are led by the Holy Spirit, who leads them to do the will of the Father.

Most church leaders do not explicitly teach that believers need not do the will of God. Almost all church leaders teach that believers should do the will of God, but they seldom teach the full truth of scripture. Failure to do God's will is strong evidence of a lack of saving faith, as explained further in Chapter 16, "Saving Faith." Church members "understand" what it means when church leaders quote the "faith alone" sound bite in isolation. It tells them that it makes no difference whether they do the will of the Father or not, no difference if they refuse to obey, no difference if they are all about engaging their flesh, since they are all "saved" and will enter the kingdom of God no matter how they live. We see the evidence of the results of this errant teaching all around us.

"Faith alone" (as a sound bite in isolation) is not what the breadth of scripture teaches. Like other misuses of scripture, this also creates a lukewarm Laodicean Church with a dead faith, because it renders as optional, the desire to do the Father's will. Misunderstanding what "faith alone" means causes too many to neither seek, nor submit, to the Holy Spirit's will. It encourages us to sow to the flesh, not the Spirit, contrary to scripture: "For he that soweth to his flesh shall of the flesh reap corruption; but he that soweth to the Spirit shall of the Spirit reap life everlasting" (**Galatians 6:8**). The contrast of corruption with eternal life leads us to clearly understand that those who continue to sow to the flesh will be lost.

The Modern Church is divided over the usage and meaning of the phrase "faith alone." Some use this phrase as justification to support the doctrine that a person, after accepting Christ, can live any type of life and remain saved. In fact, as we look at how Christians behave as a group, we can easily come to the conclusion, supported by statistical analysis that many subscribe to that doctrine. Others understand that faith is more than simple intellectual belief.

So let us ask ourselves what this phrase really means. Does it mean that once we intellectually accept (meaning "believe in") Jesus Christ, we can live anyway we want and remain saved? That did not work out so well for either Satan and his demons, or the Israelites leaving Egypt. Both demonstrated the concept of "faith alone"; that is, they intellectually believed. Both suffered the wrath of God and will spend eternity in the lake of fire (Matthew 25:41). The Modern Church misuses the phrase "faith alone" because they operate under a secondary fallacy: the idea that if people acknowledge they must live their faith after accepting Jesus Christ it is a "works-based salvation." Nothing is further from the truth. It is another error of the Modern Church which can produce serious eternal consequences for its followers.

We truly are saved by faith. It's just that true, saving faith is not what the sound bite suggests, or what many are led to believe. We cannot have a true and saving faith that is not demonstrated unless we are in an unusual situation, such as a deathbed conversion. If we really don't understand what faith is, we are in trouble. True faith is evidenced by submission to the Holy Spirit: *"For as many as are led by the Spirit of God, they are the sons of God"* (**Romans 8:14**). This is what differentiates true believers from the world and true believers from false believers.

Unfortunately, we see more and more churches in this day and age basing their salvation message on exactly this "faith alone" sound bite premise. It almost seems like a way to indirectly present the prosperity gospel without actually acknowledging it as the prosperity gospel. Often those churches that water down the gospel in this manner are among the fastest growing. Why? It is because the doctrine appeals to the flesh. People want to believe that they can live this life any way they want and still be right with God. They want to be taught that all they need is this intellectual belief in Jesus Christ. People flock to places where church leaders espouse such doctrine. The "faith alone" sound bite allows people to live the worldly life they want in rejection of all that God teaches, with the expectation of eternal life in the kingdom of God.

Faithful church leaders have a primary goal for their flocks: to assist in enriching the relationship between God and the members of their flock and to help them become more Christ-like. They understand that is their responsibility. They will teach their flock that their relationship with God should never go through another man, and that their understanding of truth must come from the sources of truth – scripture and the Holy Spirit.

Unfortunately, there are other church leaders all too willing to indulge the fleshly desires of many attending our churches today: *"For the time will come when they will not endure sound doctrine; but after their own lusts shall they heap to themselves teachers, having itching ears"* (**2 Timothy 4:3**). What do we want to hear? Too many want to hear that we can have our relationship with God and the life we want on this earth also. This leads people to live in a manner that is often worldly and self-absorbing. But Jesus Christ taught a different way.

More often than not, we can tell what that person truly believes by observing his behavior. This is exactly the point made by James: "Yea, a man may say, Thou hast faith, and I have works: shew me thy faith without thy works, and I will shew thee my faith by my works" (**James 2:18**). If our faith is true and living, we will be led by the Holy Spirit, who guides our actions to do God's will. There is no doubt about it. However, if our faith is only intellectual and shallow, we may or may not act in a manner consistent with our professed faith, demonstrating that we really don't believe from the heart. It is hard to fake submission to the Holy Spirit.

Consider examples from life. If we truly believe we can fly, we should have no trouble in jumping off a tall building when someone challenges us to do so. If we refuse to, the conclusion is that we really don't believe we can fly (and conversely, if we jump off, even if we crash to the ground, others would surmise we truly believed we could fly). This is the same nature of our brethren with dead faith; they say they believe but the evidence of that belief does not exist. If we *really* believe something, we try to act consistent with that belief.

The same exists for the stock market. If we *truly* believe the stock market will really crash tomorrow, we take our money out. If we believe a prescription will heal us, we take it. Yet for all of these examples in our existing lives, we see Christians living in a manner which is inconsistent with what they claim to believe. The Modern Church often serves to reinforce this hypocrisy. Christ spoke very directly what will become of hypocrites when He addressed His servant who changed his behavior: "And shall cut him asunder, and appoint him his portion with the hypocrites: there shall be weeping and gnashing of teeth" (**Matthew 24:51**). The hypocrisy revealed in this example directly addresses the difference between belief and actions. If we truly believe, we truly act.

What we believe and the way we act should be consistent. Faith works the same way. If we truly believe, we are committed to act in a faithful manner that tries to please God by submitting to the Spirit, even as we acknowledge that we will still fail from time to time. Our works bear witness to what we truly believe. That is what the Bible teaches. It does not teach the abstract idea that we can claim to believe and act however we want. That type of behavior demonstrates an intellectual faith, lukewarm faith, or outright hypocrisy, which is not a saving faith.

"Little children, let no man deceive you: he that doeth righteousness is righteous, even as he [God] is righteous" (**1 John 3:7**). God praises men for doing righteous things. The same is true in Hebrews 11, where God extols the virtue of many exercising their faith through action. This does not mean we can be righteous on our own: "For there is not a just man upon earth, that doeth good, and sinneth not" (**Ecclesiastes 7:20**). We are to be led by the Spirit, to abide in Christ (John 15:5). This is the righteousness God is seeking. But we all are stuck with our free will, and occasionally disregard His lead and succumb to temptation. We all do sin (1 John 1:8). That is why God gave us a path to forgiveness (1 John 1:9). But the concept that a Christian can never do righteous things is not biblical either, because God can do His righteous work through us (John 15:5). We must be careful to understand the context of verses used by the Modern Church to in effect, justify that we are always sinners.

> "What then? are we better than they? No, in no wise: for we have before proved both Jews and Gentiles, that they are all under sin; As it is written, There is none righteous, no, not one: There is none that understandeth, there is none that seeketh after God. They are all gone out of the way, they are together become unprofitable; there is none that doeth good, no, not one. Their throat is an open sepulchre; with their tongues they have used deceit; the poison of asps is under their lips: Whose mouth is full of cursing and bitterness: Their feet are swift to shed blood: Destruction and misery are in their ways: And the way of peace have they not known: There is no fear of God before their eyes. Now we know that what things soever the law saith, it saith to them who are under the law: that every mouth may be stopped, and all the world may become guilty before God. Therefore by the deeds of the law there shall no flesh be justified in his sight: for by the law is the knowledge of sin" (**Romans 3:9–19**).

The context of this is varied depending on the OT verses from which they come. For example, the idea that none do good, comes from Psalm

14. But what is the context of that verse? It is applied to the fool that says there is no God. It is *not* applied to those living by the Holy Spirit, nor is it a condemnation of all Christians who truly believe. It is an example of how context across books of the Bible is important. When the Old Testament is cited, we must look at the context of those passages also.

The real purpose of Romans 3 is to establish the need for salvation through faith; that no one can be saved by his own works (which is true) because the law shows us that we all sin. This passage is clearly describing unbelievers. Sin separates all unbelievers from God. Because of their sin, no amount of apparently righteous acts, by themselves, will justify unbelievers before God. We all need Christ. Period.

But the religious dogma of the Modern Church tries to apply this passage (and similar passages) to Christians. This dogma portrays Christians as completely sinful, never doing anything righteous, and as actually being incapable of escaping the bondage of sin. All this does is create an environment where too many Christians don't even try to do what is right, because they believe nothing they do has any value to God. This totally contradicts the message to Christians in scripture. We are the hands and feet of God on this earth. We bring glory to God through our actions; those actions that He tries to lead us to do.

And so faith is not some abstract intellectual or lukewarm belief. Saving faith is a living faith which manifests itself in action. This is what the breadth of scripture teaches. Although we are not saved by works, that which we do, bears witness to what we truly believe. This is true in an earthly context and in a spiritual context. So if our works are largely inconsistent with what our Lord teaches, it is absolutely fair to ask if our faith is a true and saving faith (2 Corinthians 13:5). If we truly believe that Jesus is both God and Messiah, we want to please Him. We want to submit to the Holy Spirit so we can both know and do His will. The evidence we see in our churches, and as shown in the introduction, compels us to ask, "How many are true followers of Jesus Christ?"

Accepting Christ is no different. Once we really believe and are convicted by the Holy Spirit, there is a change in our life. If we submit to the Holy Spirit and walk with Him as scripture commands, our desires for fleshly pleasures are lessened, and our desire to please and obey our Lord is enhanced. Worldly desires and godly desires are mutually exclusive.

Evidence of a Holy Spirit-led life exists and can be discerned in true believers. What is that evidence?

First, it is love for the lost. We have to realize that individuals leaving this earth and not knowing Christ are destined for an eternity of torment apart from God. They are spiritually dead. Therefore, our priorities ought to include sharing the gospel with people and helping them to know Christ. This priority aligns with the will of God (1 Timothy 2:3–4). How can we say we have the love of Christ and desiring to fulfill the second most important commandment as defined by Christ ("love others as ourselves") if we are unwilling to try to help them avoid a place called the "lake of fire"?

Second, we will want to help new believers truly understand the scriptures and where to go for truth, so "That we henceforth be no more children, tossed to and fro, and carried about with every wind of doctrine, by the sleight of men, and cunning craftiness, whereby they lie in wait to deceive" (**Ephesians 4:14**). The mature Christian, one who is committed to God and His ways, examines what comes from the pulpit and challenges those who misrepresent scripture. He or she helps those who are less mature, as Jesus commanded in Matthew 28:19–20. The world has too many church leaders and religious leaders who, either purposefully or inadvertently, lead people away from God through sound bites and unsound doctrine. Only through listening to the Holy Spirit, as He provides witness to the Word of God, can we come to recognize false doctrine and false teachings and be equipped to help others do the same.

Third, it is hatred of our sin. If the Holy Spirit is in us, we should hate sin as much as God does and not live a life of sin or excuse sin with statements about constantly sinning. Yes, all of us do sin, but the mark of a committed Christian is being led by the Spirit, who leads us to avoid sin. The true believer does not excuse sin or constantly sin ("sin all the time"). This is consistent with an understanding of what Jesus Christ went through for us. Yet God has granted each of us free will. We can use that will to try to please Him, or use that same free will to anger him:

> "Or despisest thou the riches of his goodness and forbearance and longsuffering; not knowing that the goodness of God leadeth thee to repentance? But after thy hardness and impenitent heart treasurest up unto

thyself wrath against the day of wrath and revelation of the righteous judgment of God; Who will render to every man according to his deeds: To them who by patient continuance in well doing seek for glory and honour and immortality, eternal life: But unto them that are contentious, and do not obey the truth, but obey unrighteousness, indignation and wrath, Tribulation and anguish, upon every soul of man that doeth evil, of the Jew first, and also of the Gentile; But glory, honour, and peace, to every man that worketh good, to the Jew first, and also to the Gentile: For there is no respect of persons with God" (**Romans 2:4–11**).

Think about what Jesus himself taught about sin and those who lead others into sin. Our God does not joke around. He is totally serious about sin. Jesus Himself taught his disciples (followers), "But whoso shall offend one of these little ones which believe in me, it were better for him that a millstone were hanged about his neck, and that he were drowned in the depth of the sea" (**Matthew 18:6**). We must be careful that our sin does not lead others into sin. The gravity of sin before God is manifest in this passage and others.

Even more convicting is what Jesus followed it up with:

"Woe unto the world because of offences! for it must needs be that offences come; but woe to that man by whom the offence cometh! Therefore if thy hand or thy foot offend thee, cut them off, and cast them from thee: it is better for thee to enter into life halt or maimed, rather than having two hands or two feet to be cast into everlasting fire. And if thine eye offend thee, pluck it out, and cast it from thee: it is better for thee to enter into life with one eye, rather than having two eyes to be cast into hell fire" (**Matthew 18:7–9**).

While the overall effect of the passage may be an appeal to extremes, God is making the point to us that we are to live in such a manner that we do our best to avoid sin. We must never be cavalier about sin because of what our Lord went through for us, and we know how much it offends Him. Aversion to sin is one of the marks of a true believer. Yet many Christians refuse to earnestly seek to be led by the Spirit to be aware of and reject sin; some actually embrace sin. They believe they can do this without fear of eternal consequences because of what they are taught from the pulpit.

Fourth, we should have an active prayer life. There is much to be thankful for. But there are also many tragedies throughout the world: the brethren whose faith is waning, the lost, the sick, the persecuted, and the poor; we can take all our concerns to Him. If we consider others, we quickly come to realize we cannot pray enough. The question is whether we are involved enough in understanding what is happening to people in this world to care and lift them up. There is virtually no limit to what can be prayed for. We know that the man after God's own heart, David, regularly prayed three times a day. This is time with our Creator who desires to have a relationship with us. What better way to commune with our God than spending time with Him in prayer, bring Him your praise and petitions and seeking His guidance?

Fifth, is a sincere concern for people and the problems that they face in their lives. Acts of love will do miracles, bearing witness to whom we serve. Even if we only start small, by reaching out and providing assistance to a family whose breadwinner was martyred, helping those who cannot make ends meet, purchasing Bibles for distribution, or visiting a sick friend, we are doing something. There are many channels to help others even if we don't see that many around us who need help. Over time, God will use this faithfulness to lead us to do more.

It is not necessary to focus on trying to save the whole world. Over time God will use our increasing desire to serve others to bring glory to Him. We should use what God has provided us (our faith and resources) to help someone in whatever manner is appropriate and needed. If most of the focus we have is on ourselves (and that is easy to do), clearly we are not heeding the Holy Spirit's leading. We can be pretty sure that the Holy Spirit is not consistently leading us to do things for ourselves. If that is our focus, then we are probably not walking with the Holy Spirit.

Sixth and finally, there is a Holy Spirit-filled desire to study and memorize the Word of God. One of the things we can pray for is greater understanding of scripture: "Howbeit when he, the Spirit of truth, is come, he will guide you into all truth: for he shall not speak of himself; but whatsoever he shall hear, that shall he speak: and he will shew you things to come" (**John 16:13**). Do not read scripture to confirm your preconceptions, but to know and understand what is actually in the Bible. Many Christians would be surprised that much of what they have been taught does not fully align with scripture.

Can other men be guides? Yes, but they can also be false prophets. How will we know the difference except by continually reading the Word of God in context and prayerfully seeking the understanding revealed to us by the Holy Spirit? *Remember that God routinely allows men of other religions to mislead their people, and God also allows false prophets to mislead those who have accepted Jesus Christ.* Truth comes from the Holy Spirit. Listening to Him reflects our genuine interest in understanding what God says, and He will guide us in applying what it says to our lives. But here is the most condemning aspect of listening to men. Many church leaders tell us what we want to hear, not what we need to hear. Scripture does both.

Many Christians either refuse to read (or selectively read) the Bible because they believe they cannot be held accountable for that which they do not know, but this is not the mark of a true Christian. Neither is skimming through it out of some sense of "duty," such as reading through the Bible in a year. God leads us through the Spirit to desire to know Him better, and one of the ways is through the *careful study* of scripture. Although there are different gifts that each of us receive, these six points are evidence of a Holy Spirit-filled life which should be common to all believers.

The Proper Relationship of Works

Although we are not saved by works, it is axiomatic that works are a part (a result) of a true, living faith. Let no one tell you otherwise. Those who claim that we can believe in Jesus Christ and live anyway we want are misleading us, whether it is under the "faith alone" sound bite or a more insidious teaching. It is not a matter of legalistic counting of works, but is a matter of submitting to the Holy Spirit and not the flesh. We can see pretty clearly that the Holy Spirit does not lead many who name Christ as Lord, because not many submit their will to His will.

The Holy Spirit will lead us to do righteous works if we will listen to Him. We all will fail at this from time to time, but the trajectory of our actions as Christians should always be towards greater and greater Holy Spirit-filled lives, not more and more fleshly lives. Just as a man cannot serve two masters, one cannot serve the flesh and the Holy Spirit. God will try to lead us, but we still have our free will to decide whether or not to submit to the Holy Spirit.

Most Christians are familiar with this passage in James 2: "For as the body without the spirit is dead, so faith without works is dead also" (**James 2:26**). We cannot over-emphasize the point: *Faith without works is dead.* This verse reinforces the point that a true and living faith is *always* accompanied by works, which present evidence of that faith (See James 2:14–26 for the full discussion). In clear contradiction of scripture, many in the evangelical church have been taught that there are no eternal consequences for those who, while "believing" in Jesus Christ, refuse to obey the Holy Spirit on a regular basis.

How did Paul address this? "But [Paul] shewed first unto them of Damascus, and at Jerusalem, and throughout all the coasts of Judaea, and then to the Gentiles, that they should repent and turn to God, *and do works meet for repentance*" (**Acts 26:20**). What did Paul tell them? That they should repent and turn to God and do works that are "meet" (Greek *axios*), meaning "congruous with, or befitting of," repentance. Holy Spirit-directed works are a natural outcome of a true faith.

There is no such thing as a heart dedicated to God which lives in rebellion to the leading of the Holy Spirit. We can claim we love God while living in disobedience, but the Bible tells us otherwise (*e.g.,* 1 John 2:3). God tries to help us avoid sin. God has even told us He will provide a way out of temptation: "There hath no temptation taken you but such as is common to man: but God is faithful, who will not suffer you to be tempted above that ye are able; but will with the temptation also make a way to escape, that ye may be able to bear it" (**1 Corinthians 10:13**). How many of us, sinning too often, forget this?

Too often we hear from Christians that their lifestyle doesn't matter because "God knows my heart." While it is true that God knows our hearts, if we are not committed to loving God, bringing God glory, and loving our fellow man, we are deceiving ourselves about the condition of our own hearts, and believing things about our own hearts that God knows are not true.

Here is a description of a heart not led by the Holy Spirit: *"The heart is deceitful above all things, and desperately wicked: who can know it?"* (**Jeremiah 17:9**). The heart that God desires is the heart that loves Him and submits to the Holy Spirit (which leads us to work for Him). Those who believe they have the right heart before God, but rebel against His teachings, are deceived (James 1:22). Faith alone, and without works, often suggests there is either false or compromised faith.

Remember that if we look at the Bible as a whole, we will find that almost all descriptions of judgment concerning eternal destiny focus on one thing: works. For example, consider these words of Jesus: "Marvel not at this: for the hour is coming, in the which all that are in the graves shall hear his voice, And shall come forth; they that have done good, unto the resurrection of life; and they that have done evil, unto the resurrection of damnation" (**John 5:28–29**).

Note that this passage is tied contextually with judgment on where a person will spend eternity. God could have inspired John to write that those who know Jesus Christ will be delivered unto the resurrection of life and those who do not know Jesus Christ will be delivered unto the resurrection of damnation, but that is not what the passage says. It would seem to teach works-based salvation, but that is not what it is teaching either. It is making the point that those who truly had the faith, who truly believed, produced fruit (John 15:5–6). This is the theme of scripture; it is not that once we accept Christ we can live any way we want, as much of the Modern Church indirectly teaches doctrines leading to that conclusion.

The theme is repeated in Romans 2: "Who will render to every man *according to his deeds*: To them *who by patient continuance in well* doing seek for glory and honour and immortality, eternal life: But unto them that are contentious, and do not obey the truth, but obey unrighteousness, indignation and wrath, tribulation and anguish" (**Romans 2:6–9a**). Christians who are committed to performing deeds of unrighteousness will receive "indignation and wrath, tribulation and anguish."

Remember, these passages are not about rewards, but about eternal life for those doing God's will, and the opposite of it, God's wrath, for those who do not obey God's commands and do not submit to the leading of the Holy Spirit. Remember, the judgment of the sheep and the goats that Jesus describes in Matthew 25 (discussed above) also focuses on deeds and does not mention belief in Christ. Most judgments of God described in the New Testament determining who will enter the kingdom of God are based on works. But we must be clear on this point. *These are works done while abiding in Christ* (being led by the Spirit) (John 15:5), not works done on our own in the flesh. Yet God has given us the choice as to whether we will submit to the Holy Spirit or not.

Please do not read this as suggesting salvation is based on works; it is not. We have already cited verses that make it clear that God is not pleased by people who think their works done in the flesh have any merit with God. Just look at John 15:5, for example. There is a marked difference between works-based salvation and God's expectation that those who have truly accepted Christ will perform works consistent with the true and living (genuine) faith. While faith in Christ is the required foundation, works (fruit) naturally come from the man who has been ransomed from death and realizes what God has done to reach down to us. Again, for more on this point, see Chapter 16, "Saving Faith."

To God these are inseparable. *Hear this again: to God, faith and works are inseparable.* This is what the Bible teaches. Someone once said it is faith alone that justifies, but the faith that justifies is *never* alone. This is what we find in both the Old and New Testaments. So do you have a true and saving faith?

To God, it is only natural that those with true faith produce such works (fruit). If God came back tomorrow and judged us, He would be well within His right, and consistent with scripture, to say that He will judge us *only on our works;* specifically, *only the works we allow Him to do through us.* How can this be? It is because a true and living faith results in works. If we have a true and saving faith, it becomes evident, both to us and to those around us.

The Modern Church has made a serious error in completely dissociating faith and works, which is contrary to the larger picture of scripture. It has led "Christians" to reject what God teaches, to focus on themselves, and to invest in the world. This is also the reason that we see so many in the Modern Church adapting to the world rather than maintaining their light in an ever more evil world.

Many in the Modern Church camp out on Ephesians 2:8–9 and mistakenly assume that everything is binary (either faith alone, which they assume is correct, or anything else, which they assume is incorrect). They elevate that passage over all other scripture rather than looking for harmonious understanding of all the passages about salvation in scripture. A study of those passages reveals that works provide *evidence of our faith*, because it shows we are being led by the Holy Spirit (which leads us to do the Father's will).

God cannot be fooled, as we discussed earlier. If we do works from time to time to check boxes, He knows our heart in the matter. If we are trying to do the minimum we can to demonstrate some aspect of faith, He knows this also. Our hearts, indeed our lives are to be committed to Him. He knows if we are truly submitting our will to His Holy Spirit.

The same is true with over-engaging our flesh. That is a form of "bad works." We are taught not to use our freedom to engage our flesh (Romans 6:3–13). Here is the question to ask ourselves if we are unsure as to whether we are engaging our flesh: Is what I am contemplating what the Holy Spirit is leading me to do? We should pray about whatever we are considering. We would find that if we prayerfully sought an answer to this question before we engaged our flesh, we would be engaging our flesh a lot less often, to the glory of God.

Key Thoughts

Faith and works are all a part and parcel of the same belief system. Those who try to convince themselves (and others) that it is possible to have faith without attempting to obey and without producing fruit as led by the Holy Spirit are deceiving themselves. We are to walk with the Holy Spirit who leads us to *do* what is right before God.

The idea that "God knows my heart" (and He knows I believe and am therefore saved), but that we are not committed to loving Him, bringing Him glory and loving our fellow man, actually reveals a deceived heart. This deception will result in many being lost when the Lord confronts them with the same question quoted earlier "And why call ye me, Lord, Lord, and do not the things which I say?"(**Luke 6:46**).

Producing works (fruit) should be natural as we mature, because the key element of our maturation process in Christ is listening to the

Holy Spirit. But we must make the decision to submit to the Holy Spirit. Although we cannot know where the Holy Spirit leads each person, we can know the types of things the Holy Spirit leads us to do. Scripture frames the behaviors that please our God. Yet we have it within the free will granted to us by God to refuse to follow the Holy Spirit. Sadly, as Romans 8:14 teaches, only those actually being led by the Holy Spirit are the sons of God.

Virtually all faith that consists of developing an intellectual belief in the saving work of Jesus but which does not manifest itself in terms of action, is a dead faith (James 2:17). We can deceive ourselves that we have a living and active faith, when in fact it is not producing any Spirit-led works. Dead faith does not result in the desired salvation. An active and living faith produces works. We may be justified by faith alone but the true faith that justifies is never alone.

Chapter 7

Sinning and Obedience

Misleading Christian sound bite(s): Obedience has nothing to do with salvation. We can have faith but be committed to disobedience and still be saved. Following any set of rules or commands is legalism. Christians "sin all the time." Our obedience adds nothing to what Christ did on the cross.

One of the greatest deceptions of the Modern Church is the idea that once we accept Christ, we can live anyway we want and remain saved. Rarely is this directly stated, but it is an indirect, yet obvious conclusion, of preached doctrines. Obedience is often downplayed, discounted and disassociated from salvation. In some cases, outright disobedience is preached. Yet this is inconsistent with what our Lord teaches in scripture.

Why Obedience is Still Required
Somehow in the Modern Church, obedience has become either disassociated with, or anecdotal to, salvation. Many teach that after coming to Christ, a person need not obey (read: try to obey) to be saved. Yet many scriptural teachings reinforce our requirement to obey. Stated plainly, we are commanded to obey God. This has not changed since the Old Testament. God does not change: "For I am the Lord, I change not; therefore ye sons of Jacob are not consumed" (**Malachi 3:6**). The obedience God demanded of His followers in the Old Testament He demands of His

followers today. Otherwise, Jesus would not have demanded obedience from His disciples (John 14:15, John 15:10, and Matthew 7:21).

Do not be fooled into thinking that God changed because we are now living "in the age of grace." True faith in God in the Old Testament always produced obedience (Hebrews 11). The same is true today. The grace given through Jesus Christ does not allow us to disregard sin or live in willful disobedience. Remember that God extended grace in the Old Testament as well. People in the Old Testament were saved through their faith in God and His promised Messiah, just as we are (Hebrews 11). No one was ever saved by works. When we recognize, perhaps with tears, what our Lord and Savior went through for us, it is truly sad and almost inconceivable that we continue to discount the consequences of sin.

Obedience is not "works." Obedience is the outcome of being led by the Holy Spirit, and thus disobedience is the result of being led by our own flesh or a spirit other than the Holy Spirit. However, the Modern Church misuses scripture, interpreting it to say that anything that man does as a part of the process of salvation is worthless and unscriptural. Nothing is further from the truth. It was reinforced by John both in the gospel and his epistles.

Obedience is still expected of us; it demonstrates that we are listening to the Holy Spirit. It is the result of a true and saving faith. Even legal terminology used in the scripture (for example, "*deposit*") which describes the giving of the Holy Spirit, demonstrates that both parties are involved in the process. Yes, God's part in our salvation is much greater than ours, but there is nowhere does scripture say that salvation is exclusively God's decision and responsibility, for if it was, would not all be saved, since the Bible tells us that is His will? Paul, speaking of God, wrote, "*Who will have all men to be saved, and to come unto the knowledge of the truth*" (**1 Timothy 2:4**). We also see this thought expressed in Ezekiel 18:23, Matthew 23:37, and 2 Peter 3:9.

Since Jesus died for the sins of the whole world, everyone's sins are paid for (1 John 2:2). But only those who truly "receive Him" (John 1:12) ever have their sins forgiven. This is man's first step (entering in the "strait gate") in seeking forgiveness from God. The Modern Church often equates payment with forgiveness, leading to teachings like "OSAS" on the false assumption that because all sins are paid for, all our "past, present and future sins are forgiven." Even Jesus' last words, "it is finished" (Greek *tetelestai*) reflect payment, not forgiveness.

There is no place in scripture where we see God forgive a sin before it is committed. If payment equaled forgiveness, all mankind would be saved according to God's will as expressed in 1 Timothy 2:4, because Jesus paid for the sins of all mankind. Indeed some Christian Universalists believe that everyone who has ever lived will be saved because Jesus Christ paid for all sins on the cross. In fact, there is concern this is where the Modern Church is heading.

But verses like Matthew 7:13 tells us that this is not so. Why? Because "paid for" does not equal "forgiven." Forgiveness requires a true and saving faith on our part along with a humble heart. Yes, God gives us that faith (Ephesians 2:8–9), but we must apply it (see the parable of the talents in Matthew 25).

Faith is what pleases God. Think about Moses for a minute. God called Moses out as faithful when He said "My servant Moses is not so, who is faithful in all mine house" (**Numbers 12:7**). Moses was committed to obey God, even though at times he stumbled, as we all do. But Moses' faith almost always resulted in obedience.

As we look over the revealed parts of Moses life, we do not see a man committed to sin; in fact, we see just the opposite. It is true that Moses did not enter the Promised Land because of one sin he committed at Meribah (Numbers 20:8–12), but we know he is in heaven with the Lord, because of his appearance at the transfiguration (Matthew 17:3). Moses is just one of the many Old Testament saints whose obedience to God is given as evidence of their faith in Hebrews 11. God demands a committed, heart-felt level of faith that produces obedience, not a "lip service" faith similar to the rote observance of sacrifices and festivals described in Isaiah 1:11–15 and other places throughout the Old Testament.

Because of this errant teaching, along with the OSAS doctrine, we have many "Christians" living in sin. We have those that support (and even engage in) abortion, homosexual lifestyles, pre-marital sex, drunkenness, envy, selfishness, greed, pride, gluttony, materialism, etc., etc. We have those that don't think twice about divorce. We have those that steal from the government, and the list of sins goes on and on. In short, the fruit of the Modern Church's errant teaching on salvation and obedience produces unrighteousness because they reassure "believers" it makes no different how they live.

The apostle John wrote "And hereby we do know that we know him, if we keep his commandments. He that saith, I know him, and keepeth not his commandments, is a liar, and the truth is not in him. But whoso keepeth his word, in him verily is the love of God perfected: hereby know we that we are in him. *He that saith he abideth in him ought himself also so to walk, even as he walked*" (**1 John 2:3–6**). The Holy Spirit leads us to follow the letter and spirit (as defined by Jesus Christ) of the law, which biblically is a reflection of true love for both God and man.

The Bible is very clear: obedience is part of love and the result of a saving faith. When we disobey God and His moral laws, we are resisting the Holy Spirit. When we sin, the Holy Spirit in us hates our sin. If we are listening to the Holy Spirit, we should also hate our sin. We are to walk with the Holy Spirit. Paul wrote, "Therefore, there is now no condemnation for those who are in Christ Jesus" (**Romans 8:1**) (many versions based on Greek versions other than the Textus Receptus) but if we look at the same passages in the KJV and others that are based on the Textus Receptus, it says "There is therefore now no condemnation to them which are in Christ Jesus, *who walk not after the flesh, but after the Spirit.*"

Virtually all other versions of the Bible that are based on a literal translation of the Greek texts make the same point just a couple of verses later: "That the righteousness of the law might be fulfilled in us, who walk not after the flesh, but after the Spirit. For they that are after the flesh do mind the things of the flesh; but they that are after the Spirit the things of the Spirit. *For to be carnally minded is death; but to be spiritually minded is life and peace.* Because the carnal mind is enmity against God: for it is not subject to the law of God, neither indeed can be. So then they that are in the flesh cannot please God" (**Romans 8:4–8**). The removal of condemnation applies to those who walk according to the Spirit, not Christians who are walking according to the flesh.

We must remember that being indwelt by the Holy Spirit is not the same as being led by the Holy Spirit. Paul, *writing to believers* in the church in Rome, wrote, "Therefore, brethren, we are debtors, not to the flesh, to live after the flesh. *For if ye live after the flesh, ye shall die: but if ye through the Spirit do mortify the deeds of the body, ye shall live.* For as many as are led by the Spirit of God, they are the sons of God" (**Romans 8:12–14**).

Paul also wrote in that same epistle, "Know ye not, that to whom ye yield yourselves servants to obey, his servants ye are to whom ye obey; whether of sin unto [spiritual] death, or of obedience unto righteousness?" (**Romans 6:16**). This thought is extended through, "But now being made free from sin, and become servants to God, ye have your fruit unto holiness, and the end everlasting life" (**Romans 6:22**). These passages in Romans are consistent with the teaching of Jesus in Matthew 7:21; only those who do the Father's will, shall enter the kingdom of heaven. This description of death here is describing spiritual death contrasted with spiritual (everlasting) life. It cannot refer to physical death because the contrast is with spiritual life, not physical death. Doing the Father's will is evidence of a saving faith leading to spiritual life.

John made the point very bluntly: "Little children, let no man deceive you: he that doeth righteousness is righteous, even as he [Christ] is righteous. He that commiteth [habitual] sin is of the devil" (**John 3:7–8a**). We see similar sentiment in 1 John 2:3–4, and in many other passages in the New Testament. What does the Holy Spirit lead us to do? Obey God's will.

The evidence of how Christians act in too many cases demonstrates a clear refusal to follow the Holy Spirit's leading. Paul made a clear distinction between those who are walking by the Holy Spirit and those who simply have the indwelling of the Holy Spirit.

> "This I say then, Walk in the Spirit, and ye shall not fulfill the lust of the flesh. For the flesh lusteth against the Spirit, and the Spirit against the flesh: and these are contrary the one to the other: so that ye cannot do the things that ye would. But if ye be led of the Spirit, ye are not under the law. Now the works of the flesh are manifest, which are these; Adultery, fornication, uncleanness, lasciviousness, Idolatry, witchcraft, hatred, variance, emulations, wrath, strife, seditions, heresies, envyings, murders, drunkenness, revellings, and such like: of the which I tell you before, as I have also told you

in time past, that they which do such things shall not inherit the kingdom of God. But the fruit of the Spirit is love, joy, peace, longsuffering, gentleness, goodness, faith, meekness, temperance: against such there is no law. And they that are Christ's have crucified the flesh with the affections and lusts. *If we live in the Spirit, let us also walk in the Spirit"* (**Galatians 5: 16–25**).

This passage is clearly written to Christians, since unbelievers do not have the indwelling Holy Spirit. Consider carefully this last verse, where a clear distinction is made between those who live in the Holy Spirit (*i.e.*, are indwelt by the Holy Spirit) and those who walk in the Holy Spirit. They are not the same. The same issue is foreshadowed in Romans 8.

We are neither led by, nor walking with, the Holy Spirit if we are living in a manner inconsistent with where the Holy Spirit leads. The same would be true of a bandleader. We are led if we follow where the bandleader goes. But we are not led if we go places the bandleader is not leading. Simply having the Holy Spirit live in us does not qualify us as being led by the Holy Spirit. Scripture teaches that we, through our free will, can ignore, grieve and/or quench the Holy Spirit. We see it all too routinely in some who call themselves Christians.

Verse 24 of Galatians 5 (above) is even more disconcerting. It says that those who have crucified the flesh belong to Christ, with the implication that those who do not crucify the flesh may not belong to Christ. How do we do this? We crucify the flesh with our God-given free will by being obedient to the Holy Spirit. We cannot do this without submitting our will to His leading; by walking with Him, listening to and obeying His guidance.

One cannot serve two masters. When verse 24 is combined with Romans 8:1–6 and Romans 8:11–13, it becomes clear that those who refuse to walk with the Holy Spirit are subject to condemnation, even if they have the indwelling of the Holy Spirit. We have, through our God given free will, the ability to reject the guidance of the Holy Spirit. Indeed, if we are living in sin, we are not allowing the Holy Spirit to lead us.

But this is where we in the Modern Church, especially in America, have departed from the New Testament commands to love God, obey His commandments (John 14:15), and be led by the Holy Spirit (Galatians 5:25).

The Modern Church says that we can be fully engaged in the flesh and yet be of Christ in contradiction to the passage in Galatians 5. Why? Because according to the teaching of the Modern Church, nothing we do after accepting Christ can cause us to lose our salvation. So what do many believers in the Modern Church do? They "live after the flesh" (Romans 8:13) because of the errant teaching.

Romans 8:1–6, makes the point that condemnation-free living applies to believers who are led by the Holy Spirit. The test for a true believer is his or her walk, not because salvation is based on works, but because a true and saving faith results in a sincere desire to obey. This is done through actual submission to the leading of the Holy Spirit, which produces obedience. Obedience produces works (fruit).

> The test for a true believer is his or her walk, not because salvation is based on works, but because a true and saving faith results in a sincere desire to obey.

Let's ask ourselves what the Holy Spirit of God leads believers to do. If we are truly led by the Holy Spirit and are thereby walking with the Holy Spirit, we are under no condemnation because *we are doing the will of God*. The Holy Spirit does not lead us to constantly engage the flesh, but to obey God's commands. Woe to the man who believes that he can ignore the Holy Spirit without eternal consequence.

Yet this is exactly what much of the Modern Church teaches, largely because its leaders equate being indwelt by the Holy Spirit to walking with the Holy Spirit. They are different and are scripturally a false equivalency. More importantly, we see the adverse effect of this teaching on those who claim to be (and think they are) Christian. We presented evidence to this effect in the "Introduction" section.

Think for a moment about Hebrews 11. Much of it addresses this very thing; the nature of faith and what it produces. Anyone can claim they believe in something, but only when that faith or belief is turned into action does it manifest itself. Yet there are some who will say "God knows my heart and that I believe in spite of my disobedience."

Yes, God does know the heart and scripture tells us that He weighs it. God knows that those who are not committed to following the lead of the

Holy Spirit do not truly believe, even though they claim they do. Jesus put it this way: "Not every one that saith unto me, Lord, Lord, shall enter into the kingdom of heaven; but he that doeth the will of my Father which is in heaven" (**Matthew 7:21**). They have an intellectual or lukewarm belief, not a committed belief. They are like the chicken, who is involved in the breakfast by laying the egg. God is more interested in the pig. The bacon is evidence of his full commitment.

A Simple Example of Disobedience: Baptism

Let's just consider one simple example of how the Modern Church often leads people away from what God commands: baptism.

The Bible is very clear. We are commanded by God to be baptized. We have already established scripturally that in order to love God we are to obey God: "If ye love me, keep my commandments" (**John 14:15**). We have also established that we are to obey as a part of our salvation, "Son though he was, he learned obedience from what he suffered and, once made perfect, *he became the source of eternal salvation for all who obey him* and was designated by God to be high priest in the order of Melchizedek" (**Hebrews 5:8–10**).

We don't know of a single place in the New Testament where a believer was not baptized, with the possible exception of the thief on the cross. There are many scriptures that teach about water-based baptism. These include:

- "Go ye therefore, and teach all nations, baptizing them in the name of the Father, and of the Son, and of the Holy Ghost: Teaching them to observe all things whatsoever I have commanded you: and, lo, I am with you always, even unto the end of the world. Amen" (**Matthew 28:19–20**).
    - Commentary: A clear command from Jesus to make disciples and to baptize them, not to tell them they do not need to be baptized.
- "He that believeth and is baptized shall be saved; but he that believeth not shall be damned" (**Mark 16:16**).
    - Commentary: The underlying Greek emphasizes belief. However, the case is clear that those who truly believe

will be baptized. Those who reject baptism may never truly have believed. Remember, as we have shown true and saving faith is demonstrated by obedience.
- "Then Peter said unto them, Repent, *and be baptized* every one of you in the name of Jesus Christ for the remission of sins, and ye shall receive the gift of the Holy Ghost" (**Acts 2:38**).
  - Commentary: A direct commandment to new believers to be baptized.
- "Then Philip opened his mouth, and began at the same scripture, and preached unto him Jesus. And as they went on their way, they came unto a certain water: and the eunuch said, See, here is water; what doth hinder me to be baptized? And Philip said, If thou believest with all thine heart, thou mayest. And he answered and said, I believe that Jesus Christ is the Son of God" (**Acts 8:35–38**).
  - Commentary: One of the examples of baptism in the New Testament. Even the eunuch knew that he must be baptized and demonstrated his faith by obedience in asking to be baptized.
- "Can any man forbid water, that these should not be baptized, which have received the Holy Ghost as well as we?" (**Acts 10:47**).
  - Commentary: Peter, after witnessing the outpouring of the Holy Spirit, confirming the gentiles had received the gospel (consistent with John 1:12), asks if any man would deny them the chance to be baptized. While some may see this as a case that one can be saved without baptism, there was no doubt what followed – their submission and being baptized. Having the indwelling Holy Spirit is not a guarantee of salvation; it is clear evidence that you have come to Christ (entered through the strait (narrow) gate, but the journey down the narrow way that leads to eternal life does not end until physical death or rapture.
- "And they said, Believe on the Lord Jesus Christ, and thou shalt be saved, and thy house. And they spake unto him the word of the Lord, and to all that were in his house. And he took them the same hour of the night, and washed their stripes; and was baptized, he and all his, straightway" (**Acts 16:31–33**).

- ○ Commentary: Consider the urgency the jailer and his family felt that they be baptized right away. The jailer and his family demonstrated a faithful heart of obedience before God.
- "And now why tarriest thou? arise, and be baptized, and wash away thy sins, calling on the name of the Lord" (**Acts 22:16**)
  - ○ Commentary: Ananias told Paul that he was to arise and be baptized. While we clearly believe one is forgiven at the time a person believes in His Lord and Savior, it is normative that a person is also baptized; this obedience is part of what comprises a true and living faith. Saying we believe and the rejecting what our Lord commands is not a true and living faith (John 14:15).

Some may cite the example of the thief on the cross, but there is no definitive evidence as to whether he did or did not know Christ as his Lord before being crucified. In fact, there is evidence in scripture that the thief did know something of Jesus Christ before being crucified because he recognized that Jesus was an innocent man. But regardless, there is no definitive evidence as to whether he had been baptized beforehand. We must remember that Jesus' disciples baptized many disciples following Him. To assume that the thief on the cross is an example of someone who was saved without being baptized reads into scripture things that are not there.

Even if he was not baptized, he did not really have the chance to be baptized, very similar to a person who accepts Jesus Christ on his deathbed. However, it is a far different situation for a person who has ample opportunity to submit to the Lord's commandment to be baptized and then refuses. But much of the Modern Church teaches that disobeying God by refusing to be baptized makes no difference. When we accept Jesus Christ, we are to step out in faith, submit to the leading of the Holy Spirit and obey His commandments.

The only place in the New Testament where we specifically know baptism was applied after receiving the Holy Spirit involved Cornelius and his relatives and close friends, who received the Holy Spirit before baptism. But we must remember that this was a special situation. God was teaching Peter that no man should be called unclean. Through the outpouring of the

Holy Spirit, God witnessed to Peter first-hand that gentiles were allowed into the kingdom of God, something heretofore unconsidered:

> "While Peter yet spake these words, the Holy Ghost fell on all them which heard the word. And they of the circumcision which believed were astonished, as many as came with Peter, because that on the Gentiles also was poured out the gift of the Holy Ghost. For they heard them speak with tongues, and magnify God. Then answered Peter, *Can any man forbid water, that these should not be baptized*, which have received the Holy Ghost as well as we? *And he commanded them to be baptized in the name of the Lord.* Then prayed they him to tarry certain days" (**Acts 10:44–48**).

Cornelius and his family submitted to baptism. Some might raise the possibility that baptism was unimportant because they had already received the Holy Spirit, but the question is clear: would refusing to be baptized be a good way to persist in the Holy Spirit? Refusing to be baptized is a clear indication that one is not walking with the Holy Spirit, is grieving the Holy Spirit, and on one's way to quenching the Holy Spirit. It is making a personal commitment to refuse to be led by the Holy Spirit. Saving faith, as discussed earlier, manifests itself in obedience. To be baptized is to obey Jesus Christ our Lord.

Even passages which seem to downplay baptism are not often understood. When Paul says, "I thank God that I baptized none of you, but Crispus and Gaius; Lest any should say that I had baptized in mine own name" (**1 Corinthians 1:14–15**), Paul was referring to baptism as a potentially divisive issue because members of the church in Corinth had started following different men based on who baptized them, and Paul wanted them to follow Christ, not men. But Paul was in no way offering a commentary or a command against what Christ commanded.

Consider those that had already been baptized by John the Baptist. They were re-baptized into Christ: "And he said unto them, Unto what then were ye baptized? And they said, Unto John's baptism. Then said Paul, John verily baptized with the baptism of repentance, saying unto the people, that they should believe on him which should come after him, that is, on Christ Jesus. *When they heard this, they were baptized in the name of the Lord Jesus"* (**Acts 19:3–5**). These followers of Christ clearly had the right heart before God. Remember that during Jesus' time, the religious leaders led the people away from God and towards their human-centric brand of religion, which they created misusing the scriptures as a base. Elements of this are occurring in the Modern Church.

Church Leader Malfeasance Concerning Baptism and Obedience

Jesus' final commandment to his eleven faithful disciples ("the Great Commission"):

"Go ye therefore, and teach all nations, baptizing them in the name of the Father, and of the Son, and of the Holy Ghost: Teaching them to observe all things whatsoever I have commanded you: and, lo, I am with you always, even unto the end of the world" (**Matthew 28:19–20**).

We find no evidence in the New Testament that believers are not called to be His disciples; quite the contrary in fact. Consider the words of Jesus in Luke 14. We would submit that all believers, but especially church leaders, teachers and pastors are under the same commandment Jesus gave the eleven in the Great Commission. Note that the great commission has several components:

- "Go" - Don't keep your faith to yourself; put it out there.
- "Teach all nations" - Teach what? The gospel.
- "Baptizing them in the name of the Father, the Son, and of the Holy Ghost [Spirit]" - This is referring to immersion, water baptism.
- "Teaching them to observe all things whatsoever I have commanded you" - Teaching them to *observe Jesus' commandments* (including this one).

The third point clearly puts the burden upon Christ's disciples to baptize those who have come to Christ. The leaders of the Modern Church, especially church leaders, are in the forefront of this role, literally following in the footsteps of the faithful eleven. Their failure to command those who have come to Christ to be baptized is in direct disobedience to our Lord's command, with nothing to justify that disobedience. This is a place where too many pervert the spirit of the gospel. The faithful minister of the gospel of Jesus Christ simply repeats what Jesus commands: be baptized. Anything else brings into question whether they are being faithful disciples. A church leader or pastor who argues against the requirement of baptism is, quite simply, leading his flock away from obedience to Christ.

Remember what Jesus said, "But whoso shall offend one of these little ones which believe in me, it were better for him that a millstone were hanged about his neck, and that he were drowned in the depth of the sea" (**Matthew 18:6**). Offend (Greek *skandalizo*) means to entice to sin. When church leaders tells their flocks they need not be baptized (or it matters not), they are enticing them to sin; that is, to reject a command of our God. A faithful minister of the gospel should never try to lead others into sin.

The fourth point above ("teaching them to observe all things") puts another responsibility on all believers (disciples), with a greater responsibility on those who have assumed positions of leadership in the church, especially teachers and pastors. Christ's disciples are commanded to teach fellow believers to observe Christ's commandments (including this one). We are both Bible teachers, and take this command very seriously. For those who have truly acknowledged Jesus Christ as their Lord and Savior, no other reason than His command should be necessary to convince a believer to be baptized.

> For those who have truly acknowledged Jesus Christ as their Lord and Savior, no other reason than His command should be necessary to convince a believer to be baptized.

Unfortunately, we have all too often heard church leaders and pastors indirectly telling people they don't need to do what God says. This is not humility before God, but rather a dangerous arrogance and direct, willful disobedience to Christ's direct commandment in the Great Commission. So when a church leader tells his flock that they are not required to do something that God has commanded, they put themselves in God's judgment seat. This is a prime example of how those who are shepherds can mislead their flocks. We genuinely fear for those church leaders and pastors.

Here are two worrisome examples: church leaders in effect telling their congregations that baptism is optional and church leaders proclaiming that obedience to Christ's commands is good, but unnecessary to salvation, since believers cannot lose their salvation after coming to Christ. How will they be able to answer when they stand before Him, and He asks them why they found it unnecessary to obey His Great Commission?

> *"Not everyone that saith unto me, Lord, Lord, shall enter into the kingdom of heaven; but he that doeth the will of my Father which is in heaven.* Many will say to me in that day, Lord, Lord, have we not prophesied in thy name? and in thy name have cast out devils? and in thy name done many wonderful works? *And then will I profess unto them, I never knew you*: depart from me, ye that work iniquity. Therefore whosoever heareth these sayings of mine, and doeth them, I will liken him unto a wise man, which built his house upon a rock: And the rain descended, and the floods came, and the winds blew, and beat upon that house; and it fell not: for it was founded upon a rock. And every one that heareth these sayings of mine, and doeth them not, shall be likened unto a foolish man, which built his house upon the sand: And the rain descended, and the floods came, and the winds blew, and beat upon that house; and it fell: and great was the fall of it" (**Matthew 7:21–27**).

This is specifically written in condemnation of those who claim Christ as Lord but live in rebellion to His teachings. But what is almost unbelievable is that those who claim they are shepherding God's people are too often leading people to disobey the Lord. In the passage above, Jesus Christ did not say, "You never knew me." He said, "I never knew you." The Modern Church misses again the difference between willful and unintentional sin, taught in the Old Testament. Refusing to be baptized and teaching others there is no need to be baptized is willful sin (intentional disobedience of a clear commandment of Christ); it is rebellion. It is not "freedom in Christ" as some may claim.

Continual Sinning

One of the most damning things that we routinely hear from Christians is "I sin all the time" or "I sin every day." When we hear this I [Gregg] will often respond "Can you tell me the sins you've committed today?" In most cases they look at me with a blank stare. In fact I [Gregg] cannot remember a time when someone could tell me their last sin. This is a problem for a Christian on multiple fronts.

First, if a person if really sinning all that much and is not aware of it, they are not listening to, or being led by the Holy Spirit. This is something expected and commanded in scripture. According to scripture this can affect our salvation "For as many as are led by the Spirit of God, they are the sons of God" (**Romans 8:14**). Not being aware of our sin demonstrates a callous indifference to what Jesus Christ went through for us as well as being tone deaf to the Holy Spirit.

If a person really is sinning all the time and has no recollection of those sins, how can that person really confess his sins to God? True Christians are aware of their actions and their sin and make a sincere effort to avoid sin. The Holy Spirit convicts them. When they do sin, they confess it to God seeking His forgiveness as taught in 1 John 1:9, and attempt to avoid repeating the sin.

Second, if a person is claiming they "sin all the time" but are not really sinning, then we have a different problem. When people start to accept such dogma, they start to believe it. They quote it whether it is true or not. If they really are not sinning that often (and we all do sin from time to time), then they are under a delusion that they are constantly walking around and continually sinning, but that is not the reality.

This can only serve to demoralize them and make them think "sin is no big deal" and is the standard of behavior. This mindset turns sinning into a commonplace event. In this case, it is of equal concern if the claim is not representative of their lifestyle, but rather an acceptance of what is often taught in churches. We are called by God to be holy. We are to try. Jesus told the woman caught in adultery *"go, and sin no more."* Did this mean she was to be perfect henceforth? No, but rather she should do her best to avoid sin. Jesus emphasized this on many occasions. We are told to be holy: "As obedient children, do not be conformed to the passions of your former ignorance, but as he who called you is holy, you also be holy in all your conduct, since it is written, 'You shall be holy, for I am holy'" (**1 Peter 1:14–16**). We are told to be holy in our thought and conduct, but we can't do it on our own. God gives us the Holy Spirit to lead us to control our thought and conduct. But we must submit to His will. We must follow where He leads.

God clearly teaches us that sinning is not okay, and continually sinning is especially wrong. Believers are told they must confess their sins to God to receive His forgiveness and be "cleansed from all unrighteousness (1 John 1:9). If sin is truly "no big deal," then why are there the commands for confession, forgiveness and cleansing from unrighteousness? Continual and intentional sin clearly puts our eternal destiny at risk (Galatians 5:21b). The entire Bible is written to sentient beings to whom God has given the power to choose; the nature of the Bible testifies to it. This warning to Christians in the Galatian Church is clear, and yet it is ignored by many in the Modern Church.

God teaches us that we are to pluck out our eye rather than sin (Matthew 18:9). *We are to go to great lengths to avoid sin.* Yes, we do sin, but we should never try to minimize its seriousness, we should never practice it, and we as Christians should be spiritually aware enough to strive to avoid sin by submitting to and being led by the Spirit. There is no place in scripture where God either expects or approves of any sin.

It has been said that "sin is not the issue" for the believer. This is a half-truth and highly misleading. Consider a doctor who takes our temperature and finds the reading well above normal. The doctor knows that the temperature itself will generally not kill the patient, but the high temperature signifies a larger problem. Sin operates the same way.

Frequent sin may not directly destroy us because of the sin itself, but it demonstrates a compromised faith that indicates an uncertain eternal destiny. *It shows we are not living our faith and that we are not relying on the Holy Spirit.* One of the reasons that God gives us the Holy Spirit is to live in the power of the Holy Spirit. When we are living in sin or "sinning all the time" we are living in our flesh.

This has happened in the past and it is happening now. Compromised faith destroyed the Israelites. True faith results in a commitment to obedience and to serving God and man. This is why God tells us that a person who willfully sins that they, "hath trodden underfoot the Son of God" and "counted the blood of the covenant, wherewith he was sanctified, an unholy thing" (**Hebrews 10:29**).

This is not some self-righteous or arrogant argument about our righteousness. It is plain speaking about the faith that God requires us to have and demonstrate. God requires a level of faith that will compel us to strive to be righteous and obedient (even though we will sometimes fail), and even gives us His Spirit to lead us in obedience. Even though our righteousness comes through Jesus Christ (because we cannot be fully sinless), it is errant doctrine to suggest that God does not expect us to do our best to avoid sin.

Unfortunately, many leaders in the Modern Church teach that any commitment to obedience (Matthew 10:38) is needless, because our righteousness comes only through Christ. We must not buy into the argument of some in the Modern Church that believers "sin all the time." This just trivializes sin. If we had to be crucified to pay for our sin, how hard would we try to avoid sin? This is the perspective we should have.

It is understood there are times we will struggle with sin. Paul describes his battle with sin in his epistle to the Romans, "For that which I do I allow not: for what I would, that do I not; but what I hate, that do I. If then I do that which I would not, I consent unto the law that it is good. Now then it is no more I that do it, but sin that dwelleth in me. For I know that in me (that is, in my flesh,) dwelleth no good thing: for to will is present with me; but how to perform that which is good I find not. For the good that I would I do not: but the evil which I would not, that I do. Now if I do that I would not, it is no more I that do it, but sin that dwelleth in me" (**Romans 7:15–20**).

Sadly, this passage is often misused by Christians to justify habitual sin. If this were a general statement designed to remove our responsibility to avoid sin, the other passages where God calls us to righteous living would be disingenuous. Furthermore, the context of this passage is clear. It addresses Christians (with Paul as the example) *wanting to do the right thing, but struggling to actually do the right thing.* These verses do not in any way excuse or address those who are committed to disobey God's commands or commandments by willfully living in sin. Paul did not write this as a license to sin. He wrote it to comfort and encourage those Christians struggling in their battle with sin by reminding them that he waged the same battle with his own flesh.

But note that God understands, because He knows the heart as to whether our attempts to avoid sin and repent are heartfelt and sincere. Consider God's discourse with Jeremiah about the people in Jerusalem when He says, "Thou hast forsaken me, saith the Lord, thou art gone backward: therefore will I stretch out my hand against thee, and destroy thee; I am weary with repenting" (**Jeremiah 15:6**). God knows if we are sincere in our repenting.

Let us be clear about this. Those who "sin all the time" are not being led by the Holy Spirit; indeed, they are grieving the Holy Spirit. It is surprising that those who claim to belong to Christ could make this claim. Are they not hearing from the Holy Spirit through their consciences about their sin? It is true we do sin and should be humble about this, but the idea that we "sin all the time" simply says we are not listening to the Holy Spirit, who hates sin as much as God the Father does.

This teaching also indicates we may not have enough appreciation for what our Savior went through for us. Our innocent Savior paid the price of our sin for us. Paul wrote, "Let love be without dissimulation. Abhor that which is evil; cleave to that which is good" (**Romans 12:9**). Take note: "The fear of the Lord is to hate evil: pride, and arrogancy, and the evil way, and the froward mouth, do I hate" (**Proverbs 8:13**). Sin is evil; lawlessness is evil. God hates both. We are to hate and avoid sin. If we don't, we are not being led by the Holy Spirit (although we may still be indwelt). All of these commands and admonitions are for us as Christians, not for unbelievers.

Yet many "Christians" often cavalierly proclaim that they sin all the time, as if it is no big deal. It is a huge deal. American society was originally created largely by Christians. How well does our society today reflect God's values? Remember that this country has been Christian from the start, but we are now at a moral low point because Christians are refusing to be led by the Holy Spirit. We have the responsibility to use our God-given free will to try to avoid sin, as the Bible instructs us. Why would God instruct us to avoid sin if we cannot? God wants our hearts to be focused on His ways and His will, not ours.

If we are being led by the Holy Spirit, God will provide a way for us to escape temptation.

> "There hath no temptation taken you but such as is common to man: but God is faithful, who will not suffer you to be tempted above that ye are able; but will with the temptation also make a way to escape, that ye may be able to bear it" (**1 Corinthians 10:13**).

Some would say there is a scriptural basis for living in sin; that we are unable to live any other way. One passage cited to make that point is in James 4 which is often misinterpreted by much of the Modern Church. James states, "Therefore to him that knoweth to do good, and doeth it not, to him it is sin" (**James 4:17**).

But this cannot mean exactly what much of the Modern Church often interprets it to be. The Modern Church uses this verse to show we live in sin all the time because we are not always doing the good we should for there is *always* good that we can do. So some in the Modern Church teach we live in sin based on this verse. It is also used to justify not striving to avoid sin in their own lives since they are already sinning anyway (based on their interpretation of this verse).

But this interpretation conflicts with other scripture, so the verse cannot mean what many claim. If it means what much of the Modern Church teaches us it means, this passage would conflict with the variety of scriptures telling us to avoid sin. Consider what Paul writes on the subject in Romans 6:

> "What shall we say then? Shall we continue in sin, that grace may abound? God forbid. How shall we, that are dead to sin, live any longer therein? Know ye not, that so many of us as were baptized into Jesus Christ were baptized into his death? Therefore we are buried with him by baptism into death: that like as Christ was raised up from the dead by the glory of the Father, even so we also should walk in newness of life. For if we have been planted together in the likeness of his death, we shall be also in the likeness of his resurrection: Knowing this, that our old man is crucified with him, that the body of sin might be destroyed, that *henceforth we should not serve sin.* For he that is dead is freed from sin. Now if we be dead with Christ, we believe that we shall also live with him: Knowing that Christ being raised from the dead dieth no more; death hath no more dominion over him. For in that he died, he died unto sin once: but in that he liveth, he liveth unto God. Likewise reckon ye also yourselves to be

dead indeed unto sin, but alive unto God through Jesus Christ our Lord. *Let not sin therefore reign in your mortal body, that ye should obey it in the lusts thereof.* Neither yield ye your members as instruments of unrighteousness unto sin: but yield yourselves unto God, as those that are alive from the dead, and your members as instruments of righteousness unto God. For sins shall not have dominion over you: for ye are not under the law, but under grace. What then? Shall we sin, because we are not under the law, but under grace? God forbid. Know ye not that to whom ye yield yourselves servants to obey, his servants ye are to whom ye obey; whether of sin unto death, or of obedience unto righteousness?" (**Romans 6:1–16**).

There is no biblical basis for believing that God will deliver from punishment those committed to sin. When we don't care enough to focus on avoiding sin and following the leading of the Holy Spirit, we are in effect committed to sin and rebelling against God. We are not acting as true sons of God. Ephesians 2:8–9 was designed to remind us that we cannot somehow achieve righteousness apart from Christ (*i.e.,* through our own works). It was never meant as a free pass to sin.

It is not the Spirit that is leading us to spend large sums of money on ourselves and live extravagantly. It is not the Spirit that leads us to refuse baptism and it is not the Spirit that leads us to sin regularly by disobeying God. It is not the Holy Spirit that leads us to put ourselves first. It is not the Spirit that leads us to be quiet about our faith, and it is not the Holy Spirit that leads us to follow false teachers. We have so desensitized ourselves to the Holy Spirit that we miss where God is trying to lead us.

Willful Sin versus Unintentional Sin

Scripturally, there is a huge difference between intentionally and unintentionally sinning. This is another place where God's knowledge of the condition of our heart is important. The Old Testament even prescribes different penalties for intentional and unintentional sin. More and more "Christians" in the Modern Church believe the grace of God allows us to intentionally engage in sinful lifestyles.

A believer (indwelt by the Holy Spirit) can only willfully engage in sin by refusing to listen to the Holy Spirit. Certainly this attitude and behavior is not present in a person being *led* by the Holy Spirit. Yet we see "Christians" regularly engaging in all different types of sin, and still believing they are truly saved Christians. We sin enough unintentionally and even occasionally intentionally (although we are led by the Holy Spirit to avoid such), without intentionally leading a sinful lifestyle. The grace of God was never designed to cover those who intentionally and regularly live in sin.

> The grace of God was never designed to cover those who intentionally and regularly live in sin.

> "But the soul that doeth ought presumptuously, whether he be born in the land, or a stranger, the same reproacheth the Lord; and that soul shall be cut off from among his people. Because he hath despised the word of the Lord, and hath broken his commandment, that soul shall utterly be cut off; his iniquity shall be upon him" (**Numbers 15:30–31**).

It is inconceivable that one of Jesus' true followers intentionally lives in sin:

> "Whosoever abideth in him sinneth not: whosoever sinneth hath not seen him, neither known him. Little children, let no man deceive you: he that doeth righteousness is righteous, even as he is righteous. He that committeth sin is of the devil; for the devil sinneth from the beginning. For this purpose the Son of God was manifested, that he might destroy the works of the devil. Whosoever is born of God doth not commit sin; for his seed remaineth in him: and he cannot sin, because he is born of God. In this the children of God are manifest, and the children of the devil: whosoever doeth not righteousness is not of God, neither he that loveth not his brother" (**1 John 3:6–10**).

We are taught to avoid sin whenever possible, especially willful sin. Our view of right and wrong should be the same as God's view. We are not allowed the "freedom" to choose right and wrong for ourselves. When we intentionally choose to disobey God or believe that which is wrong is right, we are willfully sinning. God addresses willful sin in Hebrews 10:

> "For if we sin wilfully after that we have received the knowledge of the truth, there remaineth no more sacrifice for sins, But a certain fearful looking for of judgment and fiery indignation, which shall devour the adversaries. He that despised Moses' law died without mercy under two or three witnesses: Of how much sorer punishment, suppose ye, shall he be thought worthy, who hath trodden underfoot the Son of God, and hath counted the blood of the covenant, *wherewith he was sanctified*, an unholy thing, and hath done despite unto the Spirit of grace? For we know him that hath said, Vengeance belongeth unto me, I will recompense, saith the Lord. And again, The Lord shall judge his people. It is a fearful thing to fall into the hands of the living God" (**Hebrews 10:26–31**).

This carries with it the idea of not only willful sin, but also continuing in that willful sin. God tells us here specifically that "no more sacrifice for sins is left" for those who continue to sin willfully. Willful, continual sin is essentially rejection of Christ. Notice this addresses a man who was sanctified. Clearly, if all future sins were forgiven at the cross, the necessary sacrifice, even for willful sin, would have been made. But they weren't forgiven, as explained above; they were all paid for, but not all forgiven.

Again, nowhere in the Bible does God forgive a sin before it is committed. We are again reminded that continual, willful sin (which is rebellion against God) leaves us without a sacrifice. There is no sacrifice to tap into when we intentionally sin against a holy and righteous God, especially when we continue in sin as discussed in Galatians 5:21b. Can God forgive even continual and willful sins? Yes, but the heart is important to God. If we are continually and willfully sinning are we relying on the Holy Spirit? Are we being led by the Holy Spirit? Do we really want to tempt God (Matthew 4:7)? Remember that God knows the heart. Indifference towards sin can be eternally fatal.

We are creatures of instinct and the flesh far too often. We need to be more thoughtful and respectful of God's commands. We still need to confess (1 John 1:9) and be sorry for these sins, even though they are unintentional. God knows our heart and how much we desire to avoid sin. God commands us take captive to Christ even unintentional, thought-based sins: "Casting down imaginations, and every high thing that exalteth itself against the knowledge of God, and bringing into captivity every thought to the obedience of Christ" (**2 Corinthians 5:10**).

For those who do not obey by faith, but rather live in sin, there are consequences that much of the Modern Church does not acknowledge. For example:

> "And if some of the branches be broken off, and thou, being a wild olive tree, wert grafted in among them, and with them partakest of the root and fatness of the olive tree; Boast not against the branches. But if thou boast, thou bearest not the root, but the root thee. Thou wilt say then, The branches were broken off, that I might be grafted in. Well; because of unbelief they were broken off, and thou standest by faith. Be not highminded, but fear: For if God spared not the natural branches, take heed lest he also spare not thee. Behold therefore the goodness and severity of God: on them which fell, severity; but toward thee, goodness, if thou continue in his goodness: otherwise thou also shalt be cut off. And they also, if they abide not still in unbelief, shall be grafted in: for God is able to graft them in again" (**Romans 11:17–23**).

When we live in sin, we are not standing by faith. We are to have humble hearts before God, acknowledging and confessing our sin (1 John 1:9). God will not give up on us for an un-confessed sin if we have the right heart before Him. It is a different thing to be callous about our sin and not confess it. The Bible clearly says that God will be faithful to forgive our sins if we confess them (1 John 1:9). This also indicates the converse:

God may not forgive our sins if we are arrogant before Him and refuse to confess our sins.

Although human wisdom is often challenged when compared to scriptural truths, we do appreciate a quote from Dietrich Bonhoeffer, who said "When all is said and done, the life of faith is nothing if not an unending struggle of the *spirit with every available weapon* against the flesh." We are to do all we can to oppose sin; not willingly submit to it or be apathetic towards the commission of sin. Yet the Modern Church has enabled, through errant doctrine, this toleration of sin, even willful and continual sin; it is enables the flesh rather than constrain it.

Convicted or Deceived?

When we claim we are Christians and are not committed to following the Holy Spirit, we deceive ourselves (James 1:22). But the insidiousness of the message coming from the Modern Church leads many of its followers to believe that they are now, and will always remain saved (unconditional eternal security), *regardless of the state of their faith.* This teaching reinforces sinful lifestyles. Individuals are aware. They recognize that when a church leader tells the congregation they need not be baptized to be saved, what the church leader is really saying is that we need not obey God to be saved. As our Lord said, we have men teaching as doctrine the rules of men.

God understands the heart disposed to Him, the heart opposed to Him, and the heart that does not really care. God's word (by itself) is able to discern the thoughts and intents of the heart. So if your thoughts and intentions are to disobey God (by living in sin) or to consider as inconsequential the sin for which His Son suffered and died, you will be convicted by His word, but only if you faithfully study it while submitting your will to the Holy Spirit, who will "guide you into all truth" (John 16:13). The Holy Spirit, through scripture, will reveal your true heart to you, if you let Him.

Paul warned the Christians in the church at Galatia that their failure to "walk in the Spirit" could have dire eternal consequences:

> "This I say then, Walk in the Spirit, and ye shall not fulfill the lust of the flesh. For the flesh lusteth against the Spirit, and the Spirit against the flesh: and these

are contrary the one to the other: so that ye cannot do the things that ye would. But if ye be led of the Spirit, ye are not under the law. Now the works of the flesh are manifest, which are these; Adultery, fornication, uncleanness, lasciviousness, Idolatry, witchcraft, hatred, variance, emulations, wrath, strife, seditions, heresies, envyings, murders, drunkenness, revellings, and such like: *of the which I tell you before, as I have also told you in time past, that they which do such things shall not inherit the kingdom of God"* (**Galatians 5:16–21**).

Paul specifically stated that *if we are led by the Holy Spirit, we are not under the law.* Why is this? Because the Holy Spirit leads us to do God's will instead of our will. The only reason we are not under the law is because we submit to the Holy Spirit. Remember that the moral aspects of the law are repeated in the New Testament to Christians. Paul left no ambiguity in his warning that those who live in rejection of the Holy Spirit will not enter the kingdom of God (Galatians 5:21). Being led by the Holy Spirit leads us to keep the law in both spirit and letter, to love God, and to love others.

Today we have mature Christians (think long time Christians) who refuse to submit to the Holy Spirit. In the Modern Church, there are many Christians who do not understand the proper role of the Holy Spirit in their lives. The concept of being led by the Spirit is foreign to them. We are to live in the power of the Holy Spirit which leads us away from sin, and towards obedience. This is largely the failing of the Modern Church because of its focus on making disciples while neglecting the maturation of disciples. They tend to observe the first half of the Great Commission: "Go ye therefore, and teach all nations, baptizing them in the name of the Father, and of the Son, and of the Holy Spirit" (**Matthew 28:19**), but neglect the second half, *"Teaching them to observe all things whatsoever I have commanded you"* (**Matthew 28:20a**).

The Modern Church is doing a woefully inadequate job of equipping Christians to obey God by being led by the Spirit. A large part of this is due to the Modern Church's increasing acceptance of the tenets of Calvinism, aided perhaps by their desire to assure rather than to alarm their congregations. Church leaders will have to answer for that failure before

God. However, Christians themselves bear the ultimate responsibility for learning God's Word. How do you think God will treat "believers" who refuse to learn what God wants, because they refuse to prioritize God and His Word?

Paul directed his disciple Timothy to "Study to show thyself approved unto God, a workman that needeth not to be ashamed, rightly dividing the word of truth" (**2 Timothy 2:15**). As true believers, we should make it our goal to find out our Lord's will and make every attempt to submit to it. We should spend time in prayer seeking the Holy Spirit's guidance. God will not let us blame our failure to obey His commands on our church leaders. He gave us His word and His Holy Spirit. We have all we need to understand and obey His will (Romans 12:2).

Make no mistake; this is not works-based salvation, but rather the proper response of a truly repentant heart before God. We must remember that all the letters to the churches in Revelation address actions. It was not the actions that saved them per se, but rather they were condemned because the actions which gave evidence of a saving faith were missing, compromised, or not done with a sincere heart. Run, don't walk, away from those who say that when a believer insists the Bible demands obedience, it means a works-based salvation; it does not.

Led to Disobey

Remember what Jesus taught, "Then said he unto the disciples, It is impossible but that offences will come: but woe unto him, through whom they come! It were better for him that a millstone were hanged about his neck, and he cast into the sea, than that he should offend one of these little ones" (**Luke 17:1–2**). Think about this for a moment. We have church leaders in the Modern Church who openly say a believer's behavior after coming to Christ cannot affect his salvation, even though the Bible clearly says otherwise. They are actually leading their followers into rebellion and encouraging sin! This is a place where many church leaders are "teaching for doctrine, the commandments of men" (**Matthew 15:9**), in rebellion to what Christ commanded. This is the reason for Christ's warning in Luke 12:

"And I say unto you my friends, Be not afraid of them that kill the body, and after that have no more that they can do. But I will forewarn you whom ye shall fear: Fear him, which after he hath killed hath power to cast into hell; yea, I say unto you, Fear him." (**Luke 12:4–5**). This scripture, with a command to fear God, comes with a warning. The context in which this is written is clear. As used here, the word "fear" (Greek *phobeō*) does not mean respect (although we should respect God also), but means we are to have an actual, healthy fear of God. That should be our natural reaction when we consider who God is and who we are. The fear of God serves to help us maintain a good conscience before God. That is the point Jesus is making. The same point is made in the Old Testament as well: "The fear of the Lord is a fountain of life, to depart from the snares of death" (**Proverbs 14:27**).

Remember that in Acts 4, Peter rejected the commands of the Sanhedrin because they conflicted with the commandments of God. What do we suppose the reaction of God is to people who directly or indirectly support church leaders who do not faithfully speak the Word of God? We must use our understanding of God's word, as led by the Holy Spirit, to discern truth from error. We are to call out those who would lead us away from God's teachings and desires.

We are creatures born with a sinful nature into a world where sin reigns. However, we must have the most reverent fear and respect for our God and Creator. That is the proper relationship between us and our Creator. We must recognize that we become the bondservants of Jesus Christ when we accept Him as Lord and Savior. When church leaders indirectly tell their congregations that they do not have to do what God says (because their salvation is guaranteed), they are leading their congregations into disobedience, exactly the opposite of their commission. They are dangerously close to becoming wolves instead of shepherds. We follow them at our peril; we risk leaving the narrow way for the broad one.

Remember also the final words of Solomon as he sought wisdom, "Fear God, and keep his commandments: for this is the whole duty of man" (**Ecclesiastes 12:13**). Christ's sacrifice was never designed to lead us to reject holiness. Yet, that is exactly what some current teachers of the law (church leaders) are doing by telling us we need not obey parts of scripture, or that no matter how much we disobey, we remain saved.

We all need to honor our God and understand our relationship with Him. We are His servants; He is the King. Once this relationship is clearly understood, we will have a far different view of our actions before Him.

Key Thoughts

There is no biblical basis for living in regular (or continual) sin ("I sin all the time"). If we are truly doing that, we do not share the hatred of sin that God has, nor are we being led by or walking with the Holy Spirit (and are in fact grieving the Holy Spirit). When we sin regularly, we are not using our God-given free will to oppose sin. Furthermore, we are not making use of what God said He will give us to resist sin, for God has told us He will provide a way out of temptation.

There is a marked difference between willful sin (which is dealt with biblically) and unintentional sin. A "Christian" who is living in a continually sinful lifestyle should not expect to enter the kingdom. We are called by God to be holy, just as He is holy.

This does not mean that we do not sin. But when we do, the proper response is a godly sorrow (not a worldly sorrow) and confession (1 John 1:9) which leads us to make a sincere attempt to repent and to try to avoid further sin. Reflect on the response of God (the God who does not change) to willful sin in the Old Testament.

We do live in an age of grace, but the grace extended to us through our Lord Jesus Christ was never designed to excuse or disregard sin. That is the focus of the evil one. We love the Lord's grace; we need the Lord's grace. But we have taken the concept of grace to a place it was never meant to be. We use it to trivialize the commandments of God under the banner of unlimited mercy and freedom, and as a means to justify constantly engaging our flesh.

Finally, we need be wary of any church leader who in anyway excuses sin among Christians with any doctrine claiming that those sins are somehow already forgiven by the sacrifice of Jesus Christ on the cross Future sins are not forgiven, as discussed in Chapter 8, "Forgiveness of Sins." No faithful church leader should ever directly or indirectly encourage a Christian to sin.

Chapter 8

Forgiveness of Sins

Misleading Christian sound bite(s): When we accept Jesus, all sins, past present and future are forgiven immediately. We need not ask for forgiveness when we sin.

When are Sins Forgiven?

Many in the Modern Church teach all past, present, and future sins are forgiven when we accept Jesus Christ. There can be seemingly valid reasons to believe so. However, the larger context of scripture disputes this teaching. Here is the simple truth: there is nowhere in the Bible where God forgives a sin in advance of its commission. Nor is there any passage which, understood in context of the rest of scripture, supports the concept that future sins have been forgiven.

The teaching that all future sins are forgiven is a necessary doctrine to support the Modern Church's doctrine of OSAS ("unconditional eternal security"), which claims that there is nothing a person can do after receiving Christ that will cause him to lose his salvation. The doctrine teaches that intentional sin, rebellion and even abandoning the faith have of no eternal consequences, because those sins have already been forgiven.

Therefore, to support that doctrine, obviously all future sins have to be considered forgiven at the moment of first belief. This demonstrates how church doctrine has evolved to support the foundational (and erroneous) doctrine of OSAS. However, both willful and regular sin committed by

Christians after they have received Christ is dealt with scripturally, as discussed in previous chapters, and these passages directly contradict the Modern Church teaching that a Christian's future sins are forgiven.

Here we see an example of doctrine taught by much of the Modern Church that is inconsistent with scripture. We also see erroneous doctrine spawning more erroneous doctrine. The need to support the doctrine of OSAS created the doctrine that all sins (past, present, and future) were forgiven at the moment of coming to Christ. In turn, that doctrine now has some in the Modern Church insisting that, since all sins have already been forgiven, believers need not confess and ask for forgiveness for sin, even though God expressly commands it (1 John 1:9).

Some take it even further, suggesting that it is fact *an insult to God* for believers to ask forgiveness for the sins they commit, since they have already been forgiven! The language in 1 John 1:9 indicating that confession of sin is necessary to receive forgiveness for that sin is explained away: "This sin can only affect a believer's relationship with God (in fellowship or out of fellowship); it cannot affect a believer's salvation (because of OSAS)." Like a malignant tumor, the error keeps growing larger in the Modern Church, endangering the eternity of more and more followers.

These beliefs are based on inappropriate usage of the word "all" and differences between sins being paid for and forgiven. For example, consider the Old Testament where God says, "For on that day shall the priest make an atonement for you, to cleanse you, that ye may be *clean from all your sins* before the Lord." (**Leviticus 16:30**) Scripture clearly says that "ye may be clean from *all* your sins before the Lord" but we know from context that these are all previous sins, not all sins ever committed. If the atonement included future sins there would never be a need for that person to atone for sins again. Yet the Israelites were commanded to observe this Day of Atonement annually for the forgiveness of all sins of the previous year (Leviticus 16:29–34). *Again, there is no recorded instance in the Bible of God forgiving a sin before it is committed.*

In discussing forgiveness of sins as that concept appears in the Bible "all sins" refers to sins committed up to the moment in time they are forgiven. This is the only interpretation that makes all scripture true. A quick look at 1 John 1:9 tells us this is so, but there are many other scriptures that make it clear that sins are not forgiven before they are committed.

Once we truly accept Christ, we are justified *at that moment*. We have been given a clean slate for all past sins and appear righteous before God. But justification cannot be singularly permanent. It must be part of an ongoing process (often described using the present tense Greek verb) *because it relies on the foundation of faith, and that faith must endure.* We have seen in scripture that a person's faith is not always stable or permanent. Justification by faith must be maintained because we still have a life to live before God (the narrow way).

This is also consistent with the legal concept on which justification is founded. If a defendant commits a crime and appears before a judge, that judge may acquit or declare the defendant innocent of all previous infractions. But no judge would ever say to the defendant that not only have your past crimes been expunged (erased), but all future crimes are expunged (erased) as well. Yet this is the thinking that is embraced.

Future sins are not forgiven. We are told this explicitly in 2 Peter 1:9, quoted below. There are also many passages that speak specifically to Christians regarding the eternal outcome of leading sinful lives and of not acting consistently with our claimed faith, as discussed in previous chapters. If we were justified once *and permanently*, the way we live would have absolutely no impact on our justification; we would remain righteous before God no matter how much sin we live in.

But this is not scriptural, even though it is taught in many Modern Churches. We know from scripture that those who sin willfully and continually after receiving Christ are not justified in God's sight (Galatians 5:16–21 and Hebrews 10:26). Those verses would make no sense if future sins are forgiven at the moment of first belief. There is plenty of supporting evidence that these verses are written to believers.

Because we know that justification means we are declared righteous before God, 1 John 1:9 cannot make sense if we are *permanently* justified at the moment we come to Christ, because the passage (1 John 1:9) tells us that being faithful to confess our sins results in being cleansed from all unrighteousness. Unrighteousness is sin. *There is no need for a man who is fully and permanently justified at acceptance of Christ to be cleansed from sin.*

"He forgave us all our sins, having canceled the charge of our legal indebtedness, which stood against us and condemned us; he has taken it away, nailing it to the cross" (**Colossians 2:13–14**). "All our sins" is translated by some theologians to mean here all past, present, and future sins, but that is not the context of the rest of scripture. The verb tense is past, not future. This is reinforced by the language. The term "which stood" describes a past sin, something already in existence, not a future sin that has not yet occurred.

Even more direct is Peter's statement about immature believers: "But he that lacketh these things is blind, and cannot see afar off, and hath forgotten that he was purged from his *old* sins" (**2 Peter 1:9**). Only his *old sins* were purged when he came to Christ, not sins that he may commit after the purging. If present (ongoing) and future sins were also forgiven, why would God inspire Peter to limit the purging to "old sins?"

In Hebrews 10, we must read the full context of what is being taught, for this could seem to teach all sins are forgiven for all time.

> "For the law having a shadow of good things to come, and not the very image of the things, can never with those sacrifices which they offered year by year continually make the comers thereunto perfect. For then would they not have ceased to be offered? Because that the worshippers once purged should have had no more conscience of sins. But in those sacrifices there is a remembrance again made of sins every year. For it is not possible that the blood of bulls and of goats should take away sins. Wherefore when he cometh into the world, he saith, Sacrifice and offering thou wouldest not, but a body hast thou prepared me: In burnt offerings and sacrifices for sin thou hast had no pleasure. Then said I, Lo, I come (in the volume of the book it is written of me,) to do thy will, O God. Above when he said, Sacrifice and offering and burnt offerings and offering for sin thou wouldest not, neither hadst pleasure therein; which are offered by the law; Then said he, Lo, I come to do thy will, O God. He taketh away the first, that he may establish the second. By the which will we are sanctified through the offering of the body of Jesus Christ once for all. And every priest standeth daily ministering and offering oftentimes the same sacrifices, which can never take away

sins: But this man, after he had offered one sacrifice for sins forever, sat down on the right hand of God; From henceforth expecting till his enemies be made his footstool. For by one offering he hath perfected for ever them that are sanctified. Whereof the Holy Ghost also is a witness to us: for after that he had said before, This is the covenant that I will make with them after those days, saith the Lord, I will put my laws into their hearts, and in their minds will I write them; And their sins and iniquities will I remember no more. Now where remission of these is, there is no more offering for sin. Having therefore, brethren, boldness to enter into the holiest by the blood of Jesus, By a new and living way, which he hath consecrated for us, through the veil, that is to say, his flesh; And having an high priest over the house of God; Let us draw near with a true heart in full assurance of faith, having our hearts sprinkled from an evil conscience, and our bodies washed with pure water. *Let us hold fast the profession of our faith without wavering*; (for he is faithful that promised;) And let us consider one another to provoke unto love and to good works: Not forsaking the assembling of ourselves together, as the manner of some is; but exhorting one another: and so much the more, as ye see the day approaching" (**Hebrews 10:1–25**).

The reasoning of many in the Modern Church seems to be that since Christ died for *all* the sins of the world, then *all* a person's sins, including future sins, are forgiven at the moment he comes to Christ. The error in that reasoning is that it equates "paid for" with "forgiven." Yes, Christ died for the sins of the entire world; He paid for every sin that has ever been, or ever will, be committed. But we know from scripture that not all sins are forgiven. If they were, all mankind would spend eternity with God (and some suggest this whether they accept Jesus Christ or not).

However, a fair reading of the Bible reveals that the vast majority of people will spend eternity in the lake of fire (*e.g.*, Matthew 7:13). Their sins were paid for on the cross, but they were not forgiven because they never came to Christ in faith. Obviously, *payment does not equal forgiveness*. When we consider passages like this one, we must be careful to distinguish whether it is talking about payment for sin, or forgiveness of sin. The difference has eternal consequences. This passage is talking about *payment* for sin.

There are several other things to consider with this passage. First, the use of the word sanctified. In the passage, the word for sanctified (Greek *hagiazo*) means to be "freed from the guilt of sin." That is exactly happens when we accept Christ. However, our God-given free will remains in force. We are freed from the guilt we have about sin, but we retain the ability to choose to sin or not sin.

But here is the compelling point. Even if we sin after accepting Jesus Christ as our Lord and Savior and are truly sorry, confessing that sin to God (1 John 1:9), we need not carry the guilt around any longer. Jesus need not do anything else since He has already paid for all sins, and we Christians can be forgiven in Him by means of confession. But passages like the one in Hebrews quoted above were never designed to suggest that one may live in guilt-free sin because of what Jesus did. The New Testament is full of passages, written to Christians, admonishing them stop sinning (with warning of eternal consequences if they fail to stop).

Note the part of the passage quoted above which says, "And every priest standeth daily ministering and offering oftentimes the same sacrifices, which can never take away sins. But this man, after he had offered one sacrifice for sins forever, sat down on the right hand of God" (**Hebrews 10:11–12**). Jesus Christ is once and for all time, the permanent sacrifice (payment) for sins, but we must tap into that sacrifice through initial belief followed by continued demonstrated faith and confession of our sins. That is how receive forgiveness of sin. This interpretation makes all scripture true, not the understanding that all sins have been forgiven for all time at the moment of first belief.

It also aligns with the verses immediately following, "For if we sin wilfully after that we have received the knowledge of the truth, there remaineth no more sacrifice for sins, but a certain fearful looking for of judgment and fiery indignation, which shall devour the adversaries." (**Hebrews 10:26–27**). In plain language, the passage is saying that prior acceptance of Christ's gift of salvation will not prevent eternal damnation for a believer's future willful, habitual sin. Paul makes the same point in

Galatians 5:19–21, saying that "those who practice such things (habitual sins of the flesh) will not inherit the kingdom of God. This passage in Hebrews 10:26–27 and the passage in Galatians 5:19–21 directly address future willful, habitual sin by believers and refutes the idea that all sin (including future) is forgiven as soon as we accept Jesus Christ.

The Bible specifically addresses how to receive forgiveness of a Christian's sins after acceptance of Jesus Christ: "But if we walk in the light, as he is in the light, we have fellowship one with another and the blood of Jesus Christ his Son cleanseth us from all sin. If we say that we have no sin, we deceive ourselves, and the truth is not in us. *If we confess our sins*, he is faithful and just to *forgive us our sins*, and to cleanse us from all unrighteousness" (**1 John 1:7–9**).

The Modern Church often teaches that this is relational repair or relational forgiveness (to put us back "into fellowship" with God), but this requires reading into scripture things that are not there. The text states quite categorically that if we confess our sins, He is faithful to forgive our sins. That does not necessarily mean that we must confess sin that don't come to mind when we go before God in prayer, but that we should have the right heart before God, and be faithful in confessing our sin. But there is more to be learned here, so let's take a closer look at this passage.

The first thing we notice is the entire passage is conditional, *"But if we walk in the light."* We have already seen that one who believes in Christ does not necessarily walk in the light. Paul draws this distinction in Galatians 5:25 where he acknowledges the difference between walking in the Holy Spirit and having the indwelling of the Holy Spirit.

Remember that in the letter to the Galatians, Paul is talking to Christians (those who have accepted Christ). Paul had to warn them on multiple occasions about their sinful lifestyle, telling them their actions would prohibit them from inheriting the kingdom of God. The Galatians 5:19–21 passage expressly precludes the idea that all future sins will be forgiven. If all future sins are forgiven at the moment a person accepts Jesus Christ, Paul's warning (that they will not inherit the kingdom of God) is not only empty, but a flat out lie. A person who relies on the doctrine of men instead of the Word of God on this point should rethink his position.

The second thing we notice is that the passage clearly states that the promise of forgiveness of the sins of a believer is conditional: "*If* we confess our sins." Only after we confess our sins does God promise to forgive those sins. Once we are forgiven, we no longer need feel guilty about our sin: "As far as the east is from the west, so far hath he removed our transgressions from us" (**Psalm 103:12**).

The third thing we notice is that following forgiveness, God will *"cleanse us from all unrighteousness."* It is our unrighteousness, our sin, which separates us from God. God equates sin and unrighteousness later in this epistle, "All unrighteousness is sin" (**1 John 5:17a**). This part of the passage alone specifically tells us the passage in 1 John 1:9 is more than relational repair. It is the actual forgiving of sins.

If all our future sins were forgiven, there is no way we would need to be cleansed of our sins (or unrighteousness), nor could we ever break our fellowship with God by sinning, because all our sins would already be forgiven. Our separation from God comes because sin equals unrighteousness, which is abhorrent to a holy God. There are other verses that also seem to indicate that only our past sins are forgiven at the moment we accept Christ. A small sampling of these includes:

- "Whom God hath set forth to be a propitiation through faith in his blood, to declare his righteousness for the remission of *sins that are past*, through the forbearance of God" (**Romans 3:25**).
    - Commentary: The context is clearly unpunished sins, not present, and not future sins, and that God, through His forbearance (patience) did not punish those sins at the time they were committed. If this really meant future sins why would these not have been included? Why would the passage expressly say "past sins?"
- "And when ye stand praying, forgive, if ye have ought against any: that your Father also which is in heaven may forgive you your trespasses" and "But if ye forgive not men their trespasses, neither will your Father forgive your trespasses" (**Mark 11:25, Matthew 6:15**).
    - Commentary: Note the requirement that we must forgive others *before* the Father will forgive our sins. A heart harboring un-forgiveness is a present (ongoing) sin. Jesus makes it clear that present (ongoing) sin is not

forgiven, whether it is confessed or not. (This passage is Jesus' comment on "Forgive us our trespasses" in the Lord's Prayer). Jesus Himself makes it clear that only past sins are forgiven, both at the moment of coming to Christ and at times of later confession. God's forgiveness is withheld until you put that sin in the past and then confess it to Him (1 John 1:9). God does not forgive our present (ongoing) or future sin. Only when we put that sin behind us, in our past, will He accept our confession and bestow His forgiveness (1 John 1:9). There is an old bumper sticker that reads, "Christians aren't perfect; just forgiven." True to a point. We aren't perfect, but only our past sins are forgiven when we confess them. Since we aren't perfect, we will occasionally sin in the future. This verse tells us we have to put our sins in the past before we bring them before God in heartfelt confession if we are to be forgiven (**1 John 1:9**).

- "Blotting out the handwriting of ordinances that was against us, which was contrary to us, and took it out of the way, nailing it to his cross" (**Colossians 2:14**).
    - Commentary: Note the tense of the passage – that is blotting out that *which was against us* but not in any way suggesting the blotting out of that which we have not yet committed or what will be against us in the future.
- "For if we sin wilfully after that we have received the knowledge of the truth, there remaineth no more sacrifice for sins, But a certain fearful looking for of judgment and fiery indignation, which shall devour the adversaries" (**Hebrews 10:26–27**).
    - Commentary: As noted above, this is written to Christians, to warn them that those who sin willfully after receiving the truth (coming to Christ as in John 1:12) are no longer covered by Christ's sacrifice on the cross, and face eternal punishment. This demonstrates clearly that all future sins are not forgiven. Verse 29 of Hebrews 10 also makes it very clear that this applies to those sanctified, not unbelievers.

Paul emphasized the nature of those who are committed to sin: "Know ye not, that to whom ye yield yourselves servants to obey, his servants ye are to whom ye obey; whether of sin unto death, or of obedience unto righteousness" (**Romans 6:16**). Six verses later he wrote, "But now being made free from sin, and become servants to God, ye have your fruit unto holiness, and the end everlasting life" (**Romans 6:22**). It is clear Paul is talking about spiritual death or life. The book of Romans was written to Christians, and Romans 6:2 confirms that this chapter in Romans is addressed to believers. How could a believer's continual yielding to sin lead to his spiritual death, if all sins, past, present, and future were already forgiven?

God knows that some Christians will choose sin over Him. For that reason, He inspired many warnings in the gospels and epistles to make it clear that those who do so willfully or habitually will not spend eternity with Him. So it seems that, biblically, our past sins have been forgiven at the moment we accept Christ. Going forward in our Christian walk, we have Christ's perfect, eternal sacrifice available to us when we do sin, through true confession and repentance (1 John 1:9). Unfortunately, many, many passages in scripture warn us that His sacrifice does not guarantee entrance into the kingdom of God to those Christians who continue in willful or habitual sin.

We have not even talked about those Christians that take the mark of the beast. Wouldn't that sin also be forgiven if all future sins were forgiven? Yet God does not tell us that. Instead, we read, "And the smoke of their torment ascendeth up forever and ever: and they have no rest day nor night, who worship the beast and his image, and whosoever receiveth the mark of his name" (**Revelation 14:11**). Their eternal destiny seems clear.

What about later denying Christ? Jesus said, "But whosoever shall deny me before men, him will I also deny before my Father which is in heaven"(**Matthew 10:33**). How can this be so, if all a Christian's future sins are forgiven at the moment he receives Christ? Obviously it can't. And we know that Jesus is truth.

Sin without Confession

The inevitable questions that come up are "What happens if I sin before death without confession?" or "What happens if I refuse to confess a sin?" The answer to the same is both. God is able to judge the thoughts and attitudes of the heart as shown in scripture: "For the word of God is quick, and powerful, and sharper than any two-edged sword, piercing even to the dividing asunder of soul and spirit, and of the joints and marrow, and is a discerner of the thoughts and intents of the heart" (**Hebrews 4:12**). Jesus is the Word. These are His words.

God is able to discern the thoughts and attitudes of the heart, something we humans have a tough time doing, even with our own heart. If we die, having been a faithful servant, God knows our heart. If we have been faithful, doing our best to confess our sin and attempting to avoid sin, God knows this. God is able to forgive a faithful, obedient believer's non-habitual yet un-confessed sin through Christ's sacrifice, because He looks at the heart. In multiple places, we read, "Every way of a man is right in his own eyes: but the Lord pondereth the hearts" (**Proverbs 21:2**).

But the issue remains the heart. If we sin intentionally, if we are arrogant before God and refuse to confess our sins (even knowing how much he hates sin and how much it cost Him to pay for those sins), if we don't care enough to try to avoid sin, God also knows that heart as well. Christians who are committed to living in sin, or who refuse to try to avoid sin, or even refuse to confess their sins before God, should be concerned. That is arrogance before a holy, just and righteous God. We are called to be holy as God is Holy.

But the Modern Church teaches that no matter how callous we are, no matter how committed to sin we are, no matter if we refuse to forgive others, or fail with a contrite heart to seek forgiveness for ourselves, we are still saved. Don't believe it! Those who do are tempted to lead a sinful lifestyle that could endanger their eternity. This is exactly the type of apathy towards God that Jesus criticized in the Laodicean church.

Paying for Sins versus Forgiveness of Sins

There is a great difference between paying for sins and forgiveness of sins which apparently is not understood (or is ignored) by the Modern Church. Jesus is the once and for all time final sacrifice for sin, for not only Christians, but for the whole world. "And he is the propitiation for our [Christians'] sins: and not for ours only, but also for the sins of the whole world" (**1 John 2:2**). Think about this for a moment. He paid for every sin that mankind has committed or will ever commit.

Jesus Christ actually died for the sins of the whole world, but only those that have a relationship with Christ will actually be saved. Why? It is because forgiveness of sins in Christ is still the basic requirement for salvation. As discussed briefly above, we have a part in forgiveness; we have to accept God's gracious gift of salvation. Our acceptance is met with His forgiveness of our (past) sins.

True forgiveness comes with a sorrowful and contrite heart before the one against whom we have sinned. Thus, our contrite heart before God is important to the process. *Our desire to be forgiven is critical*; this is what we seek when we come to the cross. It is actually God's forgiveness we seek when we accept His gift of salvation. That forgiveness can only be granted by a just and holy God because Christ paid for those sins on the cross.

How do we receive forgiveness for our sins? We seek the forgiveness of God for past sins when we accept Jesus Christ, and He is faithful to do this if we are sincere. After we know Christ, we are to confess our sins and God is then faithful to forgive us: "If we confess our sins, he is faithful and just to forgive us our sins, and to cleanse us from all unrighteousness" **(1 John 1:9)**.

Again, since we know from scripture that Christ paid for the sins of the entire world but the whole world is not being saved, we must conclude there is a difference between what Christ did (payment for all sin) and forgiveness of sin. Forgiveness is not automatically imputed to everyone.

In 1 John 2:12 the word "forgiven" (Greek *aphiēmi*) is a present form verb indicating an action in the past with continuing action. However, it is a stretch to interpret this to mean all future sins are forgiven. Rather, the effect of the action is that those sins that were forgiven at our acceptance of Jesus Christ remain forever forgiven; we need not revisit them. Yet this is insufficient to ensure our entrance into the kingdom, because we will continue to sin even after we know Jesus Christ. That sin erects a new barrier between us and God, which we discuss below.

Forgiveness is something requiring action on our part, but which relies on the eternal sacrifice of Jesus Christ: "But this man, after he had offered one sacrifice for sins forever, sat down on the right hand of God" **(Hebrews 10:12)**.

Scripture teaches however, that there is no sacrifice for sins remaining for those believers who are willingly and continually sinning: "For if we sin wilfully after that we have received the knowledge of the truth, there remaineth no more sacrifice for sin" (**Hebrews 10:26**). This latter verse confirms that the sacrifice of Christ is eternal *and is required for future sins to be forgiven*. Otherwise, there could never be a situation where "no more sacrifice for sin" exists, if the Modern Church's interpretation of 1 John 2:12 (that all future sins are forgiven) is correct. It is amazing what infeasible and errant explanations some offer for this passage of scripture to try to discount its teaching.

While it is clear that Christ does not have to offer Himself as a sacrifice over and over, we must tap into that sacrifice, and this must be done over and over, any time we catch ourselves in a sin. Stated another way, does a person have to repent and seek forgiveness for sins to tap into Christ's sacrifice, or are a believer's sins automatically forgiven regardless of what he does after accepting Christ? The larger picture of scripture clearly seems to indicate there is no automatic forgiveness of a Christian's sins committed after coming to Christ. The condition of our heart is what is critical, yet Modern Church doctrine often builds callous and apathetic "Christians."

Scripture gives clear guidelines of the lifestyle of the believer (the narrow way) that leads to eternal life. Several verses in the Bible talk about God removing sin. An example includes, "For I will be merciful to their unrighteousness, and their sins and their iniquities will I remember no more" (**Hebrews 8:12**). These verses are talking about sins that have already been committed and are already forgiven. There is nothing to indicate that they apply to all future sins. Once we receive forgiveness for sins we have committed, we can know that God has been faithful and removed those sins from us. We need not deal with them again, even though we may continue to regret them. God understands if we are truly sincere in seeking forgiveness.

Key Thoughts

There is no place in the Bible where God has forgiven the sins of an individual before they are committed. Under certain circumstances, God has taken away the sin of some people after they commit them. Jesus' sacrifice on the cross provided the continuing and eternal sacrifice for sins of not just Christians, but of the whole world. However, to have our sins forgiven, we must first come to Christ (John 1:12–13).

To have sins forgiven which are committed after we come to Christ, we are to confess these to God after we have committed them. He is then faithful to forgive us (1 John 1:9) if we are sincere about our repentance and are not engaged in a willfully sinful lifestyle. He does not forgive present (ongoing) or future sins. If we forget or fail to confess our sins but with a heart of integrity, God is able to forgive unintentionally, unconfessed sins of those in Christ and are trying to live in obedience to His commandments. However, those who engage in patterns of willful sin, or those who willfully refuse to seek forgiveness, along with those who refuse to forgive others (an example of ongoing present sin), should be seriously concerned. These behaviors demonstrate the wrong heart before God.

We should never be in a position of regularly sinning and confessing things to God with an insincere heart. God knows our hearts, and we are unable to fool or mislead Him. To have our sins forgiven, we must be faithful, submit to the Holy Spirit, and try to obey His commandments.

Chapter 9

God's Promises

Misleading Christian sound bite(s): God will always fulfill His promises. Only if there are stated conditions on a promise are they conditional. God will do what He has promised regardless of man's decisions or efforts. God cannot change His mind once he has made a promise. All promises in the Bible are to Christians. Everything that God says is a promise.

Because this topic has the potential to be highly contentious, it is important to read the whole chapter. Rather than explore each sound bite, contrast with scripture, and then come to a conclusion, we will state the conclusion first: *God is faithful* to fulfill His promises, but 1) *He only fulfills the promise to the person or group to whom it is made*, and 2) *He only fulfills His promise after all stated and unstated conditions have been met. Too many in the Modern Church teach that if God says something, it is an unconditional promise and will happen no matter what.* Yet this is not what scripture teaches.

What is a Promise?

A promise is defined as "a declaration or assurance that one will do a particular thing or that a particular thing will happen." In some cases, the word guarantee is also used in place of the word promise. However, the understanding of what constitutes a promise, including a promise made by God, as presented from many Modern Church pulpits, often misses a critical element.

Misunderstanding God's promises gets many Christians into trouble. Because of the way God's promises are represented from the pulpit, many believe they have God boxed into a corner and that God must act to fulfill His promises, regardless of what happens or what a Christian does. The understanding often perpetuated throughout the Modern Church is that when God makes a promise to us, He will fulfill it or act upon it regardless of any other factors. This is a part of the mythology of God created by the Modern Church, but it is not consistent with scripture.

Indeed there are even some church leaders who will refuse the plain teaching of scripture demonstrating God has not fulfilled some promises in the past. They are not committed to the scripture but to the vision of God they have created in their own minds. It is not hard to see how we can end up with doctrine not on a firm scriptural footing.

This false understanding is part of the reason that we have the prosperity gospel. It is part of the reason that we have the OSAS doctrine. *There is a difference between God being faithful to a promise and God acting to fulfill a promise.* We can count on God's faithfulness, but we cannot necessarily count on God to act on a promise. Why? Because most of God's promises are conditional, not unconditional as many in Modern Church pulpits proclaim. For example, some of the promises of God are dependent on our obedience and our faith; that is the condition that must be met for the promise to be in effect. Furthermore, some of His promises are not even made to today's Christians.

If a church leader tells us God has given us a promise and quotes a verse or two out of context, how would we know if 1) the promise was given to us, and 2) the promise is unconditional or contains an explicit or implicit (unstated) condition? To get the answers, we must examine scripture with the aid of the Holy Spirit. Sermons on God's promises are often incomplete and misleading because these two elements of the promise are either ignored or misunderstood.

Does God always fulfill His Promises?

God does not always fulfill His promises by acting as He originally indicated He would because stated or unstated conditions are not met. God did not, for example, fulfill his promise to the Israelites leaving Egypt. God told the Israelites, "And I have said, I will bring you up out of the affliction of Egypt unto the land of the Canaanites, and the Hittites, and the Amorites, and the Perizzites, and the Hivites, and the Jebusites, unto a land flowing with milk and honey" (**Exodus 3:17**). While God did bring the Israelites out of Egypt, he did not deliver all those to whom He made the initial promise into the Promised Land. Even Moses did not enter the Promised Land.

God Himself explained in several scriptural passages why He did not fulfill His promise of Exodus 3:17 to all the Israelites who originally received the promise: "For the children of Israel walked forty years in the wilderness, till all the people that were men of war, which came out of Egypt, were consumed, *because they obeyed not the voice of the Lord*: unto whom the Lord sware that he would not shew them the land, which the Lord sware unto their fathers that he would give us, a land that floweth with milk and honey" (**Joshua 5:6**). God tells us point blank that He did not show them the land which He had promised their fathers to give them because they did not trust (have faith to obey) Him.

We know that God was capable, through His power, of bringing them into the Promised Land, but He did not do that because of the compromised faith of the Israelites. God explained His decision to Moses this way: *"Because all those men which have seen my glory, and my miracles, which I did in Egypt and in the wilderness, and have tempted me now these ten times*, and have not hearkened to my voice; Surely they shall not see the land which I sware unto their fathers, neither shall any of them that provoked me see it"* (**Numbers 14:22–23**). God tells us explicitly that He did not act on what He promised to do for those to whom He made the promise. Why?

It was because the promise was based on the faith of the nation of Israel in God, demonstrated through obedience. God actually led them to the Promised Land, and Joshua and Caleb pleaded with the people to trust God to fulfill His promise by going in and trusting Him to give them the land. The people showed their continuing lack of faith in God by talking of stoning them, until God Himself intervened (Numbers 14:6–10). All the men of war (the ones who displayed their lack of faith by refusing to trust God, as Joshua and Caleb had urged) were therefore denied the fulfillment of the promise, and died in the wilderness over the next forty years.

Did God kill the Israelites after they tempted God once? No. Tempted

God twice? No. Tempted God five times? No. Ten times the Israelites continued to tempt God through their disobedience. The grace of God, even in the Old Testament was on display. But the grace of God is not without limits. He had patience with "His treasured possession" (Israel) yet the Israelites kept on testing God. When God actually put the Promised Land right in front of them, they lacked the faith to go in and take it. They didn't trust God to fulfill what He had promised, and finally God said enough.

What is compelling about this event is that we are reminded three times in the New Testament that the Israelites did not enter the Promised Land as God had promised (1 Corinthians 10, Hebrews 3–4, and Jude). Furthermore, we are warned not to follow their example. But there is a reason why this does not nullify God's faithfulness. Let's look at a few more examples before we analyze that reason.

We have a similar situation where a man of God told Eli, "Wherefore the Lord God of Israel saith, I said indeed that thy house, and the house of thy father, should walk before me forever: but now the Lord saith, Be it far from me; for them that honour me I will honour, and they that despise me shall be lightly esteemed" (**1 Samuel 2:30**). Lightly esteemed (Hebrew *qalal*) means of "trivial value" or "cursed." God made a promise that they would walk before Him forever, but later God, based on their behavior, had apparently changed His mind.

Another example occurred with the Ninevites: "So Jonah arose, and went unto Nineveh, according to the word of the Lord. Now Nineveh was an exceeding great city of three days' journey. And Jonah began to enter into the city a day's journey, and he cried, and said, Yet forty days, and Nineveh shall be overthrown. So the people of Nineveh believed God, and proclaimed a fast, and put on sackcloth, from the greatest of them even to the least of them" (**Jonah 3:3–6**).

God did not end up doing the harm He stated He would to Nineveh because the Ninevites repented of their evil. God's stated course of action changed based on the behavior of the Ninevites. But He did not explicitly tell the Ninevites that they would be saved if they repented; He gave no condition at all that we can see in scripture. He simply told them, through the prophet Jonah that Nineveh would be overturned in 40 days. The king responded, "Who can tell if God will turn and repent, and turn away from his fierce anger, that we perish not?" (**Jonah 3:9**).

If the king of Nineveh had assumed, as many modern day Christians do, that God's statements (promises) of His future action are irrevocable, regardless of the subsequent behavior of the objects of the promise, there would have been no reason for him to advise his subjects to repent, for he would have believed their fate had been sealed.

But the king and his subjects understood that their subsequent behavior might prevent fulfillment of God's promise of destruction. The sinning Ninevites understood this about God, but the Modern Church does not seem to. God knows and sees the past, present, and future with equal clarity. He knew the Ninevites would repent, but went through the process to motivate them to repent. What He said did not happen because of the sincere repentance of the Ninevites, an unstated condition to avoid destruction.

Consider another example where God specifically sent Isaiah to tell Hezekiah, the King of Judah, "Set thine house in order: for thou shalt die, and not live" (**Isaiah 38:1**). God specifically sent Isaiah to Hezekiah to tell him he was going to die and to put his affairs in order. But what happened? Hezekiah tearfully prayed to God and God sent Isaiah back to Hezekiah, telling Isaiah, "Go, and say to Hezekiah, Thus saith the Lord, the God of David thy father, I have heard thy prayer, I have seen thy tears: behold, I will add unto thy days fifteen years" (**Isaiah 38:5**). Our God, praise to Him, is moved by both rebellion and by prayerful entreaties offered with soft hearts.

We thank God for His grace and His mercy but we as Christians must understand this about our God: He is faithful, but He will not necessarily act as stated if *we* refuse to act faithfully.

Are God's Promises all Unconditional?

Most of God's promises (but not all), are conditional. The same is true on this earth. If I promise to buy your house, this does not relieve you of your responsibility to attend the closing, pay fees, and sign over the house. These are assumed conditions, even though they may not be explicitly stated. The same is true with most of God's promises.

God has an expectation of us that must be fulfilled to realize His promises. That expectation is *faith*. Not faith in the promise, but faith in God. Nor is it the faith that is some intellectual exercise. It is the faith that manifests itself in action; that is, a genuine faith. Faith in a promise itself means nothing, just as Jesus taught the Pharisees the hypocrisy of their belief about what made the gold in the temple sacred. Faith in God means everything.

We must have faith in the one making the promise, just as we do when we lend people money expecting repayment. We trust the borrower to repay. However, the modern-day idea that we can expect to receive (or *claim*) a promise from God when we are committed to disobeying or ignoring Him is both illogical and unscriptural. This is another of the failings of the Modern Church. The idea that we can "stand on a promise of God" no matter how we act is clearly not scriptural, yet because of the shallow presentations of many church leaders, people's actions testify to their belief that God's promises will be fulfilled no matter how they act.

It is the specific reason we are reminded three times in the New Testament of the example of the adult male Israelites leaving Egypt not entering the Promised Land. Almost all of God's promises are conditioned on a true and living faith and a committed heart before God, whether or not that condition is stated. We see that in the examples cited in the preceding section. Even though scripture shows the opposite, the Modern Church commonly teaches that God will fulfill His promises no matter how we act. This is either implied or explicitly stated by many Modern Church leaders. There is no explanation to believers of what a promise of God is, to whom the promise is given, and, if the promise is to us, or what is required of us to make us eligible to receive the promise. Often, the Modern Church teaches we need only "claim" a promise, believe a promise, and God has no choice but to fulfill the promise.

The idea that we can believe in something and then ignore the conditions upon which the promise is based (acting contrary to what God wills) is errant and frankly, dangerous. It is another approach to interpreting scripture that builds the Laodicean Church. Too many believers try to "rest on the promises of God" without ever considering the conditions accompanying the promise, and refusing to acknowledge that their actions have anything to do with God's fulfillment of the promise. The Israelites leaving Egypt learned this the hard way.

We can fail to receive a promise of God when we do not meet the stated or unstated condition upon which the promise is based: "Let us therefore fear, lest, *a promise being left us of entering into his rest, any of you should seem to come short of it. For unto us was the gospel preached, as well as unto them: but the word preached did not profit them, not being mixed with faith in them that heard it*" (**Hebrews 4:1–2**). God Himself warns believers not to "fall short" of His promise, indicating clearly that *we* have responsibility to fulfill in order to partake of that promise. The condition mentioned here is faith. Yet this is rarely explained from the pulpit. It is much simpler and more compelling to tell congregations that God will act to fulfill His promises no matter how they act.

When God does not act to fulfill a promise to those whom He gave it, does this mean that God is untrustworthy? Absolutely not! Does this mean that God lies? No. Does it make God unfaithful? No!

God is faithful to His promises, but most of His promises are conditioned upon the faith in God and subsequent behavior of the recipient. If the person or group to whom the promise is made fails to meet the (stated or unstated) condition(s), God's promise will not be fulfilled *for those who fail to meet the condition(s).* Why? It is because the promise was made to those who meet God's condition(s) for receiving the promise. The promise was never directed to those who would not meet the condition(s). This is demonstrated over and over in the Old Testament, where we see the things that God says to man often linked to the faith (and subsequent behavior) of man.

But church leaders often assume and present the promises of God as unconditional, when they are actually conditional. It is a teaching from the pulpit that often leads believers to act in an unfaithful manner because they believe that they have a promise from God they can rely on no matter how they act. As a result, many cling to a dogmatic and incomplete understanding of God's promises. Many make claims about the promises of God which are not consistent with scripture.

How do we come short of God's promise of entering His rest? *We come short if we don't receive the promise by a true and living faith,* an express condition for receiving the promise, as detailed in earlier chapters. Faith that saves, faith that results in the receiving of God's promises, is not faith characterized as a simple belief, but rather an engaging faith *in God* that manifests itself in action.

Many want to believe the promises of God on their terms, without examining the underlying explicit or implicit conditions. The concept of

God's promises being unconditional is applied to salvation, prosperity, and many other things. Stated differently, people want to believe the promises of God apply to them even though they continue to act in an unfaithful and disobedient manner towards God. But in most cases, God's promises are conditioned upon the faith of the recipient. *The faith required to realize those conditional promises of God is an obedient faith, a fruitful faith, and a lasting faith.*

Some Modern Church preachers even teach that God's promises are not like man's promises, and are therefore not conditioned on our faith. Scripture paints a different picture. Almost all of God's promises are conditioned (stated or unstated) on us having an obedient faith.

May God grant us grace? Yes. God showed grace to the Israelites leaving Egypt because He did not destroy them the first nine times they were unfaithful, but eventually God said "enough." The grace of God is elastic, not unbreakable. We should never harbor the evil thought "sinning is no big deal because I have the grace of God to cover it." That is pure evil before a holy God. Yet this idea is starting to surface more and more in the Modern Church.

Paul warned the believers at Corinth: "Moreover, brethren, I would not that ye should be ignorant, how that all our fathers were under the cloud, and all passed through the sea; And were all baptized unto Moses in the cloud and in the sea; And did all eat the same spiritual meat; And did all drink the same spiritual drink: for they drank of that spiritual Rock that followed them: and that Rock was Christ. But with many of them God was not well pleased: for they were overthrown in the wilderness" (**1 Corinthians 10:1–5**). God specifically draws the parallels between us and the Israelites to show us we are in the exact same position they were.

Some might teach that the Israelites dying in the wilderness were simply disciplined and are with God in eternity even now. But looking at it this way is very temporal (or earthly) perspective. If we believe such, what we are really saying is that God rewarded them for their sin. We must remember that it is always better to be with the Lord than here on earth.

Paul specifically noted this in Philippians 1:23. Paul said it was *far* better. Even on the best day, the Promised Land is a much worse place than being with the Lord. Do you really think God rewards people for disobedience by taking them into the kingdom? We see no evidence of that in scripture. An examination of the underlying Greek, along with the context of the passage in Hebrews 3, strongly suggests the "rest" being discussed is eternal rest.

So we see that it is completely unbiblical to teach a person that all of God's promises are unconditional and apply to him. We discuss this point further in Chapter 12, "The Temporal versus the Eternal: the Prosperity Gospel." The Modern Church's teachings on God's promise of salvation are especially dangerous. Many Modern Church leaders tell their followers they can simply believe the promises of God concerning salvation at one point in time and be forever saved, no matter how they may live after accepting Christ. This is often what is implied or expressly taught from the pulpit.

Many millions of church-goers have been taught and believe this to their peril. But like almost all of God's promises, the promise of salvation also has conditions. Always carefully examine any promise of God you find in scripture to see if it applies to you, and determine the conditions that must be met to be eligible to receive the promise. Faith is a requirement for almost all of God's promises to us.

Are God's Promises for All?

Church leaders also make the mistake of assuming all of God's promises apply to the church, even when the context indicates that they apply to the nation of Israel or to other groups. This often results in the church leaders making unilateral promises on God's behalf that are not fully supported by scripture. This is especially dangerous on the question of salvation because many church leaders are mistakenly or deliberately misapplying scriptural promises to the church.

Consider this commonly stated example: God told the exiled nation of Israel, "For I know the thoughts that I think toward you, saith the Lord, thoughts of peace, and not of evil, to give you an expected end" (**Jeremiah 29:11**). An examination of **Jeremiah 29:4** reveals that this promise is made "unto all that are carried away captives, whom I have caused to be carried away from Jerusalem unto Babylon." It was never made to the church. Nothing could be more explicit.

Yet this verse is often appropriated by church leaders preaching a prosperity gospel message, applying it to say that God is somehow obligated to bless their flocks with earthly financial and health prosperity, when in fact the promise was never made to them.

Another well-known example is found in Jesus' discourse with Nicodemus, "And as Moses lifted up the serpent in the wilderness, even so must the Son of man be lifted up: That whosoever believeth in him should not perish, but have eternal life. For God so loved the world, that he gave his only begotten Son, that whosoever believeth in him should not perish, but have everlasting life. For God sent not his Son into the world to condemn the world; but that the world through him might be saved" (**John 3:14–17**).

Who is this promise written to? To those that have, at one moment in time, believed? Not exactly, although this is what some in the Modern Church teach. As we discussed earlier, "believeth" (Greek *pisteuō*) is in the present tense (commonly called the continuous present tense), so the promise is actually made to those that believe now and continue believing, not those that believed at one time and have abandoned their belief (or failed to endure in their faith).

It is of note that some church leaders will camp out on the concept that, "For all the promises of God in him are yea, and in him Amen, unto the glory of God by us" (**2 Corinthians 1:20**). But they only want to talk about God's promises that seem to benefit their congregations, and never seem to state that God's promises of punishment may also apply to their flocks.

Apparently they believe they are called to "sell" God as a God of love, mercy and forgiveness, rather than faithfully speaking the whole and balanced truth of scripture. Their approach to scripture is often unbalanced. They want to apply the positive promises of God to their flock regardless of whom the promises are written to, but do not apply the negative promises (warnings of the consequences of disobedience) that clearly apply to today's Christians.

In reality, what Jesus promised today's believers is the opposite of the promise in Jeremiah 29:11: "If the world hate you, ye know that it hated me before it hated you. If ye were of the world, the world would love his own: but because ye are not of the world, but I have chosen you out of the world, therefore the world hateth you. Remember the word that I said unto you, The servant is not greater than his lord. If they have persecuted me, they will also persecute you; if they have kept my saying, they will keep yours also" (**John 15:18–20**). A similar teaching is, "Yea, and all that will live godly in Christ Jesus shall suffer persecution" (**2 Timothy 3:12**). Jesus told his disciples (and by extension all believers living after his ascension) that they would be hated and persecuted by the world. This is God's promise to His true disciples. They are not promised health, wealth and prosperity.

Key Thoughts

Our God is not untrustworthy in any way. *God is faithful.* But we have misunderstood God and His promises. We have developed a false mythology of who our God is especially as relates to the promises of our God. There are passages in scripture where God's promise was not fulfilled, based on man's actions of obedience based on faith or disobedience grounded in a lack of faith in God. *This tells us that those promises were conditional; not that God was unfaithful.*

We find no instance where God did not keep His promise to those intended recipients who met the conditions accompanying the promise. Most of God's promises are tied to one condition, often not explicitly stated; that condition is the *living and demonstrated faith* of the intended recipient. Believing a promise applies to us, and then acting unfaithfully toward God, doesn't lead to realization of the promise, because the condition of faithfulness has not been met. The promise only applies to those who meet the condition.

Therefore, it is a mistake to simply assume that God's promises will all be fulfilled regardless of what we do or do not do. Again, most of God's promises are conditional, usually conditioned on a faith resulting in obedience.

The context of promises made in the Bible must be considered before stating their applicability to modern-day Christians. It is not reasonable for Christians to assume they can appropriate promises made to others. We must apply an understanding of the context in which a promise is made to know if it is meant for us.

Scripture teaches this: If you personally want to receive one of God's promises, 1) make sure you are in the category of those to whom He made the promise, and then 2) make sure you meet God's stated and unstated conditions to be eligible to receive the promise.

Chapter 10

The Sovereignty of God

Misleading Christian sound bite(s): God is in control

The subject of God's sovereignty contrasted with man's free will is such complex and deep subject matter that it alone could warrant its own set of books. But the "God is in control" mantra we often hear from the pulpit is too simplistic and does not capture the truth, at least not the whole truth. So we must be wary of using that sound bite to justify doctrine or decisions.

The world and the events that occur within it do not reflect fully deterministic control by God because the things that happen in this world do not reflect God's will *as revealed in the Bible.* Nor do the choices and actions of the people in the Bible. Usually, we have an idea of what is, and what is not, within God's will because of His Word and what He tells us. That does not mean we understand all of God's plans or purposes, or know of all His efforts. But we do know what pleases Him and what angers Him, and consequently, much of what is within His will and what is not within His will. Indeed this is the focus of much of scripture.

The Bible itself may be the single greatest testament to the free will that God has granted us. Throughout the Bible, we see people who are confronted with choices and provided guidance on how God wants them to respond to those choices. We also see God's reactions to those choices. If the entire world reflected God's good and perfect will (*i.e.,* if God actually does exercise His control over everything that happens in the world), then not only would the Bible itself be disingenuous, but what the Bible tells us about God's will would be at odds with what happens in this fallen world.

The sound bite "God is in Control"

There is a difference between someone explicitly in control (actually controlling someone or something) and someone implicitly in control (having the ability to control someone or something but not actually doing it). For example, we can control our children's actions because of our larger size and greater strength (explicitly control them) but we generally tell them what they should and should not do and trust them to do the right thing (implicitly control them).

God has provided us a moral framework (commandments and commands) and ceded free will to mankind, expecting us to exercise our free will to submit to His will because of who He is and the love He has shown us. This is the reason that we are commanded to do and not do certain things in the Bible. However, as we know, man often makes decisions, both corporately and individually, that are contrary to God's will.

The Bible is full of examples of God's will not being done on earth. Jesus' lament over Jerusalem is one example: "O Jerusalem, Jerusalem, thou that killest the prophets, and stonest them which are sent unto thee, how often would I have gathered thy children together, even as a hen gathereth her chickens under her wings, and ye would not" (**Matthew 23:37**). We see that God desired to gather His people to Himself, but Jesus said "ye would not," demonstrating that God allowed His people to choose to oppose His will. In this case, disobedience was followed by the destruction of the city in 70 A.D.

We see this time and time again throughout the Bible; God tells people His will and subsequently allows men to use their God-given free will to obey or oppose His will. Disobedience is followed by punishment, temporal and/or eternal. Consider God's commandment to Moses: "Take the rod, and gather thou the assembly together, thou, and Aaron thy brother, and speak ye unto the rock before their eyes; and it shall give forth his water, and thou shalt bring forth to them water out of the rock: so thou shalt give the congregation and their beasts drink" (**Numbers 20:8**). What did Moses do? We are told a few verses later: "And Moses lifted up his hand, and with his rod he smote the rock twice: and the water came out abundantly, and the congregation drank, and their beasts also" (**Numbers 20:11**). Moses disobeyed God, and as a result did not enter into the Promised Land with the next generation of Israelites.

If God forced people to do evil, He would be open to the charge of being the source of evil (which He is not). Calvinists sometimes argue that God is the source of evil because He created beings which do evil (fallen angels and humans). Their reasoning is flawed. Just as our justice system does not hold parents accountable for what their kids do after they become adults, God is not responsible for what His sentient beings do with the choice God gives them. We are accountable before God, and should be examining ourselves, not Him, as the source of evil.

If God forced people to do something He told them not to do, and then punished them for it, then God would not be a just God. If God commanded them to do something and they refused, and allowed them to make the choice to submit to His will or disobey, then punishment is warranted. Moses, as we cited above from Numbers 20, falls into this category. The Bible is clear about how righteous and just our God is. We are taught, "He is the Rock, his work is perfect: for all his ways are judgment: a God of truth and without iniquity, just and right is he" (**Deuteronomy 32:4**).

When we make a simplistic claim that God is in control and leave it at that, we give the impression that God does actually control everything. If God is in control, we wonder why God is "causing" 20,000 children a day to starve to death. We wonder why there is terrorism and war. We wonder why women and children are forced into prostitution. We wonder why adults abuse children. The list goes on and on and on.

God is not the cause of any of these – man is. It is people that make the choices that cause these things to happen. God has given us the free will to choose to obey or disobey. God does not desire those things to happen. It is not His will for these to occur. Furthermore, just because God does not intervene to stop such evils does not mean that He want them to happen. No, evil in this world is the product of the free will of man as led by the evil one and his own sinful nature.

Even though we have a sinful nature, God has told us how to avoid evil. Perhaps the best example of this truth is the choice God gave the nation of

Israel in Deuteronomy Chapters 28–30. God clearly spells out the blessings of obedience and the dire consequences of disobedience. As we know, the Israelites ultimately choose disobedience and suffered all the promised consequences. But God is not disingenuous or insincere. God earnestly wanted the Israelites to adhere to the covenant He made with them.

Yet many of us refuse to come to God on His terms. Jesus talked about what it really cost to be His follower: "Or what king, going to make war against another king, sitteth not down first, and consulteth whether he be able with ten thousand to meet him that cometh against him with twenty thousand? Or else, while the other is yet a great way off, he sendeth an ambassage, and desireth conditions of peace. So likewise, whosoever he be of you that forsaketh not all that he hath, he cannot be my disciple" (**Luke 14:31-33**).

Back to the breakfast analogy: God wants pigs, not chickens. You may want to forget about "cheap grace." There may not be many chickens in the kingdom. Better to use our will to submit to His will. Remember, it's about Him, not about us. God teaches us that to have peace with Him we are to submit to His will, on His terms. We are to submit to His will using our own free will. Yet much of the Modern Church teaches that we can engage God on our terms.

If we lived the way God intended and followed His guidance and laws, none of the problems of evil in the world would exist. Let us again state assuredly, that per scripture, it is not God's will that the evils in this world exist. He would like us all to choose Him and His will, "For this is good and acceptable in the sight of God our Saviour; Who will have all men to be saved, and to come unto the knowledge of the truth" (**1 Timothy 2:3-4**). Yet here again, we know this is not going to happen because of man's free will. God's will is not done, further proof that He does not actually *cause* all things to happen.

All people do not choose to obediently submit to God's will. The result? Evil in the world arises out of our misuse of the free will given to us by God. Yet free will is the essence of what is required for true love. If we are forced to love God through the exercising of His will alone, the love God receives is not a freely given love. Forced love is not love; it is slavery. God wants us to love Him voluntarily, and to demonstrate that love through obedience: "If ye love me, keep my commandments" (**John 14:15**).

Now some versions of the Bible do *seem* to indicate that God controls everything. One example is the verse that teaches, "I know that thou canst do every thing, and that no thought can be withholden from thee" (**Job 42:2**). This is the rendering in the KJV but other versions render the verse as indicating no purpose of God can be thwarted. We see these are not similar.

The KJV reading is more consistent with the context of the rest of the passage and with the underlying language (Hebrew *mĕzimmah*). The underlying Hebrew suggests that no purpose or plan may be hidden from God. God knows the heart and the mind. Whatever we do is an open book before Him, but that does not mean that His will or His plans are always done. But let's be clear also: there are cases where God's purposes or plans will not be thwarted.

But there is *huge* difference between our God being *able to control everything* and *actually controlling everything*. It logically follows without need for explanation, that if God gave us the free will to choose to obey or disobey Him, God elects not to control everything. The evidence of this is all around us.

However, we make a terrible mistake when we assume that God has a plan or purpose for everything, a plan which cannot be thwarted, and thus reason that God actually controls everything. God had a plan for the Israelites leaving Egypt, "And I have said, I will bring you up out of the affliction of Egypt unto the land of the Canaanites, and the Hittites, and the Amorites, and the Perizzites, and the Hivites, and the Jebusites, unto a land flowing with milk and honey" (**Exodus 3:17**). Yet all but two of the adult male Israelites did not follow God's plan for their lives and died without entering the land they were promised.

When we view scripture through the lens of God using His sovereignty to actually control everything, we now see the evil in the world as an outcome of God's plans and purposes. It is the single greatest failing of the Calvinist's interpretation of scripture; the foundational principle of Calvinism is the mistaken assumption that God controls everything, beginning with our salvation.

This assumption is unscriptural, but very appealing to our sinful nature. The logic is obvious: it relieves us of all responsibility for our salvation. If we extend the concept that "God is in control" far enough, it frees us from any responsibility for our own actions, no matter how sinful, hurtful, or disobedient to God's commands. We are totally free to indulge our fleshly desires, not because "the devil made me do it," but because either "God made me do it." It is easy to see why this doctrine is popular and growing. Yet this is not what the broader picture of scripture teaches.

Instead, scripture is replete with commands and warnings that would not be needed if God truly orchestrated everything. The Old Testament is filled with tragic stories of the consequences of man's disobedience, but how can a just God punish anyone for disobedience that He orchestrated? The sad part is that the Modern Church is increasingly adopting Calvinistic doctrine, which indirectly relieves the members of the body of their obligation of obedience to Christ's commands.

An ever-increasing number of church leaders now focus only on preaching comforting and reassuring doctrines (many of which are misleading half-truths), instead of teaching the whole truth of scripture. A key element of this reassuring presentation is that "God is in control." Sermons in the Modern Church increasingly focus on helping us deal with worldly issues rather than improving our spiritual posture.

Because of a worldly perspective, we even misuse verses like, "And we know that all things work together for good to them that love God, to them who are the called according to his purpose (**Romans 8:28**). The problem is we want to apply a worldly perspective to such verses and treat them as promising worldly good. But that is not the way of true disciples.

Jesus taught his disciples a different message: "And ye shall be betrayed both by parents, and brethren, and kinsfolks, and friends; and some of you shall they cause to be put to death. And ye shall be hated of all men for my name's sake" (**Luke 21:16–17**). Jesus knew that there would be consequences for remaining faithful to Him. Although God could stop all members of the faithful from being persecuted or even murdered, He does not. We have lost touch with what our Lord taught us about true faith and the real cost of discipleship.

Consider just a couple of passages that are rendered untrue or disingenuous if the idea that God is exercising control over everything is true.

- "Enter ye in at the strait gate: for wide is the gate, and broad is the way, that leadeth to destruction, and many there be which go in

thereat: because strait is the gate, and narrow is the way, which leadeth unto life, and few there be that find it" (**Matthew 7:13–14**).
    - Commentary: Why would God tell *us* to enter ye in at the strait gate if we had no choice? Why would God command us to do *anything* in His Word if we had no choice? And why even mention a narrow way if we have no choice to depart from it?
- "If any man will come after me, let him deny himself, and take up his cross daily, and follow me. For whosoever will save his life shall lose it: but whosoever will lose his life for my sake, the same shall save it. For what is a man advantaged, if he gain the whole world, and lose himself, or be cast away?" (**Luke 9:23–25**).
    - Commentary: Why would God tell us that to follow Jesus we must take up our cross daily and deny ourselves if we had no choice? And why would we even bother if we are "elect" and cannot lose our salvation?

The claim of the Modern Church that "God is in control" and the misunderstanding it propagates, often encourages people to think they are not responsible for their actions before God. They interpret what they hear from the pulpit to mean: 1) they are already saved (elected before the foundation of the world); and 2) they have "unconditional eternal security," meaning that they cannot possibly lose their salvation.

Even basic teachings such as, "For even when we were with you, this we commanded you, that if any would not work, neither should he eat" (**2 Thessalonians 3:10**) would be considered inaccurate, because they place responsibility onto a person. People, including some Modern Church preachers, have taken this idea to the extreme, suggesting we need not own any responsibility in doing evil before God, because God made us the way we are and is in control of everything. Such teachings are more closely related to New Age and Asian fatalism than to the Bible. Do not be deceived. *We are responsible before our God.*

There are many passages in scripture that tell us that God *does not* control everything, and that, in fact, His will is usually *not* done on earth. For example, "For this is good and acceptable in the sight of God our Saviour; Who will have all men to be saved, and to come unto the knowledge of the truth" (**1 Timothy 2:3–4**). But we know that most of mankind takes the broad way to destruction (Matthew 7:13), in direct opposition to God's expressed will. And why would Jesus, when instructing us how to pray, pray to the Father, "Thy will be done in earth, as it is in heaven" (Matthew 6:10)? Even a brief look at scripture reveals the fallacy of the concept that God actually exercises His control over everything.

When we consider the implications of our ability to choose compared to the Calvinist doctrine related to salvation (God completely controls everything and decides who would be saved and would be lost before the foundation of the world), we seem to be left with three choices. We have to select one (and only one).

1. We believe that God's will is always done with respect to salvation, yet many will be lost according to scripture; thus the passages of scripture in 1 Timothy2:3–4 and 2 Peter 3:9 are not true; it is not God's will that all men be saved.
2. We believe that God's will is always done with respect to salvation, and since God wills all men to be saved, then all will actually be saved, even those apart from Christ, again in contradiction of scripture (Matthew 7:13).
3. God's will is not always done here on earth.

Scripture bears witness to the truth of only one of these; the last one. Remember that God *could* control everyone and force them to the salvation He wills, yet the pleas, warnings and admonitions in scripture all testify they are written to men with free will to accept or reject Christ. This is no different than the choices that God gave man many years ago.

We have seen many attempts to explain away these passages (God's desire for all to be saved) in Calvinistic soteriology, often using complex rationalization. In most cases, they use, as a foundation, that God is in control of (and therefore actually does control) everything, even though we see clearly from scripture that God does not actually control everything.

Over and over in scripture, God's will is ignored by man's choices, and often, man suffers the consequences of acting unfaithfully. There are many examples, including Joshua 5:4–6, Isaiah 24:1–5, the book of Amos, and Acts 5:1–11. Yes, God has the power to control everything, but God obviously doesn't. God allows man to make the choice to obey or disobey Him, beginning in the Garden of Eden and continuing, according to prophecy, until the end of time. This is what we term "free will."

Consider David for a moment. We know that David had the right heart before God because God specifically tells us so. David spent much time in prayer with the Lord. But it is what David wrote in his Psalms that catches our attention. In Psalm 18 for example, we see his frequent use of the pronoun "I." David wrote, "I will love thee" [**v1**], "in whom I trust" [**v2**], "I will call" [**v3**], "I have kept the ways of the Lord" [**v21**], "I was upright before Him," and "I kept myself from iniquity" [**v23**]. Psalm 26 repeats this theme where David again talks about all ways in which he has acted. You may want to go through the Psalms of David and count the number of times which David uses the word "I" to describe his faithful action.

Either such prayers of David are an offense to the Lord if God is controlling David's actions because David is taking credit for what God has done, or David clearly understands that he has a responsibility before the Lord to submit his will to God. David, through his prayers, often identifies those things he cannot control and trusts to the Lord for those things, reminding the Lord that he is acting faithfully. For example, David clearly understands that he cannot save himself; this is shown throughout his Psalms.

But David also acknowledges that he knows he has a responsibility to act faithfully before the Lord. If you read the prayers of David, it becomes clear that David does not expect, nor see, the Lord controlling everything. What we see is that David knows he has a responsibility toward God, and is committed to acting faithfully. Yet we see many pastors in the Modern Church focusing on the concept of greater control by the Lord, and less and less responsibility of man before God. It is a recipe for disaster, because it abrogates the responsibility of man before God. However in scripture, God's faithful followers often acknowledge and demonstrate their required faithful action in obedience to God.

A More Reasonable Claim

A more reasonable claim is: "God *can* control everything." This more correctly reflects, from a scriptural and experiential perspective, the truth. This does not mean that we see everything; we do not. Again, we can be assured that God does not, for example, lead or force people to do evil – that would be inconsistent with His nature: "God is love" (**1 John 4:16b**). Hence God could control those doing evil, but does not; they do evil of their own free will. James makes this point: "But every man is tempted, when he is drawn away of his *own lust*, and enticed" (**James 1:14**). We are even warned by God specifically in scripture to, "abstain from all appearance of evil" (**1 Thessalonians 5:22**).

Does God allow evil? Absolutely. It is a consequence of giving men and angels free will. But does God cause evil? Absolutely not. Failure to appreciate the difference leads many in the Modern Church to bad places theologically. Let's examine some key aspects of this apparent dichotomy which man has wrestled with over the centuries.

Much of the Bible is a series of commandments, commands, guidance, and instructions to men. Most of the Bible describes men's reactions to God's commands and the subsequent reaction of God to men using their free will. Indeed, the commands God has given us are unnecessary if we are controlled; moreover, they are disingenuous. They are disingenuous because there is no need to command us to act in a given manner when we have no choice to obey or disobey. It would be like telling a tree to stand in the place it is located. God uses His word and the love He has shown us to motivate us to love (and obey) Him. "We love him, because he first loved us" (**1 John 4:19**). Jesus told His disciples, "If ye keep my commandments, ye shall abide in my love" (**John 15:10**). Obviously, they had a choice.

If we really consider all that happens in the world today, we see that God does not actually exercise control over everything. The Bible tells us explicitly that, "In whom the god of this world hath blinded the minds of them which believe not, lest the light of the glorious gospel of Christ, who is the image of God, should shine unto them" (**2 Corinthians 4:4**). This world is permeated with the evil one's influence. God has allowed this. Not *caused* it, but allowed it.

Look at this passage from the temptation of Jesus: "And the devil, taking him up into an high mountain, shewed unto him all the kingdoms of the world in a moment of time. And the devil said unto him, All this power will I give thee, and the glory of them: for that is delivered unto me; and to whomsoever I will I give it" (**Luke 4:5–6**). Satan told Jesus that the power and glory of this world was delivered unto Him.

Note that Jesus accepted Satan's assertion that he has been given power over the world. Jesus simply countered with scripture command us to worship God only. Satan is the ruler of this world, with many under his command: "For we wrestle not against flesh and blood, but against principalities, against powers, against the rulers of the darkness of this world, against spiritual wickedness in high places" (**Ephesians 6:12**).

Consider the additional evidence presented in Job 1, Daniel 10:12–13, and Revelation 13:1–2. Many in the Modern Church are not even aware of this fact. Their pastors seldom mention it, because it is not part of the "positive" image of Christianity they want to portray. We see evil reign on this earth, as the majority of mankind, along with Satan and his fallen angels, live in rebellion against God. If we attribute the evil in the world to God, we ignore scriptural reality.

Although God's will is usually *not* done on earth, we Christians are commanded to seek and defer to His will. He knows best, and he wants all things to work together for our good if we love God and are called according to His purpose (Romans 8:28). That is why our Lord and Savior, in teaching us to pray in the Lord's Prayer, implored us to petition God, "Thy kingdom come. *Thy will be done in earth, as it is in heaven*" (**Matthew 6:10**). As a side note, notice that "Thy kingdom come" immediately precedes "Thy will be done in earth." Why? Because God's will is not going to be fully done on earth until Christ returns to rule and actually imposes His will, what evangelical theologians call "the millennial kingdom." The kingdom must come first for God's will to be fully realized.

God does try to guide those who have accepted Jesus Christ, though His Holy Spirit, to do His will, but even then He does not force us; we retain our free will. That is why the Bible is full of instructions to believers to walk with the Holy Spirit. Now, contrast that with the sinful and apathetic lifestyles of many of today's Christians. They live in direct opposition to the leading of the Holy Spirit. We must *walk* in the Spirit, not just be indwelt (Galatians 5:25). Again, this passage in Galatians 5 is also reinforced in Romans 8.

Certainly, God does influence both believers and non-believers. However, influence is not control; nor is foreknowledge control. God tries to lead us to make the right choices. God is beyond evil. He is a righteous God; He neither causes evil nor leads people to do evil. Since God is the standard for morality, our God defines what is right and wrong. We do not. Having said this, God never leads us to do evil.

The evil one does not control us (because he cannot) but he can influence us: "Wherein in time past ye walked according to the course of this world, according to the prince of the power of the air, the spirit that now worketh in the children of disobedience" (**Ephesians 2:2**). Yet even now, the evil one is seeking to devour us through his leadings; we Christians are warned to "Be sober, be vigilant; because your adversary the devil, as a roaring lion, walketh about, seeking whom he may devour" (**1 Peter 5:8**). Remember that the devil is not an adversary to those actually doing his will. In fact, it has been said that if we are not experiencing any type of persecution, we are fulfilling the will of the evil one just fine.

The Babylonian conquest of Jerusalem involving the slaughter of many of its inhabitants and burning of the city was not God's choice. God wanted them to surrender. It was their choice to refuse to surrender. They chose to ignore God's prophet and listen to their own. Earlier in their history when God made a covenant with the Israelites, He gave them a choice to obey His commandments and prosper, or suffer terrible consequences for disobedience.

In **Deuteronomy 30:19**, after explaining the choice, God urged them, "choose life, that both thou and thy seed shall live." The evil we see in this world is not caused by God. On the contrary, that evil is usually the result of disobedience to God's commands and rebellion against His will. We see how the God of the Old Testament treated those which were unfaithful to Him and realize he is the same God today: "For I am the Lord, I change not" (**Malachi 3:6**).

Unfortunately, we see the idea that everything is predestined of God not only conflicts with scripture but also produces bad behavior. Consider the following scientific study. A teacher had a group of students that he subdivided into two groups. In one group, the students were shown many messages about man having free will. In the other group the students were shown many messages that free will was an illusion. Once each group had seen these messages, they were then given a test and the teacher pretended to be called away. Before he left, he told the students to self-grade the test using the provided key and then take a $1 coin from a jar of $1 coins, for each correct answer.

What was the result? Those who saw the messages denying free will took more coins than they were entitled to based on the number of correct answers they had. Those who saw the messages reinforcing free will only took the number of coins they were entitled to based on the number of correct answers they had. This demonstrates a key concept related to our understanding of free will. The more likely we are to believe that we have no free will, the less the chance we will act in an honorable manner. If we buy into the concept that there is no such thing as free will and don't act honorably, we rationalize that it is not our fault since we are not in control.

Because church leaders in the Modern Church too often use the "God is in control" sound bite combined with promises from God presented as unconditional (independent of men and their actions), many in their congregations are led down the same path. Many of them believe that God is responsible for their choices and actions, and therefore they bear no responsibility for their sins (this is the basic problem with Calvinism). The passages about the consequences of our decisions in His Word clearly refute the sound bites (*e.g.,* Romans 6:15–22, Romans 7:25, Romans 8:12–13, and Hebrews 10:26–27). Unfortunately, the end result of this unscriptural teaching is more sin among the misled congregation, exemplified by the results of the study.

Have you ever considered why God praised people in the Bible? For example, look at what God said to Satan: "And the Lord said unto Satan, Hast thou considered my servant Job, that there is none like him in the earth, a perfect and an upright man, one who feareth God, and shunneth evil?" (**Job 1:8**). This would make no sense if God controlled Job's behavior. If that were true, God, not Job, would be responsible for Job's good behavior. The same is true for others that God commended. Throughout the Bible, God acknowledged the free will given to men, and either commended or condemned people based on how they use that free will.

In some cases, God has punished or destroyed people when they use their free will to disobey Him. In other cases, He has forgiven them. Why the difference? It is probably because God knows the heart. He knows whether the sin was intentional or unintentional; whether there is true repentance or callous indifference; whether it is an isolated sin or a pattern of sinning. But today, we see too many "Christians" living in callous indifference.

Given how many bad (disobedient) decisions Christians make after they have accepted Jesus Christ as their Lord, is there any doubt who is in control of our decisions? Being indwelt by the Holy Spirit does not mean Christians are led by the Holy Spirit. We are led by the Holy Spirit when we are following the Holy Spirit and submitting to God's will. Consider again the bandleader. If the bandleader is leading the band north and we turn east are we "walking with" or "being led by" the band leader? Of course not!

Believing God is in control and actually controlling everything is an insidious form of Calvinism growing in today's Modern Church. When we believe this, we believe that our behavior plays no part in their eternal destination. We assume, in contradiction of scripture, God has chosen the people with whom He will spend eternity (and, like all Calvinists, we assume that includes us), and nothing we can do or say will ultimately make any difference. We make no effort to share the gospel, because God has already made His choice. Is this love for our fellow man? Or it is callous indifference encouraged by the evil one?

Jesus Christ commanded us to play a part in the salvation of others: "Go ye therefore, and teach all nations, baptizing them in the name of the Father, and of the Son, and of the Holy Ghost" (**Matthew 28:19**). Do we love those who are heading for the lake of fire? Do we want to make every effort to help change their destination? Or do we disregard Jesus Christ's command under the concept that God is in control and what we do makes no difference? So what does the doctrine that God actually controls everything encourage you to do? The answer should tell you where that doctrine originates.

How God uses His Sovereignty

God can and does act in a sovereign manner. We see this most clearly when God uses His power to override the natural laws He put in place on this earth. We see His sovereignty in the creation of the universe. He flooded the earth, parted the Red Sea, stopped the rotation of the earth and even made it go backwards, and there are many more examples of His sovereignty over His natural laws in the Bible. Prophecy of God tells us that God will exert His sovereignty again in the future, just as God demonstrated His sovereignty to historically fulfill prophecy (ex: Jesus the Messiah).

But God accomplishes most of His works through people exercising their free will. Over the centuries He has worked through Abraham, Moses, Samuel, David, Peter, Paul, and many, many others. There are also places where God has directly controlled men, but these are few and far between. One of those men was Pharaoh during the ten plagues in Exodus 7–12. After the first five plagues, Pharaoh, through his own free will, hardened his own heart. But after the last five, God no longer gave him that choice; God hardened Pharaoh's heart, beginning in Exodus 9:12, in order to accomplish His purpose.

But here is the clincher. God knew in advance that Pharaoh would harden his own heart and not let His people go. How do we know? God tells Moses "And I am sure that the king of Egypt will not let you go, no, not by a mighty hand" (**Exodus 3:19**). 1 Samuel 6:6 reinforces the same thing. God gave Pharaoh a choice and Pharaoh made a choice of how he would respond to God's messenger affirmed through the plagues.

Pharaoh's pride overwhelmed his reason when each of the first five plagues abated. We are the same. We may be disciplined by God or suffer the natural earthly consequences of our own disobedience, but as soon as we are delivered, we often return to the same behavior. But there are two additional lessons from this story. First, a country enjoys the benefits of its leader's obedience to God, and suffers the consequences of his or her disobedience (In countries where we vote, this should always be a consideration). Second, God's patience is not unlimited. We like to think we have up until the moment of death to choose to accept Christ and be obedient to His will, but our continued disobedience may terminate that choice before that moment (Hebrews 6:4–8 and Hebrews 10:26–27).

Consider God's exercise of His sovereignty in the case of Nebuchadnezzar. He not only used the king to discipline Israel and Judah, He also gave him dreams of things to come which He interpreted through Daniel, and even let him see someone in the burning furnace who is probably the pre-incarnate Christ. Later Daniel told the king, "And they shall drive thee from men, and thy dwelling shall be with the beasts of the field: they shall make thee to eat grass as oxen, and seven times shall pass over thee, until thou know that the most High ruleth in the kingdom of men, and giveth it to whomsoever he will" (**Daniel 4:32**).

Even here God warned Nebuchadnezzar, through Daniel, of what would happen to him if he did not change his behavior. As a result of all God's intervention in the king's life, Nebuchadnezzar recognized the sovereignty and justice of God (Daniel 4:34–37). God put a lot of work into the king. We would not be surprised to learn he was now in the kingdom.

Jesus exercised His sovereignty literally thousands of times during His ministry, concluding with His ascension. The apostle John called them "signs," indicating they were proof of His divinity. The conversion of Saul (Paul) in Acts 9:1–19 is another example of God (Jesus) exercising His sovereignty.

Yet this is not God's normal method. Most of the men and women in the Bible exercised their free will to obey or disobey God. Our God does use His foreknowledge to choose people in the Bible that He knows will be obedient and do His will: people like Samuel, Isaiah, Jeremiah, Daniel, the apostles, and many others. But we find very few recorded instances where He overrode their free will. Ultimately, He conveys his messages and works His will through the obedience of His faithful followers. We see this over and over again in the Bible.

God chose Moses to bring His people out of Egypt, and after some grumbling, Moses obeyed God and did God's will. But God did not *force* Moses to obey; Moses *chose* to obey, putting his faith in God. God told Jeremiah, *"I the Lord search the heart, I try the reins, even to give every man according to his ways, and according to the fruit of his doings"* (**Jeremiah 17:10**). Here are a couple of additional examples:

Joshua was God's faithful servant and Moses' military general and second in command for 40 years in the wilderness. After the twelve spies returned from spying out the Promised Land, He and Caleb were the only two in all of Israel who had faith that God would fulfill His promise (Numbers 14). After Moses died, God chose Joshua to lead His people into the Promised Land. God personally directed him to assume command and gave him encouragement (Joshua 1:1–9), but Joshua exercised his own free will to obey, trusted God, and went forth and took possession of much of the territory that had been promised to the descendants of Abraham, Isaac and Jacob. He remained faithful to God until the end. Shortly before he died, he encouraged the tribes of Israel saying, "And if it seem evil unto you to serve the Lord, *choose you this day whom ye will serve*; whether the gods which your fathers served that were on the other side of the flood, or the gods of the Amorites, in whose land ye dwell: but as for me and my house, we will serve the Lord" (**Joshua 24:15**). He had a choice, and he chose God.

Isaiah recorded in Isaiah Chapter 6 that he was called into the very presence of the pre-incarnate Christ sitting on a throne. Whether he saw Him in a vision, or whether his spirit was transported to heaven is not revealed. Isaiah recorded that "I heard the voice of the Lord, saying, Whom shall I send, and who will go for us? Then said I, Here am I, send me" (**Isaiah 6:8**). Isaiah also had a choice, and chose to obey.

We don't see God forcing people to do things very often in the Bible. What we do see is the often-repeated theme of God using obedient people to accomplish His will. The Bible is essentially a book about one central choice given to all mankind: to believe and obey God or not.

Key Thoughts

As long as we are not fatalistic about things, the concept that God is in control does limited harm, because God can choose to be in control. But God does not act to control everything. If He did, He would be the source of evil or, more likely, there would be no evil. Furthermore, the world would look like a very different place, a place more like the new heaven and new earth described in Revelation 21 and 22.

We cross the line when we assign evil actions to God, or when we assume that God is the author of events which He condemns in scripture. It is errant thinking to assume that because God *can* control something, that if He allows something bad to happen, He is okay with it, or He actually approves of it. God's reactions to man's choices throughout the Old and New Testament reflect that neither supposition is true.

Scripture shows time and time again that God does not control the believer. He does influence believers (and non-believers). However, even this influence is subject to the free will to choose that God granted us. Otherwise, we as believers would not be able to grieve, ignore, or quench the Holy Spirit. God has granted us the free will to reject both our Savior and the Holy Spirit.

We as Christians must never use the concept of God's control to either intentionally or unintentionally circumvent the commands of God in scripture. Some refuse to share the gospel because "God is in control." Some refuse to help the poor because "God is in control." Some do not worry about sin because "God is in control." Today, children are starving to death across the world. Because we refuse to help, does that mean we approve of the children starving to death? Unlikely. But applying this type of thinking to God's actions or inactions is exactly where we get ourselves in trouble.

It is not that people intentionally think such things, but rather people don't worry about doing the will of the Father because they are assured that "God is in control." The rationale they use is that if they don't do it and God wants it done, it will be done anyway, so why worry about it? This is one place the simplicity of the sound bite can be dangerous. Indeed, those who believe such things have missed the essence of scripture. Others rely on the sound bite to actually support their disobedience.

Foreknowledge and predestination (explicit control) are not the same. God's will is not always done here on earth; indeed if we are honest we see many occurrences where God's stated will is not done. Even though God knows that evil things will happen, He does not cause them to happen. We are the source of evil through the free will God has granted us. He is not responsible for evil.

Our God allows men to freely choose to obey Him, or to reject Him and His commands. God is patient, and often gives us time to repent. God's desire for our lives is for us to love Him, to love our brothers and sisters, to do His will, to try to live a holy life, to bring glory to Him, all by submitting to the Holy Spirit, who will guide us to do His will. This is the use of our free will that pleases our heavenly Father and allows Him to use us to accomplish His will.

Chapter 11

Once Saved, Always Saved (OSAS)

Misleading Christian sound bite(s): Once a person has accepted Christ, his salvation is a done deal and he is assured a place in heaven.

The entire essence of the Bible has been distilled by much of the Modern Church to one message: "believe" Christ died for our sins and anything is fair game. The word "believe" is in quotes here because true belief, that is true faith, results in actions aligned with that faith, not simply intellectual acknowledgment as discussed in Chapter 16, "Saving Faith." Most churches do not directly state that the only requirement for salvation is this intellectual acknowledgment, but rather it is the underlying theme of the aggregate teachings of most of the Modern Church. Some church leaders even state such errant doctrine directly, although scripture clearly teaches the opposite.

What is Once Saved, Always Saved?
Once Saved, Always Saved (OSAS) is a doctrine that in its essence says that once a person has accepted Jesus Christ, no acts and no decisions, can ever separate that person from his salvation; in essence, *unconditional eternal security.* This doctrine is based on a misunderstanding of the interaction between the free will of man and the sovereignty of God, the variable nature of faith, or of God's demonstrated intolerance for sin. It is a doctrine, as presented, which renders many, many of the

commands and teachings of our Lord to believers, optional. This sound bite, which comes from the vast majority of evangelical church pulpits, tells people that they remain saved forever once they accept Jesus Christ, no matter what they do or what they believe thereafter. More than any other doctrine, it is one which is not rooted in the breadth of scripture, but man's teachings.

Let us consider first, the impact of such teaching on an extreme scale. In 2009, a man killed and injured a number of people. The fact the man committed murder was unfortunately, unremarkable. Yet the frame of mind established by what the man wrote before he killed people is convicting. Here is an excerpt from what he wrote[1]:

> "But this guy [the pastor] teaches (and convinced me) you can commit mass murder then still go to heaven." He continued later "Maybe soon, I will see God and Jesus. At least that is what I was told. Eternal life does *not* depend on works. If it did, we will all be in hell. Christ paid for *every* sin, so how can I or you be judged *by God* for a sin when the penalty was *already* paid. People judge but that does not matter. I was reading the Bible and The Integrity of God beginning yesterday, because soon I will see them."

He even provided the name and phone number of the pastor so that others could confirm this doctrine. These are the emphases of the original author. Now clearly, we do not have many Christians who go around killing, but the understanding that the man above had is exactly what many "Christians" are taught and believe. It is why sin is irrelevant to so many. It is why disobedience runs rampant among God's people. It is the reason for the increasing levels of spiritual apathy. The idea that every future sin is already forgiven and that a person remains saved regardless of how they act is simply not scriptural. In order for OSAS to be true, modern theologians have rationalized that all past, present, and future sins have been forgiven at the moment a person comes to Christ. The purveyor of these doctrines is much of the Modern Church, but not the Bible.

---

[1] FULL TEXT OF GYM KILLER'S BLOG, New York Post, Aug. 5, 2009

What did the murderer above write? *That every sin is paid for so he was taught he could do whatever he wanted and he would be with the Lord.* What he understood is exactly what comes from many Modern Church pulpits, whether church leaders recognize they are teaching this or not.

Is the Modern Church leading us towards or away from God with such teachings? Once we tell people with a sinful nature that nothing they do or don't do after coming to Christ matters to their salvation, they know they from that point on, they are free to ignore the Holy Spirit, ignore scripture, and ignore church leaders. The evidence presented in the introduction shows dramatically how this doctrine has led more and more people away from God instead of to Him.

It is probably the most damaging doctrine taught in the Modern Church today, because at its core, people understand they are being taught that they can continue to live their worldly lifestyle, ignoring and even rebelling against God, and continue to be saved. More than any other doctrine, it builds a lukewarm church, identified as the Laodicean Church in Revelation 3. It creates both rebellious and lukewarm disciples in our churches, who are, in all likelihood, unsaved, even though they believe they are and are told they are. Furthermore, we see church leaders reinforce this notion regardless of the behavior of the members of their congregation.

Some parts of the Modern Church have started to become aware of how far we have drifted from the foundation of the church. Some of the things we currently believe have either emerged or been radically altered and extended only in the last 500 or so years. There is no significant historical precedent for the OSAS doctrine before John Calvin. This in itself raises a very troubling question. How could a doctrine which is so central to salvation, not be referenced or written about extensively for the first three-quarters of the Church Age? The answer is simple. Most all of the early church fathers did not believe what is currently taught.

Some have termed the Modern Church's current error as "hyper-grace" or "cheap grace," but the foundational error is actually OSAS, because this is the doctrine that tells Christians they can act anyway they want or believe anything they want and remain saved. It is not just about extreme grace. It is about payment of future sins, election, predestination, and perseverance.

The doctrine of OSAS relies on New Testament statements that are interpreted as unconditional promises from God of permanent, guaranteed salvation (*unconditional* eternal security) at the moment a person truly believes in Him (John 3:16) and receives Him (John 1:12). Some proponents of OSAS also cite other verses addressing the mechanics and legal basis of salvation which they interpret as supporting the doctrine, but both neglect the larger context of scripture. Furthermore, even scriptures which seem to support the concept are often misunderstood.

The general teaching of the doctrine of OSAS in the Modern Church is that God will preserve those proclaiming Christ, regardless of what decisions they may make after becoming Christians. It is interesting that most people adhering to this doctrine believe we retain our God-given free will even after accepting Jesus Christ, but believe that the exercise of that free will to renounce our belief in Christ or live in habitual, willful disobedience of His commands cannot affect our salvation. They call this "eternal security" and since it is continually proclaimed from the pulpit, the overwhelming majority in most Modern Church congregations believes it to be true.

The outcome of the doctrine of OSAS and what it produces in too many "Christians" should be evidence enough that, as taught, it is not of God but rather originates in human rules for salvation. However, the doctrine is inconsistent with the breadth of scripture. Consider these three outcomes of what this doctrine produces:

First, the doctrine appeals to our sinful nature, allowing many (who think they are "leaning on the promises of God") to lead lives focused on themselves first (a form of idolatry), with God somewhere down the list of priorities: "Thou shalt have no other gods before me" (**Exodus 20:3**). Focusing on God *first* never enters their mind. We have already shown above in the "Introduction" Section, using evidence from professing Christians themselves, where their priorities are. We see some professing Christians regularly and heavily investing in themselves and their pleasures, but not in the lost, the starving, the homeless, the dying, or the perishing. Nor do we see them spending time in God's Word. Because the only bar, a low bar, the Modern Church has set for salvation is a one-time belief in (John 3:16) and acceptance of Jesus Christ (John 1:12). As a result, nothing else of God seems to be a priority for many. One and done.

Second, it allows professing Christians to comfortably fit in with world, something which God condemns in scripture (Romans 12:2, John 15:18–19, and 1 John 5:4). The morality of many in the Modern Church, who claim to be Christians, who should be standing firm with God and His Word, continues to degrade. The world says the homosexual lifestyle is okay. So do most professing Christians, according to surveys. Why? To be accepted by the world. And why not, since this doctrine assures them that they remain saved no matter what they believe or how they behave after that magic moment of "salvation." If a given teaching in scripture seems difficult or places responsibility on the believer, the doctrine tells them they can ignore it. Why? Because according to this doctrine, it makes no difference to their salvation. They think their "freedom in Christ" allows them to embrace all manner of sin, ignore God's commands, ignore scripture, ignore the admonitions of family, friends and church leaders, and even change their faith and yet remain saved. This is exactly what church leaders espousing the doctrine of OSAS *indirectly teach*. The sinful nature of man wants to hear one thing: their eternity is secure regardless of what they do, so they can live any type of life they want here on earth; the Modern Church engages this sinful nature. This is consistent with the OSAS doctrine, but not with God's Word. Too many church leaders sow to the flesh through this doctrine and not to the Spirit.

> The sinful nature of man wants to hear one thing: their eternity is secure regardless of what they do, so they can live any type of life they want here on earth; the Modern Church engages this sinful nature.

Satan has turned many in the Modern Church into enemies of Christ, when they should be part of the body of Christ. Yet most self-proclaimed, born-again Christians (as shown in the Introduction Section), don't even believe in the evil one. Scripture clearly describes the interaction of mankind with an omnipotent God who holds men responsible for their actions. This is the teaching of scripture: not that man can save himself, but rather that, once we have been saved, we must use our God-given free will to submit to God.

Third, the doctrine too often does not result in either true repentance or a new creation in Christ. As stated in the introduction, less than 20% of those claiming to be born-again Christians have a biblical world view.

Why wouldn't a person want to have what he thinks is the best life here and still have a "ticket to heaven" (in his mind, the "best of both worlds")? Why the need to change, since changing will have no impact on our salvation? Why not live our lives the way we want, the way we think we should (not His will, but my will be done)? Yet this denies the fundamental teaching of our Lord to deny ourselves (Luke 9:23–24).

Much of the reason for the increasing acceptance of this doctrine of OSAS is that it fulfills man's need to have a simple recipe for salvation. It also fulfills man's desire to live in the flesh and not have to worry about the eternal consequences. But the doctrine is contrary with the overall view of scripture.

In his preaching, Paul reasoned from the entire work of scripture that Jesus (Yeshua) was the Messiah. God did not name and completely identify Him as, for example, He did when He named Cyrus as the one who would free the people of Israel from the Babylonian captivity approximately one hundred fifty years before it happened (Isaiah 44:28 and Isaiah 45:13). But God did not provide this irrefutable and stated evidence that Jesus was the Messiah. Paul was forced to reason with people, using scripture, to prove Jesus of Nazareth was in fact, the Messiah.

We are to do the same thing about all biblical issues - that is, reason from the larger context of scripture, not simply take sound bites of scripture out of context. We must set aside our preconceptions to be able to truly understand the Bible. And we must trust God that His Word is true.

Biblical scholars spend so much time looking at individual verses that they may miss the larger context of scripture (that forest and trees thing). They focus on individual passages of scripture without considering the entire message of the Bible and the story it tells. Even so, there are many individual passages which clearly call into question or directly refute the OSAS doctrine. The efforts to explain away these passages occur because people want to believe the lie of what Dietrich Bonhoeffer called "cheap grace." Here is a partial list of these passages.

Exodus 32:30–35	Numbers 14:11–12	Deuteronomy 8:19–20
Deuteronomy 29:18–20	Deuteronomy 30:19	Jeremiah 15:6
Ezekiel 18:9, 21–22	Ezekiel 18:24–26	Psalms 69:28
Matthew 7:21	Matthew 13:18–23	Matthew 24:13
Matthew 24:45–51	Matthew 25:1–12	Mark 4:14–17

Mark 13:13	John 8:31	John 14:15,23
John 15:1–10	John 16:1	Acts 20:28–31
Romans 2:6–8	Romans 6:16	Romans 8:13–14
Romans 11:17–24	1 Corinthians 5:5	1 Corinthians 10:11–12
1 Corinthians 15:1–2	Galatians 5:1–4	Galatians 5:16–21
Galatians 6:7–9	Philippians 3:7–14	Colossians 1:21–23
1 Thessalonians 3:5	1 Thessalonians 5:19	2 Thessalonians 2:1–3
1 Timothy 1:18–20	1 Timothy 4:1–2	1 Timothy 4:16
1 Timothy 5:11–15	1 Timothy 6:11–12	2 Timothy 2:11–13
2 Timothy 2:15–18	2 Timothy 4:6–8	Hebrews 2:1–3
Hebrews 3:5–6	Hebrews 3:12–14	Hebrews 3:7–19
Hebrews 4:1–2, 11, 14	Hebrews 5:8–9	Hebrews 10:23
Hebrews 10:26–31	Hebrews 10:35–39	Hebrews 12:14–15
James 2:14–26	James 5:19–20	2 Peter 1:5–11
2 Peter 2:1–22	1 John 2:17	Jude 1:3–6
Revelation 2:26–28	Revelation 3:1–5	Revelation 3:10–12
Revelation 3:15–19	Revelation 21:7–8	

The entirety of God's Word is written to men with free will, commanding them to act in certain ways and not to act in other ways. If we did not have a free will, much of what God teaches us through His Word would be totally unnecessary, confusing, misleading, deceptive, insincere and/or untruthful, but we know this is inconsistent with His nature. God is truth, and He is not the author of confusion and deception. Once we have accepted Jesus Christ, we make the decision to either be led by the Holy Spirit or to walk in the flesh. Scripture after scripture tells us this. These scriptures also tell us the consequences of that decision can be eternal.

OSAS is one of the most damaging doctrines routinely affirmed in American Christianity and its adoption is as broad and sweeping as the road to destruction Jesus described: "Enter ye in at the strait gate: for wide is the gate, and broad is the way, that leadeth to destruction, and many there be which go in thereat: Because strait is the gate, and narrow is the way, which leadeth unto life, and few there be that find it" (**Matthew 7:13–14**). While there are isolated passages that seem to support this doctrine, some requiring extreme interpretations to align with the doctrine, the overall message of the Bible does not.

The doctrine continues to be taught because evangelical seminary professors and Modern Church leaders are:

- Clinging to their preconceptions based on erroneous doctrine they learned in childhood or in seminary (Some refuse to even consider studying passages of scripture that seem to conflict with their preconceptions).
- Refusing to acknowledge the promises of God must be received through faith. Modern Church teaching claims that one may believe (or stand on) the promises of God and then act in a manner which is inconsistent with what God teaches yet still receive those promises. The Modern Church in effect believes and teaches that all of the Israelites should have entered into the Promised Land even though God destroyed them for their continuing disobedience as evidenced by a compromised faith.
- Refusing to consider the broader range of scripture, the nature of God and His relationship with man as revealed in the Old and New Testament.
- Discounting the responsibility of man before God as taught throughout scripture and reaffirmed by many men of faith. They fail to accurately comprehend and explain the interaction between the sovereignty of God and man's responsibility to properly exercise his free will in obedience to God.
- Following other men rather than the breadth of what scripture actually teaches.
- Refusing to examine the underlying language to determine if supportive passages really teach what they believe it does (Remember that those translating the Bible are also subject to doctrinal biases and preconceptions).
- Understanding that it is easier to attract people when teaching a "feel good" man-made philosophy that once a person has claimed to accept Jesus Christ, no decision he makes can affect his salvation, because it allows people to live whatever type of life they want and still think they will spend eternity in "heaven."
- Failing to understand the doctrine appeals to the sinful nature of man, including those doing the preaching, and allows men to engage their sinful nature and reject the leading of the Holy Spirit.

> In essence, the OSAS doctrine teaches:
>
> People who have accepted Jesus Christ, who then use their God given free will to intentionally commit themselves to the most evil and/or selfish acts, to rebel against God by willingly ignoring what God commands, to refuse to be led by the Holy Spirit, or even to later reject Jesus Christ, will be welcomed into God's kingdom.

Does this sound like something the God of the Old and New Testaments would say, or does this sound like something the evil one would say to mislead people? Knowing the huge price paid for our sin, does it sound reasonable the God of the Bible will then welcome into His kingdom those who are committed to sin (rebellion against God)?

God specifically describes those that are the saints as follows, "Here is the patience of the saints: here are they that keep the commandments of God, and the faith of Jesus" (**Revelation 14:12**). Who are the saints? They are God's people. This verse describes what *the saints* actually do (not God, not anyone else); that is, *keep the commandments of God and the faith of Jesus.*

In the end, the fruits of the OSAS doctrine, along with breadth of scripture, reveal that this is a false doctrine which misleads believers into doing the evil one's will. Yet people are so committed to this doctrine because of its overwhelming appeal to the flesh. It promises them exactly what they *want* to hear; they can have their salvation and the world too. They can act anyway they desire and remain saved. They can believe anything they want and remain saved. They can ignore God and remain saved. The doctrine incubates lukewarm disciples who are not overly concerned about trying their best to lead a righteous and holy life by submitting to God. These are exactly the things happening in the Modern Church as a result of the OSAS doctrine.

In reality, the doctrine is designed to encourage believers by giving them "blessed assurance" of their salvation. Unfortunately, it actually fosters a lukewarm attitude in many. Too many Christians are not concerned with pleasing or obeying God; they remain focused on their earthly pleasures and pursuits. They don't need to consider God anymore, because this doctrine tells them their eternity is guaranteed. They think they have avoided the lake of fire, and that is all they really care about their eternal future. They no longer have to think about God and the eternal, so they focus on this life.

Now clearly, we don't see most believers openly engaging in the most evil or selfish acts all that often. However, if we really looked at the hearts of many Christians, we would find many intentionally living in rebellion against God. Some refuse to share the gospel, some refuse to get baptized, some refuse to obey American law, some refuse to share with the poor, some refuse to love others, some refuse to give up sin.

Many harbor pride, un-forgiveness, bitterness, selfishness and/or the love of money in their hearts. Many are focused on the world: family, friends, job, pastimes, sports and hobbies. Any thought of God is far in the background, to be thought about on Sunday morning. Maybe. That is, unless they decide to go on a family picnic on Sunday morning. And why not, since they are "already saved," and cannot lose their salvation?

The common thread is they all refuse to submit their will to God's will. They refuse to be led by the Holy Spirit. They sin presumptuously: "So I spake unto you; and ye would not hear, but rebelled against the commandment of the Lord, and went presumptuously up into the hill" (**Deuteronomy 1:43**). This becomes obvious when we ask Christians what they believe and by observing how they act. In many churches, 80% of the ministries are run by 20% of the people. The focus of too many modern Christians is on being served, not serving.

The Bible is not a "better living guide" as many treat it. It contains the actual commands of an all-powerful God. We don't avoid sin to have a better life (although it may have that effect); we do it because of the high price that was paid for our sin and our love of God: "If ye love me, keep my commandments" (**John 14:15**). However, the Modern Church, through this errant doctrine, often reinforces a message of the triviality of sinning against God. Trivializing sin, given the plan of salvation necessitated by our sin and the terrible price our Lord paid for it, also testifies to the errant nature of the doctrine. We are to try our best to avoid sin (Romans 6:15–18).

The really sad aspect to this doctrine is that it implicitly puts the Modern Church's stamp of approval on Christians living in the flesh. The Modern

Church does not directly promote overt or intentional sin, but OSAS encourages church members to focus on this world and relegate the things of God to the background. By four words not found together in scripture, this doctrine has made all of God's commands to believers optional!

Have you ever noticed that most of the false religions in the world promise earthly rewards like luxury, power and sex, especially in the afterlife? Why? Because these are things that many people of this world can relate to and desire. It is why false religions draw people to them. This doctrine works the same way. Why wouldn't a person not want the best for themselves here and still be right with God? This is the message that sells; an all too convenient doctrine to grow church attendance and coffers. One person said of this doctrine, tongue-in-cheek, that "the only difference between the saved and unsaved is that the saved have been given a license to sin" [by the Modern Church].

The doctrine of OSAS *indirectly* promises the same things these other religions do - earthly rewards. It *indirectly* promises we can believe whatever we want, act however we want, be whatever we want, and still be saved. We can have as many earthly rewards or indulgences as we desire; we can engage our flesh to whatever degree we desire and this doctrine tells us our eternal destiny remains secure. It supports a form of idolatry - worship of self and the things of this world. This is neither scriptural, nor of the Lord. Ask yourself this: Is there anywhere in the New Testament where we see Christians focusing on their flesh like American Christians do today? People I [Gregg] have shared the gospel with often point out this hypocrisy.

Christianity is supposed to be different. Our Lord denied Himself and told us to do the same: "He that findeth his life shall lose it: and he that loseth his life for my sake shall find it" (**Matthew 10:39**). Jesus echoed this thought in another of the gospels, "And he said to them all, If any man will come after me, let him deny himself, and take up his cross daily, and follow me. *For whosoever will save his life shall lose it*: but whosoever will lose his life for my sake, the same shall save it" (**Luke 9:23–24**).

Our God promises His faithful followers they will spend eternity with Him and receive spiritual rewards in eternity. Yet too many Christians are about saving their life here, not losing it. Very few Modern Church pastors who teach the doctrine of OSAS preach sermons about the cost of discipleship, the cost of truly following Jesus. Their churches may be growing in numbers, but they are not necessarily making true disciples. The pews and the coffers are filled, but the true disciples are few. And a large portion of the blame lies with the doctrine of OSAS.

Scripture is clear that Christians have a responsibility to obey God's commandments after coming to Christ. Think about all the epistles (letters) from Paul to the churches. Think about Jesus confronting the churches in Revelation. Both Jesus and Paul issued rebukes, corrections, and even threats to believers. The idea once a person accepts Christ, God takes full responsibility to ensure that all live lifestyles consistent with that claimed faith is not true scripturally. The Modern Church's focus on getting them to say "I do" to Christ *must* be followed by discipleship, "Teaching them to observe all things whatsoever I have commanded you (**Matthew 28:20**). Yet because some church leaders believe that once a person says "I do" to Christ, he can never be lost, so they don't worry too much whether that person is living his faith. It's "on to the next convert."

Not only is this doctrine creating the lukewarm Laodicean Church, but it is also ruining our Christian witness and our society, causing those outside of the kingdom to reject Christianity and label Christians as hypocrites (just what Jesus labeled the religious leaders of His day).

Although people are able to deceive one another, they cannot deceive God. No one except the Lord Himself truly knows the heart of any man. We should be concerned about any person who claims to know Christ, but does not seem to be walking with the Holy Spirit. We should pray for a person who attends church regularly but refuses to obey the commands of Jesus Christ. But we should also not reassure them with false doctrines. We should be wary of anyone who assures another, without truly knowing the other person's heart, that he is saved and guaranteed eternity with God. All of these behaviors are not of God, and are contrary to the commandments to Christians in scripture.

Those who would teach (either directly or indirectly through errant doctrine) that we can live our lives anyway we want after accepting Christ (because our salvation is "guaranteed") are doing exactly what the devil did in the Garden: encouraging people to use their free will to disobey God's direct commandments. God cares how we use our free will. If He had created us without a free will (that is without the ability to choose), the

Bible would look very different probably more like a history book. In fact, there really would be no reason for God to even give us a Bible.

Let us explore some elements of the doctrine from a scriptural perspective.

Foundations to Help us Understand the Truth

Here are some foundational principles to help us see the truth as we explore some of the issues with this doctrine.

- We serve a just God. This means that the same rules exist for all. God does not a respecter of persons; He does not arbitrarily show favoritism to some (Psalm 33:5, 2 Thessalonians 1:5–6, Romans 2:11; 9:14, and 2 Timothy 4:8).
- All scripture is true and therefore harmonizes with other scripture. We cannot simply look at a few select passages, or even a superficial overview of scripture to determine the truth. We should first consider the plain meaning of a passage within its context (Remember: a text without a context is a pretext). If apparent conflicts with other passages emerge, we must dig deeper. If we cannot reconcile the apparent difference between verses, we need to remain in prayer, asking the Holy Spirit to lead us into truth as promised by Jesus (John 16:13). Where there are two or more differing interpretations of doctrinal scripture, at least one is wrong (Psalm 119:160, John 17:17, 2 Timothy 3:16, and 2 Peter 1:20–21).
- God is holy (Leviticus 11:44); He hates sin. He hated sin so much that sent His son to die an agonizing death to provide a sacrifice for our sins. It is only natural then that those who are walking with the Holy Spirit also hate sin (Psalm 36:2), especially if we understand what Jesus Christ went through. We should never trivialize sin and never live in it, yet many Christians do (Psalm 11:5, Proverbs 15:9, Proverbs 6:16–19, Romans, 6:16, 19, and Ephesians 4:30).
- The Holy Spirit, although He will lead us if we submit to His will, does not control us. We retain our free will after we accept Jesus Christ as our Lord. We saw this in the Chapter 10, "The Sovereignty of God." Being indwelt by the Holy Spirit is not the same as walking with (or being led by) the Holy Spirit (Galatians

5:25). Being led by the Holy Spirit means we are actually following the Holy Spirit and submitting our will to His will, as discussed in the Chapter 7, "Sinning and Obedience."

- God knows and judges our hearts (1 Kings 8:39, Jeremiah 17:10, and 1 Samuel 16:7). We cannot fool God because He sees our heart. Some who claim Christ as Lord may not actually know Christ as Lord. Jesus knows those who are His, but scripture clearly teaches there are those who think they are His, but are not (Matthew 7:21).
- Most (but not all) of God's promises require faith in God to realize them. Even though God is faithful, scripture clearly shows that believing in a promise of God and then acting unfaithfully may result in that promise being personally null and void (James 1:6–8). God's promises may be relied on when received with a true and living (genuine) faith. God has specifically stated that He has not acted as He promised when those receiving the promise were subsequently unfaithful (Joshua 5:6).
- Because God gave both angels and mankind free will, God's will is often not done on earth. We see many examples in the Bible and here on earth where man disobeys God. We also see places where we are told that God wanted men to come to Him, but men were not willing (Matthew 23:37).
- We are justified by grace through faith (Ephesians 2:8–9), but that justification is not permanent, and depends on our subsequent decisions in this life, primarily but not exclusively, enduring in faith. True faith is required for salvation. True faith drives our actions. Faith can and does fail because we retain our free will after accepting Jesus Christ. The Bible speaks explicitly of compromised, shipwrecked, lost, or dead faith (Luke 8:13, James 2:17, and 1 Timothy 1:19). How many times did Israel lose faith?
- Obedience is critical to salvation, not because obedience directly saves, but true faith produces a true desire to obey. This obedience is evidence of true faith, producing what we might think of as "good works," which Jesus called "fruit" in John 15. Jesus Himself said of the Father "every branch in me that beareth not fruit he taketh away" and these removed branches were to be burned (John 15:6). Jesus taught this concerning branches that were *in Him* (John 15:1–2).

- Past sins were forgiven when we accepted Jesus Christ. Our future sins were not forgiven when we accepted Christ. The sins of the whole were *paid* for on the cross but *not forgiven* (2 Peter 1:9). Otherwise everyone would be in the kingdom, since it is sin that separates us from God. We require forgiveness of sins through Jesus Christ.
- God does not want automatons (robots); He wants individuals who truly love Him of their own free will. Only love given freely has any value. We, who are made in His image, understand the same thing. What is forced love worth? Would we try to force love from our children? Would it be any value of us if we did? This is what our God values – that we make the choices that show we love Him, not that we are coerced or forced to love Him.
- The nature of our God is never to reward or welcome into His kingdom those who are committed to disobedience or those who reject Christ. Nowhere in the Bible has He ever done this. Mark the words "committed to disobedience," which is radically different from inadvertent sin, occasional sin, or struggling with sin for a time as Paul describes in Romans 7. Again, if we are listening to the Holy Spirit, we should hate sin as much as God does.
- As discussed in the Chapter 5, "Salvation and Eternal Life" and according to scripture, complete salvation does not appear to be a single ("one and done") event that occurs at the acceptance of Christ. There are simply too many passages that refer to salvation and eternal life as a future event (such as Philippians 3:7–14). It is the reason we are given a *deposit* of the indwelling Holy Spirit "as a pledge of our inheritance" (**Ephesians 1:13–14**). A deposit is put down as a guarantee of fulfillment of a promise in the future. There is no need for a deposit or pledge on something we have already received. Salvation is a process; a process that can be interrupted by our free will. Once we are with our Lord, we will never lose our salvation.

Errors in Presentation of Once Saved, Always Saved

Most church leaders will affirm there are probably unsaved souls in their congregation, even among those that claim Christ as Lord. Scripture tells us there are those who claim Christ as Lord, yet refuse to do the Father's will, and therefore will not enter the kingdom (Matthew 7:21).

Unfortunately, relationships between church leaders and members of their congregation are often shallow in nature. Many church leaders don't know what their congregants believe or how they act away from meetings of the fellowship. This is not necessarily surprising, but it should limit what is said from the pulpit.

We are often too liberal in our assumptions about the hearts of others. This is also true of our church leaders. But we have neither the right nor the ability to make such judgments. God tells us, "The heart is deceitful above all things, and desperately wicked: who can know it?" (**Jeremiah 17:9**). We have trouble with our own hearts, much less truly knowing someone else's heart.

However, this does not stop church leaders from proclaiming from the pulpit that all within their midst who claim to have accepted Christ, regardless of the evidence, will be forever saved. This means that they essentially make a claim they have no right to make. Calvinists justify this in their minds on the Calvinist precept that all of the elect are forever saved and everyone else is forever lost, so what they say cannot impact anyone's eternal destiny. But there is dishonesty here. Both Calvinist and non-Calvinist church leaders should prayerfully consider the impact of teaching OSAS to those in the congregation who think they have accepted Christ, but are actually lost.

If these church leaders were honest with their congregations, there is a chance that those not living a lifestyle consistent with their claimed faith would repent when confronted, as many in scripture did. It is why God sent prophets to the Israelites to warn those who claimed to believe in God about their actions being inconsistent with their beliefs. The prophets warned the people of God's coming wrath, giving them the opportunity and the motivation to repent.

God told Ezekiel "But if the watchman sees the sword coming and does not blow the trumpet to warn the people and the sword comes and takes someone's life, that person's life will be taken because of their sin, but I will hold the watchman accountable for their blood" (**Ezekiel 33:6**). This spiritual principle holds today. Church leaders are, in effect, watchmen. The wrath of God is coming ("the sword").

Church leaders are to watch over and shepherd their congregations. God told Ezekiel that if he did not warn those of the error of their ways, he would be held accountable. At the very least, church leaders should not be proclaiming eternal salvation to all the professing believers in their congregation, because they don't fully know the hearts of everyone. They could proclaim such salvation if they presented it as conditional, but that is not what happens.

The OSAS doctrine does serious damage here, since church leaders are guaranteeing salvation to those that are lost (professing but not true believers), and reinforcing their sinful behavior, rather than telling them the truth so they might truly repent and truly receive Christ (John 1:12). Again, this is likely because of Calvinistic beliefs (if God has predetermined they are saved, their behavior does not matter to their salvation, and if God has predetermined they are lost, there is no way a message of repentance will matter).

This thinking demonstrates inconsistency with the heart of God and direct commands in scripture. Instead of warning these people of their eternal peril, many of today's church leaders encourage their continued self-deception by reiterating the doctrine of OSAS, and thus reinforcing their erroneous assumption that their salvation is secure.

We are not talking here about people who truly believe and later reject Christ through ceasing to believe, or through living in rebellion to God's commands. Those who are not truly Christians often pose as Christians, and many are church members who regularly attend church. Almost all of these people do not truly understand or truly accept God's plan of salvation, and think somehow attending church regularly, being a member, etc. is their "ticket to heaven." James warned such people, "But be ye doers of the word, and not hearers only, deceiving your own selves" (**James 1:22**). But again, because of the teaching of OSAS, they believe they are saved and are "eternally secure."

There are also people attending church who, after accepting Christ, try earnestly to walk with the Holy Spirit. It is not that all of the Modern Church is full of false disciples. Undoubtedly there are true disciples in many, many churches. Unfortunately, there are also many who cling to their old lifestyles after truly accepting Christ, thinking they are assured a place in heaven because they are taught, and believe, the doctrine of OSAS. They see no need for obedience or endurance, and have no desire to produce fruit because they are not submitting to and being led by the

Holy Spirit. *Their eternal destiny is in peril because they have bought into the deception of OSAS.* They understand they have been told there is no need to actually repent because their salvation is secure based on the intellectual belief in Jesus Christ.

Many of today's church leaders preach to individuals as though they all have the same faith (true and saving faith). But it is dangerous to tell entire church congregations that they are saved no matter what they do. That message imperils the eternal destiny of both true believers and the potentially lost (professing believers) in the congregation. There is reason to fear God will hold church leaders accountable for the souls of those that might have been being saved had they been honest with their congregations. This was true in Ezekiel's time and is true now.

Unfortunately, in many evangelical churches today, preaching and teaching is all about making the church members feel "loved" and "accepted." Sin is seldom discussed, except as something we have been freed from because of Christ's work on the cross. Mentioning hell or the lake of fire is now even considered offensive by many. It is considered "unsettling and upsetting" to the congregation. Too many church leaders don't want to bring up either the harsh realities of not following Christ, or the cost of following Christ (Luke 14:25–33), because they don't think it will help them increase the numbers in the pews, the earthly measure of a "successful" church.

Perspectives in Interpretation

The doctrine of eternal security of the believer is the foundation of the doctrine of OSAS even though there are a few subtle differences. As we discussed earlier in this chapter, some aspects of the doctrine of OSAS (*i.e.*, eternal security) can make sense, but only from God's perspective. Paul wrote about God's foreknowledge, "For whom he did foreknow, he also did predestinate to be conformed to the image of his Son, that he might be the firstborn among many brethren. Moreover whom he did predestinate, them he also called: and whom he called, them he also justified: and whom he justified, them he also glorified" (**Romans 8:29–30**).

There are significant issues with the concept of predestination. These are covered in slightly more detail in Chapter 13, "Calvinism and its Impact on the Modern Church." For purposes of addressing the OSAS doctrine we will deal with predestination as it is currently understood by the Modern Church. If the passage above really does mean predestination and is speaking of individuals, we can see that these are all people God *foreknew* would remain faithful. This suggests that God does not predestine or elect individual people to salvation through Christ but rather that God knows who will come to a true and saving faith. All other elements of predestination follow the knowledge of who God knows will remain faithful. As such it references a group, not an individual.

Those who would use their free will to continue to walk with the Holy Spirit after they accepted Christ would be in this group. This understanding of the passage maintains consistency with the remainder of scripture. Yet this does not violate the idea that we retain our God-given free will after salvation. It simply says that God knew how we would use our free will. But remember, we have no idea who these people are, because we cannot see across time. We should never sit in judgment telling people that they are or are not a part of that group. Nor should we let the belief system guide our decisions as to how we act. Rather we must speak the same messages scripture does to believers.

It is this understanding that takes into account the free will that God has granted man. It is this explanation that maintains consistency with the whole body of scripture and with God's nature not to reward sin. What this also implies is that many who claim to have accepted Christ will not endure, and there are also many who never really knew Christ. But God knew from the beginning who would believe and remain faithful and who would never truly believe. These are "the elect."

Again, this perspective relies on God's knowledge of people across time: who will and will not endure. But we humans do not know this. Time is linear for us and we must deal with each day as it occurs. But God is not a creature of time like we are. God created time, and exists outside it. He can see past, present and future all at once. We can scroll backwards and forwards on a DVD, but He can see it all at once. It can be hard for us, as creatures of time, to understand and appreciate this concept.

While God knows who will endure to the end, we do not, and it certainly is not all those who name Christ as Lord (Luke 6:46 and Matthew 7:21). God knows who will attempt to walk in the Holy Spirit and who will not. In short, the doctrine of OSAS can make sense in this passage

(Romans 8:28–29) *from God's perspective* because He knows the future. That is why He could write the names of the truly saved in the book of life of the Lamb before the foundation of the world – He knows. This is why we should ask proponents of the doctrine as currently taught "Have you seen the book of life? Is my name in it?"

But at the end of the day there is one inescapable fact that we must acknowledge. That is the doctrine as presented from the pulpit builds the Laodicean Church – a church which God was prepared to "spue thee out of my mouth."

Arguments for the Doctrine of Once Saved, Always Saved

There are a few arguments from isolated passages of scripture on which the Modern Church bases the doctrine of OSAS. However, the actual words "Once Saved, Always Saved" are never used together in scripture. Let's look at some of the arguments, arising from scripture and logic applied to scripture, which are used to support the doctrine of OSAS.

Argument Number One There is nothing we can do after accepting Christ which can cause us to lose our salvation because of verses like Romans 8:38–39. No degree of sin, engaging of the flesh, losing or transferring our faith to someone or something other than Jesus Christ (as Paul confronted the Galatians about), or even intentionally rejecting Jesus Christ can separate us from our salvation, and God will welcome into His kingdom all those who at one time accepted Christ, even those committed to rebellion against Him.

> **Scriptural Objection:** It must first be noted that this passage does not directly refer to salvation, but to the love of God. To apply this passage to salvation, one must first equate "the love of God" with salvation. However, many passages tell us that God's love extends to the whole world (John 3:16), yet we know that the whole world will not be saved (Matthew 7:13–14). Applying this verse to salvation is tenuous at best. Even if we do consider it as applying to salvation, this interpretation of Romans 8:38–39 ignores the possibility that we can exercise our free will to *separate ourselves* from Christ or that God can separate us from Christ, which is documented in scripture (John 15:1–2). A close examination of

the passage supports this interpretation. Romans 8:38–39 is clearly talking about things and beings *other than ourselves*. Furthermore, much of Romans 8 addresses brothers and sisters (believers) who walk in the Holy Spirit (Romans 8:1, 4–5), with many warnings and condemnations for those who don't walk in the Holy Spirit. If Romans 8:35–39 is a promise of salvation, *the context of Romans 8 indicates the promise is made to those believers who are walking faithfully with the Holy Spirit and who are doing the Father's will.*

It is scripturally inconsistent with the nature of God (who hated sin enough to send His son to pay a horrific price for our sin) that He will welcome into His kingdom those who, after coming to Christ, are committed to disobedience or later reject Jesus Christ. God does not have unlimited tolerance for sin, as demonstrated in the Old Testament. Many Christians are committed to disobedience, and some lukewarm Christians do not share the hatred of sin that they would have if they were being led by the Holy Spirit. Scripture teaches that Jesus became the author of salvation *for those who obey Him* (Romans 8:3–4), not those who rebel against Him. For a more comprehensive view of this passage and the issues with modern interpretation, see the section on Key Scriptures later in this chapter.

Argument Number Two God controls a person within the salvation process to a degree that prevents that person from doing anything that would cause him to lose his salvation, citing verses like Romans 9:14–22.

Scriptural Objection: This argument is virtually identical to (and probably derived from) the Calvinist doctrine of "Perseverance of the Saints" which we discuss further in Chapter 13, "Calvinism and its Impact on the Modern Church." Citing verses to claim that man's God-given free will plays no part in his retention of salvation ignores Old Testament references and the myriad of appeals and commands to men to use their free will to obey God. In the Romans 9 passage, Paul referred first [**v17**] to God hardening Pharaoh's heart in Exodus 7–12, but a close examination of the Exodus account reveals that after each of the first five plagues were ended, either "the heart of Pharaoh was hardened" or "Pharaoh hardened his heart." Not until Pharaoh used his free will five times in rebellion against God did God begin to harden Pharaoh's heart, beginning with the sixth plague. This is re-iterated in 1 Samuel 6:6. God hardened Pharaoh's heart *in response* to Pharaoh's exercise of his free will to rebel against God's express commands.

Paul next refers to the potter and the clay, beginning in Romans 9:20, a clear reference to Jeremiah 18. That chapter begins with Jeremiah entering the potter's house at the Lord's command. There he found the potter making a vessel on his potter's wheel, "And the vessel that he made of clay was marred in the hand of the potter: so he made it again another vessel, as seemed good to the potter to make it" (**Jeremiah 18:4**). In the next two verses, God declared Himself the potter, and the nation of Israel the clay, and then continues His warning of impending judgment (the Babylonian captivity) against the nation of Israel for its disobedience. The Lord then explained the imagery to Jeremiah: "And at what instant I shall speak concerning a nation, and concerning a kingdom, to build and to plant it; If it do evil in my sight, that it obey not my voice, then I will repent of the good, wherewith I said I would benefit them" (**Jeremiah 18:9–10**). Note that the first vessel "was marred" (**Jeremiah 18:4**) *before*, as Paul said, the potter chose, "of the same lump [of clay] one vessel unto honour, and another unto dishonor" (**Romans 9:21**). This is exactly what happened to the nation of Israel as a result of their evil. They were God's chosen people, but as He, the potter, was molding them to be a light to the nations when they became marred by their evil, and He molded them into a dishonored, defeated nation. Again, God acted *in response* to Israel's disobedience in the exercise of their free will. Far from refuting the concept that man has free will, *this passage in Romans 9 shows God's response to man's improper use of his free will.*

Furthermore, passages such as Galatians 5:16–21 (warning Christians that their repeated sinful behavior after accepting Christ can cause them to lose their salvation) tells us that this argument is not scriptural, and in fact reflects a misunderstanding of what Paul is writing in Romans 9. We see in scripture the free will of men, before and after being saved, too often being used to rebel against God, such as living in continuing sin. We are specifically taught in scripture that if we sin intentionally after coming to Christ, there is no sacrifice left for sins, and that punishment awaits (Hebrews 10:26–27). This specifically addresses one who had been sanctified.

Remember that the Israelites were disciplined by God over and over and they did not repent and were destroyed (except for the faithful remnant). We are reminded of this multiple times in scripture. In Amos 4 for example, God sent Amos to tell the northern kingdom of Israel how many times He had disciplined them, but every time God concludes with the same summation: "yet ye have not returned to me." Even after all this discipline, God gave them another chance, yet they once again refused to heed the words of God sent through Amos. God's reached down to try to correct them; they refused and most were destroyed.

We see anecdotal evidence in the world of those who accepted Christ, produced fruit for Christ, and later exercised their free will to abandon their faith in Christ. The entire Bible deals with God calling, not forcing, men to make choices that honor Him and demonstrate their love for Him. Faith, although given by God, must be used by man through his free will to obey God. If this is not true, Jesus' parable of the talents (Matthew 25:14–30) makes no sense. If this is not true, virtually all of Christ's commands to Christians would be unnecessary. This includes commands to be led by the Spirit, not to sin, to have self-control, to endure, to love one another, etc.

Argument Number Three God's promises, including the promise of salvation, can be relied on, regardless of the disobedience of a person after coming to Christ.

Scriptural Objection: This argument assumes that all God's promises are unconditional, when in fact very few are. We have seen that God did not act to fulfill His promise to the Israelites leaving Egypt who lacked the faith to obey. The point was so important that God reminds us of this three times in the New Testament and commanding us not to make the same mistake. God was faithful and had every intention of honoring His promise. The Israelites were eyewitnesses of His power and believed intellectually, but did not trust Him enough to take the land He had promised them in Exodus 23:23 (by following the advice of Caleb and Joshua in Numbers 14:5–10), as well as the other 10 times they tested God (Number 14:21–23). Their continued lack of faith in God caused their regular disobedience. They had faith in God when they crossed the Red Sea, but they failed to, "keep in memory" (**1 Corinthians 15:2**) their faith. Retaining the faith in God which would produce obedience (demonstrated faith) was obviously an unstated condition of the promise of entering the Promised Land.

The same unstated condition applies to most of the promises made to us by God today. We are commanded many times to endure and to obey, sometimes with explicitly stated eternal consequences. Indeed, we are warned that a follower of Jesus is to "deny himself, and take up his cross daily, and follow me [Jesus]" (**Luke 9:23**). If God makes us a promise, we should not assume that promise is unconditional. Almost all His promises are conditioned upon the recipient having the faith to trust Him and obey his commands. Man has taken the concept of a promise and twisted it to mean something that it does not. If we have the faith to be obedient to God and walk with the Holy Spirit, God will honor His promises (if they apply to us) because we have met His (often unstated) conditions. If we are committed to rebelling against God and do not care enough to try to obey, or we place the world ahead of God (idolatry), scripture shows us that God will not necessarily honor those promises because we did not meet the condition of true faith, which would be demonstrated through obedience.

Argument Number Four God's will is always done, and since he desires those accepting Jesus Christ as Lord to be saved, they will be, citing verses like Philippians 1:6.

Scriptural Objection: This argument denies the existence of free will, something obvious in the Bible beginning with Adam and Eve's disobedience in the Garden. Scripturally, God's will is *not* always done here on earth, beginning in Genesis Chapter 3 unless we believe that God lied to Adam and Eve by telling them not to do what He really wanted them to do. But the ability to choose is re-iterated over and over by God in the Old Testament as the Israelites will testify. We see that God's will is not done on this earth. We see it over and over in both the Old and New Testament. It is the reason we are taught to pray for God's will to be done on earth (Matthew 6:10). We see abundant evidence in scripture of things happening here on earth *as a result of man's exercise of his free will* which are inconsistent with God's desires (*e.g.,* Matthew 23:37). The Old Testament is filled with countless instances where the free will of man opposed the will of our God here on earth. God punished Israel for doing evil (the Babylonian captivity) which is neither reasonable nor just if God is controlling people. Finally, we know that God is not the source of evil. For God to state His will to His people and then force them to disobey, only to punish them, paints God as someone wholly inconsistent with how scripture defines Him. God cedes us free will and then commands us how to use that will. The idea that God will welcome into His kingdom those committed to opposing His will is a message of the evil one.

Argument Number Five The deposit of the Holy Spirit guarantees our salvation no matter how we act (*i.e.,* He is the pledge that God will fulfill His promise of salvation).

Scriptural objection: We are able to quench (Greek *sbennumi),* meaning to "put out or extinguish," or grieve (Greek *lupeó),* meaning to "vex or pain" the Holy Spirit. Again, God would not be truthful if He commanded us not to do something that we cannot do (*e.g.* quench the Holy Spirit).

Jesus told His disciples, "If ye love me, keep my commandments; and I will ask the Father, and he shall give you another Comforter, that he may abide with you for ever" (**John 14:15–16**). Some more modern versions eliminate the *"may"* replacing it with *"will,"* yet the Greek mood is clear. The subjunctive mood is used meaning there is *possibility* that the Holy Spirit, depending on circumstances (our faith), will abide with us forever. The subjunctive mood indicates something that is conditional or something that is a possibility, but *not* a certainty.

If the Holy Spirit had been guaranteed to abide in us forever without condition, a different mood would have been used. Given how much our God hates sin but still allows us to disobey His commands through our free will after we have been indwelt by the Holy Spirit, we can only conclude (and this is confirmed in scripture), that Holy Spirit does not control us, but only leads us when we submit to Him.

As discussed above, true saving faith is demonstrated through submission to the will of God (the Holy Spirit). Continuing in that submission produces obedience and what Jesus called "fruit" in John 15:5. This is the unstated condition accompanying the promise of salvation. If we fail to meet the condition, we break the agreement (covenant) with God, and God's promise of salvation is no longer applicable to us.

Reviewing our earlier illustration, if I promise to buy your house and put a deposit down on your house to guarantee that I will buy it, you must still do your part to sign the deed conveying the house to me. You must be faithful to complete the transaction to receive the benefit (completion) of my promise to buy the house. The deposit guarantees the future action only if you fulfill your part of the agreement. The pledge of the Holy Spirit guarantees that if we are faithful, God will do His part. This condition must be met. The idea that nothing we do after accepting Christ has anything to do with salvation is completely damning.

The dominant theme of the Bible is that we must be faithful, and must demonstrate that faith through obedience to God. Think about all of the teachings to Christians in the New Testament covering faith and obedience. God tells us over and over that we have a part to play in our salvation. Again, this does not mean we can in any way earn our salvation, but rather that true and saving faith will cause Christians to act in a faithful manner consistent with the life Christians are supposed to live as described in the New

Testament. This includes enduring and being faithful by earnestly trying to walk with the Holy Spirit. We will want to do this if we have the faith we claim to have. If our faith does not cause us to act in this manner, we should examine our faith (2 Corinthians 13:5). Do we really think God wants to spend eternity with those who are in rebellion against Him and His commandments? Look at what happened to Satan in Ezekiel 28:12–17.

Argument Number Six We are kept by the power of God.

Scriptural Objection: Although there is a passage that states this outright (1 Peter 1:5), it is qualified: we are kept by the power of God, *through faith*. We have already shown that faith varies from great to dead. We are not being faithful when we do not submit our will to His will, and instead routinely act in a manner inconsistent with that faith. Saving faith entails more than just belief. Intellectual faith or belief alone does not save, but rather faith which produces obedience and works (John 15:5, James 1:22, James 2:14, and 1 John 2:3). If our faith permanently fails (we refuse to endure) or we don't try to live in a manner consistent with that faith, we have a dead faith (James 2:17, 20). The Israelites did not hold fast to their faith in God because the faith did not manifest itself although they still believed in God; they rebelled and were destroyed. Satan and his angels also believed. But they did not have the faith which manifested itself in obedience. Again, the condition for salvation (true saving faith) is not fully spelled out in this short passage, but is abundantly supplied throughout the New Testament.

Argument Number Seven All our past, present, and future sins are forgiven when we accept Christ, so any sin we commit after coming to Christ cannot affect our salvation.

Scriptural Objection: We have shown scripturally that future sins were not forgiven in Chapter 8, "Forgiveness of Sins." The writer of Hebrews warns us about the eternal consequences of continuing in willful sin after coming to Christ (Hebrews 10:26):

"how much sorer punishment, suppose ye, shall he be thought worthy, who hath trodden underfoot the Son of God, and hath counted the blood of the covenant, wherewith *he was sanctified*, an unholy thing, and hath done despite unto the Spirit of grace?" (**Hebrews 10:29**). If all future sins have really been forgiven, those who sin intentionally after coming to Christ would have nothing to fear (as the Modern Church teaches), but the Bible tells us there is "no sacrifice for sins left" for such people.

Argument Number Eight Most scriptures used to question OSAS have nothing to do with salvation.

Scriptural Objection: Actually, the opposite is true. Most scriptural passages used to support the doctrine of OSAS are not referring directly to salvation; most scriptural passages contradicting the doctrine of OSAS are specifically addressing the question of whether a believer can lose his salvation. For example, there are scriptures that tell *believers* that they must endure *(hold fast to their faith)* to be saved (Matthew 10:22 and 1 Corinthians 15:1–2).

These passages clearly and specifically reference conditional salvation. God will help us strengthen our faith if we ask Him (Mark 9:24). But we cannot expect God to *force* us to endure in our faith; otherwise there would be no reason for God to command us to endure. It is not a reasonable interpretation of the passages which appear to contradict OSAS to interpret them as having nothing to do with salvation when some explicitly state otherwise. Paul knew he had a part to play in his salvation (Philippians 3:14). It is intellectually dishonest to suggest that passages which clearly state and show there are conditions on salvation to say they do not.

Argument Number Nine God will not fail; God does everything.

Scriptural Objection: While this is a comforting thought, biblical history tells us this is a human, not a scriptural, argument. There are plenty of places in the Bible where God tells us He wants something to happen and it does not. The entire Bible is written to show men with free will how to escape the wrath of a just God, and the consequences of disobedience. It is a story of man's free will and the usage of that free will in response to a loving God and His offer.

But we see that time and time again men rebel against God. There are however, men who do not rebel against God, and it is these men that God lifts up or praises. God recognizes them for their appropriate use of their God-given free will (Hebrews 11) and the faith He gave them. The idea that God will welcome into His kingdom those who use their God-given free will to oppose or rebel against God simply has no support in scripture. It is exactly the same argument the evil one offered in the Garden, getting people to sin and trivialize what God commanded.

It is far different teaching to say that God does everything in salvation than to say that we cannot be saved without Christ. We must accept Christ with God-given faith and we must remain faithful. These are what God calls us to do. We have a part in our salvation. It is not the major part. We don't initiate it because He gives us the faith (Ephesians 2:8–9 and Romans 12:3), but we have a part to play (John 1:12, John 3:16, and 1 John 2:3). Heresy?

No, this is what the Bible teaches through numerous passages. Make no mistake; no one is saved except through Christ (John 14:6), and no one is saved by his own works. What we are talking about is the biblical requirement of demonstrating that faith through obedience to the Holy Spirit. The Holy Spirit does not lead us to be lumps of clay (that is sit around doing nothing). Using Calvinist interpretation of verses like Philippians 1:6 to relieve a believer of all responsibility after coming to Christ is a dangerous misrepresentation of what Jesus expects of His disciples.

Argument Number Ten Once we are justified we are saved forever.

Scriptural Objection: This is a question of timing, as discussed in Chapter 5, "Salvation and Eternal Life." Yes, we are justified at the moment we come to Christ, but justification is not a guaranteed, permanent event. Salvation relies on justification and justification relies on faith, thus the foundation of salvation is faith, "Therefore being justified by faith, we have peace with God through our Lord Jesus Christ" (**Romans 5:1**). But faith fails; it can be lost, transferred, compromised, dead, or shipwrecked.

We can be committed to act in an unfaithful manner. This is why we must endure: "For you have need of endurance, so that when you have done the will of God you may receive what is promised" (**Hebrews 10:36**). Other verses teach the same (Matthew 10:22, 1 Corinthians 15:1–2, Hebrews 6:4–6, Hebrews 10:23, and 1 John 2:17). We receive the promise by enduring and obeying.

We see that through the teaching of James that our works serve to demonstrate our faith (James 1:22, James 2:14, and James 2:18–20). This is not because the works save, but because the works testify to a true (or genuine) faith. They prove the faith genuine and since faith justifies, works are a part of true and saving faith. We are justified before God through our acceptance of Jesus Christ. However, we must act faithfully to maintain that faith and act in a manner consistent with our faith to remain justified.

Remember that Jesus himself tells us to be watchful for His return (which logically also means to watchful and prepared for when we leave this earth) to ensure we are able to stand before Jesus Christ (Luke 21:34–36). In that passage, and in the parallel passage in Matthew 24 and 25, Jesus makes it clear that those believers living in disobedience when He returns will not enter the kingdom, but will be cast into hell (Matthew 24:45–51). Unfortunately, the Modern Church's teaching of OSAS lull many into a false sense of security which can lead them into this quicksand.

It is inconsistent with both the nature of God and the overall message of scripture to believe that once a person truly accepts Jesus Christ, he can continue living in sin, later reject Jesus Christ, or be apathetic to God's will and ignore the Holy Spirit and remain justified before God. Even the passage, "By the which will we are sanctified through the offering of the body of Jesus Christ once for all" (**Hebrews 10:10**), when examined in the original Greek, addresses a continuing action or process which is unfinished, and therefore does not guarantee that it is uninterruptable by the misuse of our God-given free will. Living by faith includes walking by the Holy Spirit (Galatians 5:25, 1 John 2:6, and John 15) which is "abiding in Christ." We do no wrong when we walk with the Holy Spirit, but we always have the choice to submit to or reject the leading of the Holy Spirit.

Argument Number Eleven "True" Believers Can Never Lose Their Salvation

Scriptural Objection: Supporters of the doctrine of OSAS, when confronted with verses stating that believers can lose their salvation, usually claim that believers who lose their salvation "were never really saved in the first place," although many of those verses make it very clear those being referenced were once true believers. These are often the same people who claim salvation is by "faith alone." If they really believe salvation is by faith alone (that is, that works are not necessary to demonstrate a saving faith) then how could they ever know that a person who does not perform works was never saved? In short, the essence of their argument which says that faith alone saves (that is, faith without works) is not consistent with their view that those who don't demonstrate their faith were never saved. Their logic is circular: "If they lost their salvation that means they were never really saved. End of story. Time to move on."

Although proponents of OSAS may claim these people were never saved, they do not see the heart as God does. They cannot possibly know the truth about another person's relationship with God. This is another attempt to support an errant doctrinal position with a baseless assumption, instead of heeding the warnings of scripture *directed specifically to believers.*

But there are also many "transition scriptures" which demonstrate that a person can go from a state of having a saving faith to having a lost (or compromised) faith. Each of these transition scriptures describe an individual with faith transitioning to an individual without faith. We discussed the Israelites as a prime example. They had the faith to leave Egypt and walk across the Red Sea (crazy according to man right?) but their faith eroded, and consequently they started to disobey, ultimately unable to enter the Promised Land. Did God cause this? No. It was the free will of the Israelites. We know this was the choice the Israelites made because God subsequently warns us not to be like them; that is it was not His will.

There are many other passages which demonstrate transitions from faithful to unfaithful, saved to unsaved. These include Matthew 25:1–12, Matthew 24:45–51, Mark 4:20–21, John 15:1–6, Romans 11:17–24, and Hebrews 3:12).

Contrary to the doctrine of OSAS, the Bible's many admonitions to believers to "endure to the end" to be saved (*e.g.*, Matthew 10:22) make it clear that a person can abandon a true, saving faith and thereby lose his salvation. The message of the entire Bible is that the choice a believer makes has eternal consequences. This was the essence of Paul's discourse to the willfully sinning Galatian believers in chapter 5 of his epistle. Why would God warn the Galatians that they could lose their salvation, if their salvation could not be lost? And why do we see similar passages in Matthew 7:21, Hebrews 10:26, Romans 8:13–14, and elsewhere?

Don't be confused by proponents of OSAS who come up with extreme explanations of why warning passages, which clearly and directly reference salvation, are really not about salvation. It is a method use to justify errant doctrine.

Many Christians refuse to walk the narrow way of being led by the Holy Spirit. The *"narrow way"* of Matthew 7:14 is not always the one taken when our free will is involved. In the preceding verse Jesus said, "broad is the way, that leadeth to destruction, and many there be which go in thereat" (**Matthew 7:13**). This verse is usually understood to refer solely to unbelievers who never come to Christ, but in reality the totality of scripture indicates that there are many who receive Christ, and later lapse into unbelief: "Yet hath he not root in himself, but dureth for a while: for when tribulation or persecution ariseth because of the word, by and by he is offended" (**Matthew 13:21**).

Although at one time receiving Christ (John 1:12), those described by Jesus in Matthew 13:21 have ultimately chosen the broad road to destruction instead of the narrow way to life. Remember that Jesus himself tells us to be watchful for His return (which logically also means to watchful and prepared for when we leave this earth) to ensure we are able to stand before Jesus Christ (Luke 21:34–36). This is again a warning which would be unnecessary if OSAS is true. Eternity is what is important; not this temporal life.

Scripture makes it clear that there will be people who accept Jesus Christ, produce fruit in keeping with their belief, and later walk away from their faith. We will look at a few of those passages below. They all tell us that the sad result is eternal damnation. Those people do not endure. Why are there are so many warnings to Christians in scripture to endure to *"to the end"* to be saved (Matthew 10:22) if their future salvation is already secure? Unfortunately, the Modern Church's teaching of OSAS lull many into a false sense of security which can lead them into this quicksand.

There are many people who have accepted Christ and lived for Christ while producing fruit, all consistent with Jesus' definition of true disciple, only to later abandon their faith. Jesus taught us, "Herein is my Father glorified, that ye bear much fruit; so shall ye be my disciples" (**John 15:8**). There are plenty of people who have done exactly this. They have produced much fruit showing themselves to be Jesus' disciples. However, some of these same people who produced much fruit have since renounced their faith and in doing so, surrendered their salvation. They did not endure as they were commanded to in Matthew 10:32 and Romans 11:22.

It happens far too often. A book was recently written about Christians who have left their faith. There is the case of a very well-known Christian pastor who, for 19 years, produced fruit for Christ consistent with the scriptural definition of true and saving faith (John 15:5). He, based on his fruit, was a good tree and apparently produced good fruit: "Even so, every good tree bears good fruit, but a bad tree bears bad fruit. A good tree cannot bear bad fruit, *nor can a bad tree bear good fruit*. Every tree that does not bear good fruit is cut down and thrown into the fire. Therefore by their fruits you will know them" (**Matthew 7:17–20**).

If this pastor was a bad tree as described in scripture, he could not have produced good fruit. However, since he did produce good fruit at one time (bringing individuals to Christ), we are forced to conclude that he was at one time a good tree. His previous actions bear witness to his faith at one time. But now he no longer believes, and has renounced his Christian faith. Indeed, this man is now trying to remove all evidence of God from the public domain. This type of story occurs over and over, and yet many Christian leaders are unwilling to honestly admit true Christians can use their free will to disobey or renounce God, because they want to hold to their worldly doctrine of OSAS. They cling to a doctrine which is neither scripturally supported, nor is manifest in this world.

There are others: a missionary from Norway, another well-known evangelical pastor and others. They abandoned their faith after bringing many to Christ. Many have become atheists and others have accepted strange "truths." These are people who were at the very center of Christianity, producing fruit and bringing people to Christ before they departed from the faith. While it is true that the eternal destiny of these individuals is not yet fixed, since they have not yet died, we understand what scripture teaches about their position with respect to the Lord now. Perhaps they will yet return to the faith (we can and should pray so). Unfortunately, there are many believers who have died in their unbelief after openly rejecting Jesus Christ, or living in willful rebellion (sin) toward God after coming to Christ.

Finally, as shown earlier in Chapter 5, "Salvation and Eternal Life", the way to eternal life only *begins* with our acceptance of Jesus Christ. Eternal life is the goal, not the present reality; scripture says we receive it in the future. If we are faithful in staying on the "narrow way," it leads to eternal life *when* we are with our Lord (Philippians 3:8–14). The nature of God is to expect His followers to submit to His will. God is not mocked. (Galatians 6:7). He is, after all, the Creator and the Master. We are His creatures, and believers are His servants (Revelation 22:3). God made His expectations and the result of disobedience clear when He said to Ezekiel:

> "Say unto them, As I live, saith the Lord God, I have no pleasure in the death of the wicked; but that the wicked turn from his way and live: turn ye, turn ye from your evil ways; for why will ye die, O house of Israel? Therefore, thou son of man, say unto the children of thy people, The righteousness of the righteous shall not deliver him in the day of his transgression: as for the wickedness of the wicked, he shall not fall thereby in the day that he turneth from his wickedness; neither shall the righteous be able to live for his righteousness in the day that he sinneth. When I shall say to the righteous, that he shall surely live; if he trust to his own righteousness, and commit iniquity, all his righteousnesses shall not be remembered; but for his iniquity that he hath committed, he shall die for it. Again, when I say unto the wicked, Thou shalt surely die; if he turn from his sin, and do that which is lawful and right; If the wicked restore the pledge, give again that he had robbed, walk in the statutes of life, without committing iniquity; he shall surely live, he shall not die. None of his sins that he hath committed shall be mentioned unto him: he hath done that which is lawful and right; he shall surely live. Yet the children of thy people say, The way of the Lord is not equal: but as for them, their way is not equal. *When the righteous turneth from his righteousness, and committeth iniquity, he shall even die thereby.* But if the wicked turn from his wickedness, and do that which is lawful and right, he shall live thereby" (**Ezekiel 33:11–19**).

Note the emphasized part of the passage. The word "righteous" in the Old Testament usually means what we call "saved," which scripturally means they have received Christ within the meaning of John1:12. In the case of Old Testament saints, their faith was looking forward to God's provision for their salvation (*e.g.*, Job 19:25–27), just as we look back on God's provision through the sacrifice of His Son. Here God is commanding Ezekiel to tell the Jewish people in exile in Babylon that they can turn their hearts back to God and live (spiritually), but if they depart from their demonstrated faith in Him, they will die (spiritually). This passage (and many quoted below) makes it very clear that a righteous man ("saved") can turn away from the faith that saved him, and consequently lose his salvation.

We are to strive for holiness and doing the Lord's will while trusting in our Lord. It is not a true faith to say we believe and then live in rebellion, not concerned about the Father's will. Such faith will not endure. True faith produces a desire to please God by obeying Him and being led by the Spirit. Such a lifestyle is draws us closer to God in a relationship that is much more likely to endure.

A Look at Some Key Scriptures

Here are some scriptures with very short commentaries designed to explore what some of the key verses really say about OSAS (unconditional eternal security):

John 3:16 "For God so loved the world, that he gave his only begotten Son, that whosoever believeth in him should not perish, but have everlasting life."

> Commentary: Teaches that those who believe in Jesus Christ will have everlasting life. The two key issues in this passage are: 1) what happens when one ceases to believe, and 2) what does the word "believes" or "believeth" really mean? Here the Greek tense of "believeth" is the continuous present tense, meaning something that we are currently doing, not something done in the past. In the Greek, present tense verbs notate duration, not a one-time event. This verse is more accurately rendered as *"For God so loved the world that he gave his only Son, that whoever goes on believing in him should not perish, but have eternal life."* Often this verse is cited as justification that those

who have truly believed (at any moment in the past) have life everlasting, regardless of whether they are currently believing or not. But a proper translation of the verse indicates that only those who continue believing have the chance of eternal life. Furthermore, there is no reason to use the Greek present tense if belief at one time is all that is required. Hence the possibility of losing faith (and eternal life) is actually raised in this passage.

John 6:39–40 "And this is the Father's will which hath sent me, that of all which he hath given me I should lose nothing, but should raise it up again at the last day. And this is the will of him that sent me, that every one which seeth the Son, and believeth on him, may have everlasting life: and I will raise him up at the last day."

Commentary: Much like John 3:16, this passage teaches that it is the Father's will that none who *go on believing in the Son* (again, Greek present tense) should be lost, and *may* (not guaranteed) have everlasting life. Jesus then promises to raise the faithful believer "at the last day" (what we call the rapture). Actually, it is God's will that everyone have everlasting life (1 Timothy 2:3–4 and 2 Peter 3:9), but we know that will not happen (Matthew 7:13). God also wills that people not murder each other or live in sin. Clearly, God's will is not done on this earth. As in John 3:16, the use of the Greek present tense on the word "believeth" actually contradicts the idea of OSAS by raising the condition of continued faith as a requirement of salvation.

John 6:44 "No man can come to me, except the Father which hath sent me draw him: and I will raise him up at the last day."

Commentary: We need look at the usage of the various verbs and mood within the verse. There is little doubt that the Father draws us; this is also taught in other scriptures. However we see that "can" is in the present tense and "draw" is in the first aorist so a more accurate representation of this is that "No one can come and keep coming to me unless the Father who sent me draws and keeps drawing him, and I will raise him up at the last day." Why would the Father stop drawing a person? It is because they have used their ability to choose against God and to refuse to bear fruit (consistent with John 15:1–2). In short, this does not address the case where the Father ceases to draw people. Clearly there are many He has not drawn.

John 10:27–29 "My sheep hear my voice, and I know them, and they follow me: And I give unto them eternal life; and they shall never perish, neither shall any man pluck them out of my hand. My Father, which gave them me, is greater than all; and no man is able to pluck them out of my Father's hand."

> Commentary: God knows the future, and therefore knows whose faith will endure (God's perspective was discussed above). Jesus calls those faithful people "my sheep." Proponents of OSAS citing this passage fail to consider that this passage is talking about believers who God knows will be faithful and endure. Note also the Greek verb "give" (as in "I give") is again in the present tense, indicating an in-process action. Even though we do not rely on men's testimony, DL Moody understood that this continuous and in-process action requires effort on the part of the sheep and the shepherd. Most people who read this verse fail to fully appreciate the implication of the verb "pluck" (Greek *harpazo*), which means to carry off by force. We do not carry ourselves off by force, and therefore this verse does not address the believer himself voluntarily leaving the hand of God (failing to endure in the faith), nor of God's removing him for not demonstrating true faith by bearing fruit (John 15:5–6). Much like other verses, the verbs reflect continuous action demonstrating our need to endure just as John 3:16 does.

2 Corinthians 1:22, Ephesians 1:13–14 "Who hath also sealed us, and given the earnest of the Spirit in our hearts" and "In whom ye also trusted, after that ye heard the word of truth, the gospel of your salvation: in whom also after that ye believed, ye were sealed with that holy Spirit of promise, Which is the earnest of our inheritance until the redemption of the purchased possession, unto the praise of his glory."

Commentary: After believing in Christ, we are sealed with the Holy Spirit. "Earnest" has the same meaning in the passage as "earnest money" has today in a real estate purchase contract. It is a deposit, or pledge, put up to assure the seller that the buyer will fulfill his promise (to purchase the property pursuant to the terms of the contract) as explained in an earlier chapter. But the contract also lists obligations to be performed by the seller. The buyer's obligation to purchase is conditioned on the seller completing his obligations (pay outstanding taxes and liens, execute a deed conveying clear title, etc.).

The actual purchase takes place sometime after the contract is signed, giving the seller the time to fulfill his obligations. In the same way, we have obligations to fulfill in order for God's promise of salvation to be consummated *in the future*. Contrary to what those advocating OSAS say, the passage indicates that salvation is *not* a done deal at the moment of belief, but that the deposit of the Holy Spirit as earnest is just the beginning of an agreement to be fulfilled by both parties in the future. For the believer, the narrow road lies ahead.

Romans 4:4–8 "Now to him that worketh is the reward not reckoned of grace, but of debt. But to him that worketh not, but believeth on him that justifieth the ungodly, his faith is counted for righteousness. Even as David also describeth the blessedness of the man, unto whom God imputeth righteousness without works, saying, Blessed are they whose iniquities are forgiven, and whose sins are covered. Blessed is the man to whom the Lord will not impute sin."

Commentary: Man is justified by faith, not works. No person who reads the Bible disputes that truth. This passage does not, however, contradict the many passages that make it clear that true saving faith will result in the believer bearing fruit (John 15:5–6), demonstrating obedience (1 John 2:3–4) through works (James 2:14, 18–26) done in the Spirit (Romans 8:3–4). It does not teach that once we have accepted Christ as our Lord, we can live any way we want as those in the Modern Church indirectly teach. Note the latter part of the passage, directly referencing Psalm 32, which shows the context to be dealing specifically with those believers (David) who confess their sins before the Lord and are therefore forgiven (1 John 1:9). Psalm 32 goes on to describe David's emotional pain before he confessed his sin to God. So the latter part of the passage is not designed to show that simple belief is a guarantee of eternal life.

Romans 8:38–39 "For I am persuaded, that neither death, nor life, nor angels, nor principalities, nor powers, nor things present, nor things to come, Nor height, nor depth, nor any other creature, shall be able to separate us from the love of God, which is in Christ Jesus our Lord."

Commentary: Teaches that no one else or any other created thing can separate believers ("us") from the love of Christ. It does not say that a believer cannot abandon his faith and thereby lose his salvation (1 Corinthians 15:1–2), or that a believer cannot lose his salvation by sinning willfully and habitually after receiving Christ (Galatians 5:21 and Hebrews 10:26). Finally, it is unclear at best that this passage is even referring to salvation. It is talking about "the love of God," and we know God loves all mankind ("the world"—John 3:16), not explicitly about salvation.

Ephesians 2:8–9, Titus 3:5 "For by grace are ye saved through faith; and that not of yourselves: it is the gift of God: Not of works, lest any man should boast" and "Not by works of righteousness which we have done, but according to his mercy he saved us, by the washing of regeneration, and renewing of the Holy Ghost."

> Commentary: Two of the key verses cited by proponents of OSAS. Both seem incorrectly interpreted by the proponents of OSAS when considered in the larger picture of scripture. While the word saved (Greek *sozo*) is in the perfect tense (meaning an action completed in the past with continuing result), it does not speak definitively to the future. It is a leap of logic to assume that the result (salvation) will be maintained regardless of how we use our God-given free will, especially in light of other scripture. Just Paul's admonitions to the believers at Ephesus in the remainder of that epistle should be enough to make it clear that believers are not free, after receiving Christ, to live any lifestyle they want and still expect to inherit eternal life (see Romans 6:15–22).

Philippians 1:6 "Being confident of this very thing, that he which hath begun a good work in you will perform it until the day of Jesus Christ."

> Commentary: Teaches that Paul believes He (God) will complete the good work that has begun in us. Confident (Greek *peithō*) indicates a hopeful belief, not certainty. It could have been written indicating certainty (Greek *asphaleia*). While Paul certainly believes that those who have accepted Christ will have God help them see it through until the day of Christ, it is stated as a belief, not fact. Indeed, this is God's plan and desire and God will do this for those that are humble, seek to obey Him, and endure. However, many scriptures indicate that those who, after accepting Christ, live in willful rebellion against God (Galatians 5:15–21) or outright deny Christ

(Matthew 10:33) will not inherit the kingdom of God. The unconditional guarantee of eternal security Calvinists and proponents of OSAS see in this verse is simply not there.

1 Peter 1:5 "Who are kept by the power of God through faith unto salvation ready to be revealed in the last time."

> Commentary: While we are kept by the power of God, the teaching is very specific that this keeping comes through enduring *faith*, not simply intellectual belief and not independent of our faith as we have already discussed. True faith is a living and active faith, not simple acknowledgment or a one-time belief. We are commanded in many places to endure in our true faith and if we obey that command, then we may know that God will keep us.

Jude 1:2 "Jude, the servant of Jesus Christ, and brother of James, to them that are sanctified by God the Father, and preserved in Jesus Christ, and called"

> Commentary: Clearly states we are preserved in Jesus Christ, but we must look at the underlying word for preserved. Preserved (Greek *tēreō*) means to watch over and guard. We all see that people in the Bible escaped their guards. Guard and prevent from escaping are not the same concepts in Greek. There is a different Greek word if the idea was to communicate that Jesus Christ would absolutely "prevent us from escaping" (Greek *phylassō*). Remember that Jesus is our greatest advocate; He desires our love and submission. He will, through the Holy Spirit, help us (in effecting, guarding us). But that does not translate to Jesus overriding our will to prevent us from doing evil, as previously discussed. Interpreted in this way, this passage is consistent with John 10:27–29. There is also the possibility that those addressed refers to those that God knows will remain faithful, not simply all that name Christ as Lord (Matthew 7:21).

1 John 5:13 "These things have I written unto you that believe on the name of the Son of God; that ye may know that ye have eternal life, and that ye may believe on the name of the Son of God."

> Commentary: There is a great deal of irony in using this passage to support the doctrine of OSAS, because it comes at the close of John's epistle which is written to point out to believers that a true saving faith results in obedience (1 John 2:3–4 and 1 John 3:10), abiding in Christ (1 John 2:24,28), and love for God and fellow believers (1 John 4:7–8), which proponents of OSAS repeatedly deny. Although know (Greek *eidō*) does tend to mean to "know" or "perceive," it is written using the subjunctive verb which is the mood of possibility and potentiality, conditional in nature. Any action (as in this case, "to know"), may or may not occur, depending upon circumstances. However, we can know that we have eternal life if we are truly seeking to do the Father's will as led by the Holy Spirit, but as for those who are committed to doing their own will, eternal life is far less certain.

There are also plenty of scriptures as we identified earlier which demonstrate the OSAS doctrine to be untrue as presented. These include:

Exodus 32:30–35 "And it came to pass on the morrow, that Moses said unto the people, Ye have sinned a great sin: and now I will go up unto the Lord; peradventure I shall make an atonement for your sin. And Moses returned unto the Lord, and said, Oh, this people have sinned a great sin, and have made them gods of gold. Yet now, if thou wilt forgive their sin; and if not, blot me, I pray thee, out of thy book which thou hast written. And the Lord said unto Moses, Whosoever hath sinned against me, him will I blot out of my book."

> Commentary: We learn elsewhere in scripture that these Israelites coming out of Egypt were believers. That is why their names are in the book. The book is God's book of [spiritual] life (called "the book of life of the Lamb"

in Revelation 13:8). When God did what he told Moses (blotted them out of the book), they died spiritually, something that cannot happen if the doctrine of OSAS is true. Again, we have a choice. We can believe what God told Moses according to scripture, or we can believe the man-made doctrine of OSAS.

Numbers 14:11–12 "And the Lord said unto Moses, How long will this people provoke me? and how long will it be ere they believe me, for all the signs which I have shewed among them? I will smite them with the pestilence, and *disinherit them*, and will make of thee a greater nation and mightier than they."

> Commentary: This passage is confirmation that the Israelites coming out of Egypt were believers (heirs of God); otherwise, He could not disinherit them. These believers are provoking God through their continual sin (disobedience), and consequently are risking eternal damnation (separation from God), something proponents of the doctrine of OSAS say cannot happen. God states otherwise.

Deuteronomy 8:19–20 "And it shall be, if thou do at all forget the Lord thy God, and walk after other gods, and serve them, and worship them, I testify against you this day that ye shall surely perish. As the nations which the Lord destroyeth before your face, so shall ye perish; because ye would not be obedient unto the voice of the Lord your God."

> Commentary: Those who follow other gods (These need not be literal gods as people worshipped in the Old Testament, but can be material possessions, family, or anything we prioritize above God) will perish. Perish (Hebrew *abad*), means "utterly destroyed by divine judgment, blotted out," indicating not physical death, but spiritual death. Compare to OSAS which says this cannot happen.

Deuteronomy 29:18–20 "Lest there should be among you man, or woman, or family, or tribe, whose heart turneth away this day from the Lord our God, to go and serve the gods of these nations; lest there should be among you a root that beareth gall and wormwood; and it come to pass, when he heareth the words of this curse, that he bless himself in his heart, saying, I shall have peace, though I walk in the imagination of mine heart, to add drunkenness to thirst: the Lord will not spare him, but then the anger of the Lord and his jealousy shall smoke against that man, and all the curses that are written in this book shall lie upon him, and the Lord shall blot out his name from under heaven."

> Commentary: God states again that He will in fact blot a believer's name out of His book, indicating spiritual death. We know God is talking about believers, because only the names of believers are in the book per Revelation 13:8. God apparently doesn't agree with OSAS.

Deuteronomy 30:19 "I call heaven and earth to record this day against you, that I have set before you life and death, blessing and cursing: therefore choose life, that both thou and thy seed may live."

> Commentary: God gives us a choice: that is the message of the entire Bible. He has always given mankind this same choice. What we do with that choice will determine our destiny, either spiritual life or spiritual death.

Jeremiah 15:6 "Thou hast forsaken me, saith the Lord, thou art gone backward: therefore will I stretch out my hand against thee, and destroy thee; I am weary with repenting"

> Commentary: These people are said to have "forsaken" (Hebrew *natash*) God meaning "left" God. The result? God will destroy them.

Ezekiel 18:9, 21–22 "Hath walked in my statutes, and hath kept my judgments, to deal truly; he is just, he shall surely live, saith the Lord God" [**v9**], and "But if the wicked will turn from all his sins that he hath committed, and keep all my statutes, and do that which is lawful and right, he shall surely live, he shall not die. All his transgressions that he hath committed, they shall not be mentioned unto him: in his righteousness that he hath done he shall live" [**v21–22**].

> Commentary: This passage gives the same requirement for spiritual life we see in the New Testament, when we examine it as a whole. The passage describes a person who trusts God and afterward demonstrates his faith by living in obedience to Him, with the result that he has spiritual life. A declaration of faith in Christ, without any commitment of obedience, does not indicate saving faith, no matter what the proponents of OSAS claim.

Ezekiel 18:24–26 "But when the righteous turneth away from his righteousness, and committeth iniquity, and doeth according to all the abominations that the wicked man doeth, shall he live? All his righteousness that he hath done shall not be mentioned: in his trespass that he hath trespassed, and in his sin that he hath sinned, in them shall he die. Yet ye say, The way of the Lord is not equal. Hear now, O house of Israel; Is not my way equal? are not your ways unequal? When a righteous man turneth away from his righteousness, and committeth iniquity, and dieth in them; for his iniquity that he hath done shall he die."

> Commentary: In this passage, the Lord God Himself is speaking to Ezekiel, warning him about the loss of spiritual life which results from turning to a life of sin and dying without repenting. The doctrine of OSAS says this cannot happen. In this passage, God disagrees.

Psalms 69:28 "Let them be blotted out of the book of the living, and not be written with the righteous."

> Commentary: David, a man after God's own heart and full of the Holy Spirit, understood that God could blot people's names of out of the book of the (spiritually) living, and asks God to do so. David had the indwelling

Holy Spirit (1 Samuel 16:13 and Psalm 51:11), and had in all probability read that God could do so in the writings of Moses that we know as Exodus 32:32. This is also consistent with the veiled warnings of God in Revelation 3:5 and Revelation 22:19. God's warning to believers is consistent: "Be not highminded, but fear; for if God spared not the natural branches [Israel], take heed lest he also spare not thee" (Romans 11:20b–21). As noted above, God does not change (Malachi 3:6). He certainly is not going to change His criteria for entrance into His kingdom because of the doctrines of Calvinism or the Modern Church.

Matthew 7:21 "Not everyone that saith unto me, Lord, Lord, shall enter into the kingdom of heaven; but he that doeth the will of my Father which is in heaven"

Commentary: Those who respond to the will of the Father (through submission to the leading of the Holy Spirit) are those who enter the Kingdom of heaven, not those that simply call Him Lord. Scripturally, the will of the Father is more than just accepting Jesus Christ.

Matthew 24:13 "But he that shall endure unto the end, the same shall be saved"

Commentary: Note that endurance *unto the end* is required. Why? Because salvation is a process *not yet complete* (note the tense: "shall be"). See Chapter 5, "Salvation and Eternal Life", for more on the timing of salvation. The word saved is the same word (Greek *sozo*) as other verses on salvation.

Matthew 24:45–51 "Who then is a faithful and wise servant, whom his lord hath made ruler over his household, to give them meat in due season? Blessed is that servant, whom his lord when he cometh shall find so doing. Verily I say unto you, That he shall make him ruler over all his goods. But and if *that evil servant* shall say in his heart, My lord delayeth his coming; And shall begin to smite his fellowservants, and to eat and drink with the drunken; The lord of that servant shall come in a day when he looketh not for him, and in an hour that he is not aware of, And shall cut him asunder, and appoint him his portion with the hypocrites: there shall be weeping and gnashing of teeth."

> Commentary: This parable is one of several Jesus told His disciples to explain how He was going to judge all mortal on the earth at His return (what we call "the second coming") to determine who would be left alive to enter the millennial kingdom (see John 3:3) and who would be killed and sent to hell (Matthew 24:36–25:46). The issue is clearly a matter of spiritual life or spiritual death. In this passage, notice the change of heart of the acknowledged faithful (believer) servant who, upon thinking that His master's (Jesus') coming was delayed, began acting as an unbeliever. This parable makes it very clear it is the same servant as it describes the change in his behavior of "that evil servant." What was the destiny of that servant? He was assigned a place with the hypocrites – those who say they believe, but by their actions deny Him (Titus 1:16), where "there shall be weeping and gnashing of teeth," clearly hell (Matthew 25:30). The servant was described as a faithful, trusted believer at the start of the parable, yet because of his subsequent unfaithful actions, he ended up doomed (lost) for all eternity. *This is Jesus Himself telling we are to remain faithful or risk losing our salvation.* Yet the Modern Church persists in teaching the opposite.

Matthew 25:1–12 "Then shall the kingdom of heaven be likened unto ten virgins, which took their lamps, and went forth to meet the bridegroom. And five of them were wise, and five were foolish. They that were foolish took their lamps, and took no oil with them: But the wise took oil in their vessels with their lamps. While the bridegroom tarried, they all slumbered and slept. And at midnight there was a cry made, Behold, the bridegroom cometh; go ye out to meet him. Then all those virgins arose, and trimmed their lamps. And the foolish said unto the wise, give us of your oil; for our lamps are gone out. But the wise answered, saying, not so; lest there be not enough for us and you: but go ye rather to them that sell, and buy for yourselves. And while they went to buy, the bridegroom came; and they that were ready went in with him to the marriage: and the door was shut. Afterward came also the other virgins, saying, Lord, Lord, open to us. But he answered and said, Verily I say unto you, I know you not. Watch therefore, for ye know neither the day nor the hour wherein the Son of man cometh."

> Commentary: In this parable Jesus explains that there will be many believers awaiting the return of our Lord but not all will be ready. Oil is a symbol of the Holy Spirit and has been throughout the Old Testament. At His return, some awaiting our Lord had the Holy Spirit; some did not. But notice the key point concerning those who had no oil when the master appeared: their lamps had gone out because they were out of oil, but *they previously had oil* (the Holy Spirit). They were believers, or they would not have had the indwelling Holy Spirit, symbolized by the oil in their lamps. The Modern Church would say they were "saved," and according to OSAS, they were guaranteed entrance into the kingdom. However, in this parable, their lamps went out because they were out of oil, indicating they no longer had the Holy Spirit. Consequently, they were not allowed to enter the kingdom. (Notice also that in this passage, unlike other passages, Jesus (the bridegroom) did not say "I never knew you" as He did in other passages, but rather "I know you not." The lesson of the parable: our free will decisions can cause us to lose the indwelling Holy Spirit and our salvation. Hold fast to the faith by which you were saved.

Mark 4:14–17 "The sower soweth the word. And these are they by the way side, where the word is sown; but when they have heard, Satan cometh immediately, and taketh away the word that was sown in their hearts. And these are they likewise which are sown on stony ground; who, when they have heard the word, immediately receive it with gladness; And have no root in themselves, and so endure but for a time: afterward, when affliction or persecution ariseth for the word's sake, immediately they are offended"

> Commentary: In explaining the parable of the sower, Jesus tells His disciples that there are those who receive spiritual life (the plant, representing spiritual life, springs up) but they endure only for a time, but not to eternity with God. They believe and have spiritual life, but only "for a time," and then the plant dies (symbolic of spiritual death). They will never receive the promised eternal life, because they did not "endure unto the end." Proponents of OSAS hold the mistaken belief that a person, once spiritually alive, "born again" (John 3:3), cannot die spiritually. They should take a closer look at what happened to the fallen angels and to Adam and Eve in Genesis 3. The word offended (Greek *skandalizō*) means to "fall away."

Mark 13:13 "And ye shall be hated of all [men] for my name's sake: but he that shall endure unto the end, the same shall be saved."

> Commentary: Jesus is speaking to His inner circle here, "Peter, and James, and John, and Andrew" (Mark 13:3). He tells them, the most devout and faithful of His followers, that they have to "endure unto the end" to be saved. "The end" can only mean physical death or rapture. Jesus clearly makes enduring (holding fast to their faith in word and deed) *their* responsibility. The idea that somehow this requirement does not apply to believers today makes a mockery of this clear teaching of Jesus. How did we (according to OSAS) become elevated to a class more valued by God than these four? The concept that somehow verses like Philippians 1:6 puts all the

responsibility on God to make sure we hold fast to our faith ("endure to the end") is an anti-biblical teaching growing out of the Calvinistic doctrine of Perseverance of the Saints. This false teaching may be leading many down the broad road to destruction, and those espousing it will have to answer to God.

John 8:31 "Then said Jesus to those Jews which believed on him, *If* ye continue in my word, then are ye my disciples indeed."

> Commentary: Jesus told Christians who believed on Him that *if* they continued in His word (kept His commandments), then (if they met that condition) they were in fact His disciples (true believers, on the narrow way to eternal life). "If" is always a conditional clause, indicating a requirement to do something to achieve the objective. Hence, we must continue in His word (keep His commandments) to be considered a true disciple, contrary to what OSAS claims.

John 14:15, 23 "If ye love me, keep my commandments" [**v15**], and "Jesus answered and said unto him, If a man love me, he will keep my words: and my Father will love him, and we will come unto him, and make our abode with him" [**v23**].

> Commentary: Action speaks louder than words with God. He literally judges our love for Him by our obedience. Jesus' point: Your love is only as strong as your faith, and true faith produces obedience. God wants to spend eternity with those who demonstrate that they truly love Him.

John 15:1–10 "I am the true vine, and my Father is the husbandman. *Every branch in me that beareth not fruit he taketh away*: and every branch that beareth fruit, he purgeth it, that it may bring forth more fruit. Now ye are clean through the word which I have spoken unto you. Abide in me, and I in you. As the branch cannot bear fruit of itself, except it abide in the vine; no more can ye, except ye abide in me. I am the vine, ye are the branches: He that abideth in me, and I in him, the same bringeth forth much fruit: for without me ye can do nothing. *If a man abide not in me, he is cast forth as a branch, and is withered; and men gather them, and cast them into the fire, and they are burned.* If ye abide in me, and my words abide in you, ye shall ask what ye will, and it shall be done unto you. Herein is my Father glorified, that ye bear much fruit; so shall ye be my disciples. As the Father hath loved me, so have I loved you: continue ye in my love. If ye keep my commandments, ye shall abide in my love, even as I have kept my Father's commandments, and abide in his love."

> Commentary: Jesus told His disciples (the faithful eleven, after Judas Iscariot had left) that there are unfruitful branches that God the Father will take away (remove), and that these branches are burned. The branches taken away are destined for the lake of fire. He says quite clearly that *these branches are believers that are in Him* [**v2**] which will be taken away because they refuse to bear fruit for Him. He is counseling His faithful (believing) disciples to continue *in Him.* By extension, Jesus commands all believers to abide in Him, a commandment we see throughout the epistles. This commandment makes no sense if we cannot ever depart from Him, as both Calvinism and the doctrine of OSAS assert. *We have the responsibility to abide in Christ, which we do by submitting to the leading of the Holy Spirit.* He concludes the passage by telling us that we are to keep His commandments in order to abide in His love. Any teaching (such as OSAS) that a believer has no responsibility for his salvation after first accepting Christ contradicts this passage.

John 16:1 "These things have I spoken unto you, that ye should not be offended."

> Commentary: Context indicates that Jesus was warning His faithful eleven disciples about the persecution they would undergo after His departure, so that they

would not abandon their faith. Most versions of the Bible, based on the underlying Greek, render the latter part of this verse as "so you will not fall away." Clearly, if even the faithful eleven disciples could lose their salvation, so can any of us. The doctrine of OSAS says that abandoning the faith does not matter, because we are already saved, once again contradicting the words of Jesus.

Acts 20:28–31 "Take heed therefore unto yourselves, and to all the flock, over the which the Holy Ghost hath made you overseers, to feed the church of God, which he hath purchased with his own blood. For I know this, that after my departing shall grievous wolves enter in among you, not sparing the flock. Also of your own selves shall men arise, speaking perverse things, to draw away disciples after them. Therefore watch, and remember, that by the space of three years I ceased not to warn every one night and day with tears."

Commentary: Paul knew, through the Holy Spirit, that the flock would not be spared. He literally was brought to tears. There is little reason for Paul to be moved to tears for loss of rewards. His concern is for those who would be forever lost from among the flock. If OSAS is true, then Paul is literally *crying for three years* about nothing. Not likely. But he also has concern for the "overseers," who were responsible for the spiritual welfare of the flock. The "overseers" of the flock today are the pastors and those in leadership positions in the local church. We fear that those leading their congregations toward complacency or outright rebellion against God with the doctrine of OSAS may be in serious trouble when they appear before God.

Romans 2:6–8 "[God] Who will render to every man according to his deeds: To them who by patient continuance in well doing seek for glory and honour and immortality, eternal life: But unto them that are contentious, and do not obey the truth, but obey unrighteousness, indignation and wrath."

Commentary: God will judge everyone after death. Here the judgment appears to be based on works (but in actuality is based on faith that manifests itself in bearing fruit through obedience to the Holy Spirit). Key to this passage (and others like it in the Bible written to Christians) is that the demonstration of their faith will be the determination of their eventual destiny, not faith that is not demonstrated by works (James 1:22 and James 2:14).

Romans 6:16 "Know ye not, that to whom ye yield yourselves servants to obey, his servants ye are to whom ye obey; whether of sin unto death, or of obedience unto righteousness?"

Commentary: Christians who are yielded to sin are headed for spiritual death (in the lake of fire), while obedient Christians (those submitting to the leading of the Holy Spirit) are deemed righteous by God, and therefore spend eternity with Him (spiritual life).

Romans 8:13–14 "For if ye live after the flesh, ye shall die: but if ye through the Spirit do mortify the deeds of the body, ye shall live. For as many as are led by the Spirit of God, they are the sons of God."

Commentary: Written to Christians, it states uncategorically that those Christians who live after the flesh will die (spiritually) and distinguishes the true sons of God as those who walk with the Holy Spirit. This is consistent with the Textus Receptus version which echoes that there is, "no condemnation to them which are in Christ Jesus, *who walk not after the flesh, but after the Spirit"* (**Romans 8:1**). A similar message is conveyed in Romans 8:2–6. Those who are part of God's family are those who are actually led by the Holy Spirit, not those that have the indwelling Holy Spirit, but are led by the flesh.

Romans 11:17–24 "And if some of the branches be broken off, and thou, being a wild olive tree, wert grafted in among them, and with them partakest of the root and fatness of the olive tree; Boast not against the branches. But if thou boast, thou bearest not the root, but the root thee. Thou wilt say then, The branches were broken off, that I might be grafted in. Well; because of unbelief they were broken off, and thou standest by faith. Be not highminded, but fear: For if God spared not the natural branches, take heed lest he also spare not thee. Behold therefore the goodness and severity of God: on them which fell, severity; but toward thee, goodness, if thou continue in his goodness: otherwise thou also shalt be cut off. And they also, if they abide not still in unbelief, shall be grafted in: for God is able to graft them in again. For if thou wert cut out of the olive tree which is wild by nature, and wert grafted contrary to nature into a good olive tree: how much more shall these, which be the natural branches, be grafted into their own olive tree?"

> Commentary: Clearly shows that God will not spare branches (believers) who don't continue to stand by faith, but will cut them off. The branches grafted in (Gentiles) were not a part of the natural tree (Israel), but could later be cut off, indicating that they could be again separated from the root, which is Christ, meaning they could lose their salvation. Again, this is another warning from Christ Himself that salvation can be lost.

1 Corinthians 5:5 "To deliver such an one unto Satan for the destruction of the flesh, that the spirit may be saved in the day of the Lord Jesus."

> Commentary: Paul wrote to the church at Corinth that he had decided to hand the immoral brother, who is acknowledged as a brother, over to the evil one, so that he might suffer and return to a true faith resulting in obedience, giving him a chance for salvation, which he apparently did not then have. Paul did not identify the man as an unbeliever. If there were no chance of Him being lost, Paul would not have to fear for his spirit. Notice also that Paul says that "the spirit *may* be saved,"

not *will* be saved. Paul is not arrogant enough to proclaim that the person will absolutely be saved regardless of his future behavior. The determination of repentance remains with the free will of the man.

1 Corinthians 10:11–12 "Now all these things happened unto them for examples: and they are written for our admonition, upon whom the ends of the world are come. Wherefore let him that thinketh he standeth take heed lest he fall."

>Commentary: Explains by the example of the Jews in the wilderness that believers can fall (*i.e.*, lose their salvation), as we have explained above. Paul's message here confirms that, contrary to what many teach, God's rules, like God Himself, do not change. The concept that enduring faith demonstrated through obedience is somehow not required is bunk, sprung full grown from the head of John Calvin. God did not turn from a God demanding strict obedience (as evidence of faith) in the Old Testament to a God of a mushy (no matter what) love in the New Testament. The Book of Revelation and Jesus' explanations of His judgments at His return demonstrate this quite clearly.

1 Corinthians 15:1–2 "Moreover, brethren, I declare unto you the gospel which I preached unto you, which also ye have received, and wherein ye stand; By which also ye are saved, *if* ye keep in memory what I preached unto you, unless ye have believed in vain."

>Commentary: Teaches us that *if* we keep our faith we are saved. If we do not keep our faith (and there are many places that talk about shipwrecked or destroyed faith) we can fall. This is again a conditional statement which identifies the condition by which we are saved.

Galatians 5:1–4 "Stand fast therefore in the liberty wherewith Christ hath made us free, and be not entangled again with the yoke of bondage.

Behold, I Paul say unto you, that if ye be circumcised, Christ shall profit you nothing. For I testify again to every man that is circumcised, that he is a debtor to do the whole law. Christ is become of no effect unto you, whosoever of you are justified by the law; *ye are fallen from grace."*

> Commentary: Written to believers, this passage tells us we can fall from grace if we start believing that we are justified by our works. This is something we must be equally wary of. True and saving faith results in works God does through us (John 15:5), based on the foundation of our faith. Paul states specifically that Christ will do nothing for those who have come to believe that the works of the law will save them.

Galatians 5:16–21 "This I say then, Walk in the Spirit, and ye shall not fulfil the lust of the flesh. For the flesh lusteth against the Spirit, and the Spirit against the flesh: and these are contrary the one to the other: so that ye cannot do the things that ye would. But if ye be led of the Spirit, ye are not under the law. Now the works of the flesh are manifest, which are these; Adultery, fornication, uncleanness, lasciviousness, Idolatry, witchcraft, hatred, variance, emulations, wrath, strife, seditions, heresies, Envyings, murders, drunkenness, revellings, and such like: of the which I tell you before, as I have also told you in time past, that *they which do such things shall not inherit the kingdom of God."*

> Commentary: Christians who live in a sinful manner after coming to Jesus Christ will not enter the kingdom of God. Paul contrasts the difference between being indwelt by the Holy Spirit and walking in the Holy Spirit four verses later in Galatians 5:25.

Galatians 6:7–9 "Be not deceived; God is not mocked: for whatsoever a man soweth, that shall he also reap. For he that soweth to his flesh shall of the flesh reap corruption; but he that soweth to the Spirit shall of the Spirit reap life everlasting. And let us not be weary in well doing: for in due season we shall reap, if we faint not."

Commentary: Paul wrote to the Galatians that what we will reap is based on what we sow (either to the flesh or to the Holy Spirit) with the two outcomes being either "corruption" (which we know is spiritual death) or "life everlasting" (eternal life). He specifically warns us not to give up, and encourages us that we will reap eternal life if we do not give up ("faint"). This is yet another conditional statement about the requirement of enduring.

Philippians 3:7–14 "But what things were gain to me, those I counted loss for Christ. Yea doubtless, and I count all things but loss for the excellency of the knowledge of Christ Jesus my Lord: for whom I have suffered the loss of all things, and do count them but dung, that I may win Christ, And be found in him, not having mine own righteousness, which is of the law, but that which is through the faith of Christ, the righteousness which is of God by faith: That I may know him, and the power of his resurrection, and the fellowship of his sufferings, being made conformable unto his death; *If by any means I might attain unto the resurrection of the dead. Not as though I had already attained*, either were already perfect: but I follow after, if that I may apprehend that for which also I am apprehended of Christ Jesus. Brethren, *I count not myself to have apprehended*: but this one thing I do, forgetting those things which are behind, and reaching forth unto those things which are before, I press toward the mark for the prize of the high calling of God in Christ Jesus."

Commentary: Paul makes it clear that he has not yet attained his own salvation, but presses on toward the prize of salvation. "Apprehend" (Greek *katalambanō*) means "to take possession of" (like apprehending a criminal suspect), which Paul is saying he is "pressing toward," but has not yet done. This is yet another passage that directly contradicts the "one and done" message of OSAS.

Colossians 1:21–23 "And you, that were sometime alienated and enemies in your mind by wicked works, yet now hath he reconciled In the body of his flesh through death, to present you holy and unblameable and unreproveable in his sight: *If ye continue in the faith* grounded and settled, and *be not moved away from the hope of the gospel,* which ye have heard, and which was preached to every creature which is under heaven; whereof I Paul am made a minister."

> Commentary: This passage is talking about Christ's Church as the bride of Christ, to be presented to Him holy and un-blameable and un-reprovable (Revelation 19:7–8). Note that the people Paul is writing to are currently believers, "reconciled" to God. Paul makes it clear that only those who "continue in the faith" and are "not moved away from the hope of the gospel" will be a part of the bride, the church. Those who do not meet these conditions will not be part of the church, which means they will not be saved.

1 Thessalonians 3:5 "For this cause, when I could no longer forbear, I sent to know your faith, lest by some means the tempter have tempted you, and our labour be in vain."

> Commentary: This passage, written to the church in Thessalonica, reveals that Paul was concerned that his work in bringing people to the Lord would be in vain. This could not be the case if those he shared the gospel with would always remain saved. If an individual is truly permanently saved as the proponents of OSAS claim, there would be no labor of Paul's that would be in vain, for none could be lost, and Paul would be concerned about something that could never happen.

1 Thessalonians 5:19 "Quench not the Spirit."

> Commentary: Paul warned the believers in the church at Thessalonica not to quench (Greek *sbennymi*), meaning "to put out or extinguish" the Holy Spirit, indicating that believers have the ability to do exactly that because of our free will. Believers who are not following the Holy Spirit

cannot know or do the will of God, putting their eternal destiny in peril (Matthew 7:21). This is another passage contrary to the doctrine of OSAS.

2 Thessalonians 2:1–3 "That ye be not soon shaken in mind, or be troubled, neither by spirit, nor by word, nor by letter as from us, as that the day of Christ is at hand. Let no man deceive you by any means: for that day shall not come, except there come *a falling away* first, and that man of sin be revealed, the son of perdition."

> Commentary: The "falling away" before our Lord returns for the church (the rapture), can only mean that some believers will leave the faith. The warning is coupled with being deceived because the words "falling away" (Greek *apostasia*) means apostasy, which is renunciation of a religious belief.

1 Timothy 1:18–20 "This charge I commit unto thee, son Timothy, according to the prophecies which went before on thee, that thou by them mightest war a good warfare; *Holding faith*, and a good conscience; which some having put away concerning faith have made shipwreck."

> Commentary: Paul wrote Timothy that we must hold to our faith and a good conscience; otherwise our faith will be shipwrecked. The term "shipwreck" (Greek *nauageō*) here references a traditional shipwreck where the ship is literally wrecked or destroyed. The passage suggests this is the case for some; their faith will be shipwrecked or destroyed. You cannot shipwreck something that does not exist. This is another passage that is problematic for those who believe in OSAS, because faith is the basis of our salvation. No faith = no salvation (1 Corinthians 15:1–2). If we abandon or destroy our faith, we are no longer secure in our salvation.

1 Timothy 4:1–2 "Now the Spirit speaketh expressly, that *in the latter times some shall depart from the faith*, giving heed to seducing spirits, and doctrines of devils."

Commentary: As in his message to the Thessalonians above, Paul wrote to Timothy as clearly as possible that some will depart the faith, based on incorrect doctrine. Belief in OSAS could produce this result if believers use it as rationalization for living in disobedience to the leading of the Holy Spirit. Faith is the basis of our salvation. Departing the faith has a clear implication: no salvation. Knowing that faith is required for salvation, we see that departure from the faith is departure from the process of salvation. We have already shown earlier that faith is described in the Greek tense as a continuing action.

1 Timothy 4:16 "Take heed unto thyself, and unto the doctrine; *continue in them*: for in doing this thou shalt both save thyself, and them that hear thee."

Commentary: Paul warned Timothy to be careful about his doctrine, and his lifestyle, stating that both were necessary for his salvation (and his Christian witness). The underlying word for saved (Greek *sozo*) is the same used elsewhere to refer to eternity with God, which we call salvation. This passage is another warning that we must continue in our faith and our actions in obedience to God's commands. Notice the implication that either errant doctrine *or* disobedient lifestyle can cause us to lose our salvation. Paul also warned the Galatians about these two dangers.

1 Timothy 5:11–15 "But the younger widows refuse: for when they have begun to wax wanton against Christ, they will marry; Having damnation, because they have cast off their first faith. And withal they learn to be idle, wandering about from house to house; and not only idle, but tattlers also and busybodies, speaking things which they ought not. I will therefore that the younger women marry, bear children, guide the house, give none occasion to the adversary to speak reproachfully. For some are already turned aside after Satan."

Commentary: Even though the context is young widows and their role in the local church, Paul clearly stated that there are those that left the faith, and "are already turned aside after Satan." How is this possible if OSAS is correct doctrine?

1 Timothy 6:11–12 "But thou, O man of God, flee these things; and follow after righteousness, godliness, faith, love, patience, meekness. *Fight the good fight of faith*, lay hold on eternal life, whereunto thou art also called, and hast professed a good profession before many witnesses."

Commentary: Why did Paul tell Timothy, obviously already a believer, to "fight the good fight of faith" if OSAS is true? If that were the case, he should have told him to relax and "lean on the promises of God," as the Modern Church teaches. And why would Timothy have to "fight the good fight of faith" to "lay hold of eternal life" if Timothy already had unconditional eternal security? The choice becomes increasingly clear: We can either believe the scriptures, or we can believe the man-made (specifically, John Calvin) doctrine of OSAS.

2 Timothy 2:11–13 "It is a faithful saying: For if we be dead with him, we shall also live with him: If we suffer, we shall also reign with him: if we deny him, he also will deny us: If we believe not, yet he abideth faithful: he cannot deny himself."

Commentary: If we deny Jesus, our Lord will deny us (Matthew 10:33). Again, this passage is written to believers, not unbelievers.

2 Timothy 2:15–18 "Study to shew thyself approved unto God, a workman that needeth not to be ashamed, rightly dividing the word of truth. But shun profane and vain babblings: for they will increase unto more ungodliness. And their word will eat as doth a canker: of whom is Hymenaeus and Philetus; Who concerning the truth have erred, saying that the resurrection is past already; and *overthrow the faith of some*."

Commentary: Notice that Paul wrote to Timothy that some believers had their faith overthrown by false teaching. Being overthrown (Greek *anatrepo*) means to overthrow, overturn or destroy. Once again, we see that existing and saving faith can be destroyed. Contrary to the Modern Church's teaching of OSAS, Paul's epistles state time and again that loss of faith = loss of salvation (On a side note, this false teaching was making the rounds. See 2 Thessalonians 2:1–3).

2 Timothy 4:6–8 "For I am now ready to be offered, and the time of my departure is at hand. I have fought a good fight, I have finished my course, *I have kept the faith*: Henceforth there is laid up for me a crown of righteousness, which the Lord, the righteous judge, shall give me at that day: and not to me only, but unto all them also that love his appearing."

Commentary: Paul says specifically, "I" have kept the faith along with a variety of other things "he" did. While the Holy Spirit undoubtedly assisted Paul, he understood that it was *his choice and his responsibility* to keep the faith, otherwise he would have written something like, "God has kept me in the faith." Yet this is not what God inspired Paul to write.

Hebrews 2:1–3 "Therefore we ought to give the more earnest heed to the things which we have heard, lest at any time we should let them slip. For if the word spoken by angels was stedfast, and every transgression and disobedience received a just recompence of reward; How shall we escape, *if we neglect so great salvation*; which at the first began to be spoken by the Lord, and was confirmed unto us by them that heard him."

Commentary: The writer of Hebrews referred to the justice of God in punishing disobedient angels to admonish his readers not to "neglect so great a salvation," lest they too receive the same punishment: eternity in the lake of fire (Matthew 25:41). Remember, those fallen angels had spiritual life (eternity in the presence of God), until they rebelled against God and died spiritually. The writer used their example to warn his believing readers that they were also subject to spiritual death, and had to be careful to avoid it. In spite of passages like this one, the Modern Church teaches that when a person "truly" comes to Christ, they are "born again" (*i.e.,* born spiritually—John 3:5–7), which is true, but then they say a person cannot die spiritually after being "born again," which flies in the face of many scripture to the contrary, including this one. The very first humans on the planet died spiritually in Genesis 3.

Hebrews 3:5–6 "And Moses verily was faithful in all his house, as a servant, for a testimony of those things which were to be spoken after; But Christ as a son over his own house; whose house are we, *if we hold fast* the confidence and the rejoicing of *the hope firm unto the end.*"

> Commentary: We learn two things from this passage: 1) we must "hold fast" our faith "unto the end (death or rapture);" and 2) we have not yet received our salvation, but have "*the hope"* of receiving it, if we hold firm. Both of these contradict the doctrine of OSAS.

Hebrews 3:12–14 "Take heed, brethren, lest there be in any of you an evil heart of unbelief, in departing from the living God. But exhort one another daily, while it is called Today; lest any of you be hardened through the deceitfulness of sin. For we are made partakers of Christ, *if we hold the beginning of our confidence steadfast unto the end.*"

> Commentary: This passage, like many others, directly refutes the OSAS claim of *unconditional* eternal security. It directly affirms a believer's ability to depart from the living God through continual sin. Also teaches we can be hardened through sin. We are partakers in Christ *if* (conditional) we hold onto our faith *until the end,* clearly

implying we are lost if we fail to hold fast, and reaffirming that salvation is a process that is not complete until our death or rapture

Hebrews 3:7–19 "Wherefore (as the Holy Ghost saith, To day if ye will hear his voice, Harden not your hearts, as in the provocation, in the day of temptation in the wilderness: When your fathers tempted me, proved me, and saw my works forty years. Wherefore I was grieved with that generation, and said, They do alway err in their heart; and they have not known my ways. So I sware in my wrath, They shall not enter into my rest. *Take heed, brethren, lest there be in any of you an evil heart of unbelief, in departing from the living God.* But exhort one another daily, while it is called To day; lest any of you be hardened through the deceitfulness of sin. For we are made partakers of Christ, if we hold the beginning of our confidence stedfast unto the end. While it is said, Today if ye will hear his voice, harden not your hearts, as in the provocation. For some, when they had heard, did provoke: howbeit not all that came out of Egypt by Moses. But with whom was he grieved forty years? was it not with them that had sinned, whose carcases fell in the wilderness? And to whom sware he that they should not enter into his rest, but to them that believed not? So we see that they could not enter in because of unbelief."

> Commentary: Note that the writer has no doubt believers can "depart from the living God, with the context indicating the result will be loss of salvation. This is yet another verse exposing the error of OSAS.

Hebrews 4:1–2, 11, and 14 "Let us therefore fear, *lest*, a promise being left us of entering into his rest, *any of you should seem to come short of it*. For unto us was the gospel preached, as well as unto them: but the word preached did not profit them, not being mixed with faith in them that heard it" [**v1–2**], "*Let us labour* therefore to enter into that rest, *lest any man* fall after the same example of unbelief" [**v11**], and "Seeing then that we have a great high priest, that is passed into the heavens, Jesus the Son of God, *let us hold fast our profession* [of faith]" [**v14**].

Commentary: The writer warns believers not fall short of entering into the rest of God described in His promise. Why the warning if there is no way that a believer can possibly lose his salvation? We as believers must keep our faith (a true faith) to receive the promises of God. We are told directly to *hold fast* to our faith, which would not be necessary if, as the Modern Church teaches: 1) we are unconditionally eternally secure (OSAS), and 2) we have no responsibility for maintaining our salvation after coming to Christ, since God takes care of it (citing Philippians 1:6).

Hebrews 5:8–9 "Though he were a Son, yet learned he obedience by the things which he suffered; And being made perfect, he became the author of eternal salvation *unto all them that obey him.*"

Commentary: Jesus Christ is the source of salvation *for those that obey Him*. Obedience is a choice we make in this life. While we cannot be perfect in this life, God is looking for the heart that hates sin and submits to the leading of the Holy Spirit. The implication is clear: Jesus is not a sacrifice (consistent with Hebrews 10:26–31) for those who are committed to disobedience after coming to Christ. This is yet another verse contrary to the doctrine of OSAS. The promise of eternal life is not made to all who believe, but "unto all them that obey him." The message is clear: no obedience = no salvation.

Hebrews 10:23 "Let us *hold fast* the profession of our faith without wavering; (for he is faithful that promised)"

Commentary: The admonition to hold fast would not be necessary if there is no way to lose our salvation. Again, this is contrary to the Modern Church's teaching of OSAS. Note that God will be faithful to fulfill His promise of salvation, but we must recognize that the promise is conditioned on more than just coming to Christ (entering through the "strait gate" of Matthew 7:14). That must be followed by submitting to the Holy Spirit in obedience to God's commands (the "narrow way" Jesus spoke of in that same verse).

Hebrews 10:26–31 "For if we sin wilfully after that we have received the knowledge of the truth, there remaineth no more sacrifice for sins, But a certain fearful looking for of judgment and fiery indignation, which shall devour the adversaries. He that despised Moses' law died without mercy under two or three witnesses: Of how much sorer punishment, suppose ye, shall he be thought worthy, who hath trodden under foot the Son of God, and hath counted the blood of the covenant, wherewith he was sanctified, an unholy thing, and hath done despite unto the Spirit of grace? For we know him that hath said, Vengeance belongeth unto me, I will recompense, saith the Lord. And again, The Lord shall judge his people. It is a fearful thing to fall into the hands of the living God."

Commentary: Christians who, after coming to Christ, continue willfully sinning establish themselves as enemies of God (the same as unbelievers in Romans 5:10), and are on the path to eternal punishment. This verse also directly contradicts current teaching on OSAS. We know this speaks to believers because it talking to those who "was sanctified."

Hebrews 10:35–39 "Cast not away therefore your confidence, which hath great recompence of reward. For ye have need of patience, that, after ye have done the will of God, ye might receive the promise. For yet a little while, and he that shall come will come, and will not tarry. Now the just shall live by faith: but if any man draw back, my soul shall have no pleasure in him. But we are not of them *who draw back unto perdition*; but of them that believe to the saving of the soul."

Commentary: This is another passage directly contradicting the doctrine of OSAS. It clearly states that drawing back (from saving faith) leads to perdition (eternal damnation) and that we can abandon our faith (confidence), with eternal consequences.

Hebrews 12:14–15 "Follow peace with all men, and holiness, *without which no man shall see the Lord*: Looking diligently *lest any man fail of the grace of God*; lest any root of bitterness springing up trouble you, and thereby many be defiled;'"

> Commentary: Note that "peace with all men, and holiness" are requirements to spending eternity with God. These can only be accomplished by submitting to the leading of the Holy Spirit, something the doctrine of OSAS says is not essential to salvation.

James 2:14–26 "What doth it profit, my brethren, though a man say he hath faith, and have not works? can faith save him? If a brother or sister be naked, and destitute of daily food, And one of you say unto them, Depart in peace, be ye warmed and filled; notwithstanding ye give them not those things which are needful to the body; what doth it profit? Even so faith, if it hath not works, is dead, being alone. Yea, a man may say, Thou hast faith, and I have works: shew me thy faith without thy works, and I will shew thee my faith by my works. Thou believest that there is one God; thou doest well: the devils also believe, and tremble. But wilt thou know, O vain man, that faith without works is dead? Was not Abraham our father justified by works, when he had offered Isaac his son upon the altar? Seest thou how faith wrought with his works, and by works was faith made perfect? And the scripture was fulfilled which saith, Abraham believed God, and it was imputed unto him for righteousness: and he was called the Friend of God. Ye see then how that by works a man is justified, and not by faith only. Likewise also was not Rahab the harlot justified by works, when she had received the messengers, and had sent them out another way? For as the body without the spirit is dead, so faith without works is dead also."

> Commentary: True and living faith produces works— not our works, but God's works done through us (by

submitting to and being led by the Holy Spirit); anything less is a dead faith that does not save. How do we end up with dead faith? We end up with dead faith by neglecting our spiritual life, living in sin, and/or refusing to submit our will to the leading of the Holy Spirit. But the doctrine of OSAS says, "Intellectual belief is all that is necessary. Any talk of living our faith is "works-based salvation." We find that very dangerous; so does scripture.

James 5:19–20 "Brethren, if any of you do err from the truth, and one convert him; Let him know, that he which converteth the sinner from the error of his way shall save a soul from death, and shall hide a multitude of sins."

> Commentary: Note the bottom line: a Christian ("Brethren") who departs from the true faith faces spiritual death. The good news is that he can come back to the truth and save his soul. The bad news is that the Modern Church tells people that this verse doesn't mean what it plainly says because there is *no way* a Christian can lose his salvation.

2 Peter 1:5–11 "And beside this, giving all diligence, add to your faith virtue; and to virtue knowledge; And to knowledge temperance; and to temperance patience; and to patience godliness; And to godliness brotherly kindness; and to brotherly kindness charity. For if these things be in you, and abound, they make you that ye shall neither be barren nor unfruitful in the knowledge of our Lord Jesus Christ. But he that lacketh these things is blind, and cannot see afar off, and hath forgotten that he was purged from his old sins. Wherefore the rather, brethren, *give diligence to make your calling and election sure: for if ye do these things, ye shall never fall: For so an entrance shall be ministered unto you abundantly into the everlasting kingdom of our Lord and Saviour Jesus Christ.*"

> Commentary: This passage makes it clear that a believer's *past* sins are purged (wiped clean) when he

came to Christ, but not his *future* sins. However, the real warning is that the believer must be diligent to preserve his hope of salvation which is something the Modern Church says is both unnecessary and is God's responsibility.

2 Peter 2:1–22 "But there were false prophets also among the people, even as there shall be false teachers among you, who privily shall bring in damnable heresies, even *denying the Lord that bought them, and bring upon themselves swift destruction*. And many shall follow their pernicious ways; by reason of whom the way of truth shall be evil spoken of. And through covetousness shall they with feigned words make merchandise of you: whose judgment now of a long time lingereth not, and their damnation slumbereth not. For if God spared not the angels that sinned, but cast them down to hell, and delivered them into chains of darkness, to be reserved unto judgment; And spared not the old world, but saved Noah the eighth person, a preacher of righteousness, bringing in the flood upon the world of the ungodly; And turning the cities of Sodom and Gomorrha into ashes condemned them with an overthrow, making them an ensample unto those that after should live ungodly; And delivered just Lot, vexed with the filthy conversation of the wicked: (For that righteous man dwelling among them, in seeing and hearing, vexed his righteous soul from day to day with their unlawful deeds;) The Lord knoweth how to deliver the godly out of temptations, and to reserve the unjust unto the day of judgment to be punished: But chiefly them that walk after the flesh in the lust of uncleanness, and despise government. Presumptuous are they, selfwilled, they are not afraid to speak evil of dignities. Whereas angels, which are greater in power and might, bring not railing accusation against them before the Lord. But these, as natural brute beasts, made to be taken and destroyed, speak evil of the things that they understand not; and *shall utterly perish in their own corruption*; And shall receive the reward of unrighteousness, as they that count it pleasure to riot in the day time. Spots they are and blemishes, sporting themselves with their own deceivings while they feast with you; Having eyes full of adultery, and that cannot cease from sin; beguiling unstable souls: an heart they have exercised with covetous practices; cursed children: *Which have forsaken the right way, and are gone astray,* following the way of Balaam the son of Bosor, who loved the wages of unrighteousness; But was rebuked for his iniquity: the dumb ass speaking with man's voice forbad the madness of the prophet. These are wells without water, clouds that are carried with a tempest; to whom the mist of darkness is reserved for ever. For when they speak great swelling words of vanity, they allure through the lusts of the flesh, through much wantonness, those that were clean escaped from them who live in error. While they promise them liberty, they themselves are the servants of corruption: for of whom a man is overcome, of the same is he brought in bondage. *For if after they have escaped the pollutions of the world through the knowledge of the Lord and Saviour Jesus Christ, they are again entangled therein, and overcome, the latter end is worse with them than the beginning. For it had been better for them not to have known the way of righteousness,* than, after they have known it, to turn from the holy commandment delivered unto them. But it is happened unto them according to the true proverb, The dog is turned to his own vomit again; and the sow that was washed to her wallowing in the mire."

Commentary: This passage is a severe condemnation of false teachers whose teaching threatens the salvation of their followers. Church leaders, Sunday school teachers and other leaders in the modern evangelical church should take the warning in this passage very seriously. With the current way many teach the doctrine of OSAS, they are perilously close to being among those who "allure through the lusts of the flesh, through much wantonness, those that were clean escaped from them who live in error." Note the italized portions reveal that the teachers being described were Christians who had "the knowledge of the Lord and Saviour Jesus Christ" before forsaking the right way and going astray. Can there be any doubt that these false teachers are on their way to hell, in direct contradiction of the doctrine of OSAS?

1 John 2:17 "And the world passeth away, and the lust thereof: but he that doeth the will of God abideth for ever."

> Commentary: Yet another verse indicating there is more involved in salvation that just coming to Christ. Christians can neither know nor do the will of God unless they are led by the Holy Spirit. The implication of verses like these is that those who do not even attempt to be obedient to God's will after coming to Christ will not inherit eternal life. This is a major theme of John's first epistle. This verse doesn't say that if a person once believes he "abideth for ever," but that "he that doeth the will of God abideth for ever"(see Matthew 7:21). This is what it means to abide in Christ, *which we are commanded to do* in John 15:4, and throughout the remainder of this epistle (1 John 2:24, 28, 1 John 3:6, 24 and 1 John 4:13, 16). How do we abide in Christ and know His will (Romans 12:2)? By submitting our will to God's will, and being led by the Spirit (Galatians 5:16, 25). What is the destiny of those who do not abide in Christ? The fire (John 15:6). This is yet another verse at odds with OSAS.

Jude 1:3–6 "Beloved, when I gave all diligence to write unto you of the common salvation, it was needful for me to write unto you, and exhort you that ye should earnestly contend for the faith which was once delivered unto the saints. For there are certain men crept in unawares, who were before of old ordained to this condemnation, ungodly men, turning the grace of our God into lasciviousness, and denying the only Lord God, and our Lord Jesus Christ. I will therefore put you in remembrance, though ye once knew this, how that the Lord, having saved the people out of the land of Egypt, afterward destroyed them that believed not. And the angels which kept not their first estate, but left their own habitation, he hath reserved in everlasting chains under darkness unto the judgment of the great day."

Commentary: Jude wrote that *we* must contend (Greek *epagōnízomai*) for the faith. "Contend" means "to struggle with and uphold," meaning that *we* have a part to play in maintaining our faith. Furthermore, the passage reminds us that God will destroy those that lose their faith, condemning them to the lake of fire (Matthew 25:41). We also note that the angels, who were once spiritually alive in heaven with God, also lost their faith to obey. We ask our friends who believe OSAS: how is this possible?

Revelation 2:26–28 "But that which ye have already *hold fast* till I come. And he that overcometh, and keepeth my works unto the end, to him will I give power over the nations: And he shall rule them with a rod of iron; as the vessels of a potter shall they be broken to shivers: even as I received of my Father."

Commentary: This passage tells Christians that we must *hold fast to the faith* we already have. Again, no such command is required if we cannot lose our salvation. It also tells us we are to keep doing the works of God (*i.e.*, saving faith produces obedience demonstrated through doing the works of God—James 2:14).

Revelation 3:1–5 "And unto the angel of the church in Sardis write; These things saith he that hath the seven Spirits of God, and the seven stars; I know thy works, that thou hast a name that thou livest, and art dead. Be watchful, and strengthen the things which remain, that are ready to die: for I have not found thy works perfect before God. *Remember therefore how thou hast received and heard, and hold fast, and repent.* If therefore thou shalt not watch, I will come on thee as a thief, and thou shalt not know what hour I will come upon thee. Thou hast a few names even in Sardis which have not defiled their garments; and they shall walk with me in white: for they are worthy. *He that overcometh*, the same shall be clothed in white raiment; and *I will not blot out his name out of the book of life*, but I will confess his name before my Father, and before his angels."

Commentary: All references in this passage are to the saints of God. We see here that those who are precariously clinging to spiritual life are in danger of dying spiritually. The phrase *"strengthen the things which remain"* demonstrate a progressively bad situation which, if not repented of, will result in loss of salvation. Those barely hanging on to spiritual life are contrasted with those that walk with Him "in white" (see Revelation 19:14) who will be saved. Those that overcome are those that the Lord will not blot out of the book of life. These believers are told to remember their faith, to *hold fast* to that faith and *repent*. It is a command to us. If OSAS is true, then believers don't need to be on the alert, and Jesus coming as a thief in the night is of no concern. Why then do we see this warning to believers here and in other passages like Matthew 24:43, 1 Thessalonians 5:2–6, and 2 Peter 3:10?

Revelation 3:10–12 "Because thou hast kept the word of my patience, I also will keep thee from the hour of temptation, which shall come upon all the world, to try them that dwell upon the earth. Behold, I come quickly: *hold that fast which thou hast*, that no man take thy crown. Him that overcometh will I make a pillar in the temple of my God, and he shall go no more out: and I will write upon him the name of my God, and the name of the city of my God, which is new Jerusalem, which cometh down out of heaven from my God: and I will write upon him my new name."

Commentary: Jesus admonished the true believers in the church in Philadelphia to "hold fast" to their faith (1 Corinthians 15:1–2) so that they would overcome and spend eternity in the new Jerusalem (see Revelation 22:4). There is absolutely no need for Him to tell them to "hold fast" to their faith if the doctrine of OSAS is true. According to that doctrine, as taught in the Modern Church today, either 1) it doesn't matter whether they retain their faith in Christ because they are already saved anyway, or 2) they don't have to maintain their faith because God will make sure they do (Perseverance of the Saints—from Calvinism). So is Jesus just playing games with these true believers? Not likely. We should all be paying attention to what He is saying.

Revelation 3:15–19 "I know thy works, that thou art neither cold nor hot: I would thou wert cold or hot. So then because thou art lukewarm, and neither cold nor hot, I will spue thee out of my mouth. Because thou sayest, I am rich, and increased with goods, and have need of nothing; and knowest not that thou art wretched, and miserable, and poor, and blind, and naked: I counsel thee to buy of me gold tried in the fire, that thou mayest be rich; and white raiment, that thou mayest be clothed, and that the shame of thy nakedness do not appear; and anoint thine eyes with eyesalve, that thou mayest see. As many as I love, I rebuke and chasten: be zealous therefore, and repent."

> Commentary: God is not favorably disposed toward lukewarm Christians. He is directly calling those who treat the relationship with Him as a side show to earthly life to repent. More than anything else, this represents the Modern Church in so many ways, especially here in America, where we embody the words "I am rich" and yet forget what our purpose really is. Yet much the Modern Church builds this perspective through their errant doctrine. There is a clear warning here: God rejects lukewarm Christianity. The warning to this church strikes home to us here in the American churches, where we think we are rich because of our material possessions, but are in great danger of spiritual poverty. Why? It is because we are distracted by those possessions and are focused too much on this world and not enough on the next. As mentioned above, we are in danger of being too earthly minded to be any heavenly good. When God is not the number one priority in our lives, we are in trouble and, according to this warning, in eternal danger, regardless of what those teaching OSAS tell us.

Revelation 21:7–8 "He that overcometh shall inherit all things; and I will be his God, and he shall be my son. But the fearful, and unbelieving, and the abominable, and murderers, and whoremongers, and sorcerers, and idolaters, and all liars, shall have their part in the lake which burneth with fire and brimstone: which is the second death."

> Commentary: Christians must overcome the temptations of the world, and those that do will be sons of God. Those who exercise their free will to do evil, whether they claim to believe or not, will participate in the second death, which is spiritual death. Not exactly the doctrine of OSAS.

The Modern Church's Misunderstanding of Works

There are many other passages in the Bible written to Christians (not unbelievers) about how to live their lives, coupled with warnings of either earthly or eternal consequences of not doing so. But please don't make the mistake the Modern Church does. This is not salvation by works, as some might contend. Today's Modern Church theology condemns any suggestion that anything a believer does after coming to Christ can affect his salvation as "Salvation by works," or "Lordship salvation."

It is a contentious generalization which does not accurately reflect what scripture teaches. There are hundreds of scriptures telling man what to do and what not to do *after coming to Christ*. What scripture really teaches is that since man cannot save Himself, God must intervene to save him, and this is a gift, unmerited (by us) favor from God, which the Bible calls grace. *We must look to Christ for our salvation, but we must never think that we are therefore somehow relieved from our responsibility to act faithfully towards God.*

Man's participation in his own salvation does not end when he first comes to Christ. God gives us the gift of salvation, but we still retain our free will. How we use that gift is up to us, using the free will given to us by God. The fact that God requires a believer to be led by His Spirit and obey His commands does not mean that he can save himself; he is saved through the gift of Jesus Christ. His faithful obedience to God's commands after salvation *is evidence of his faith*, the means whereby God bestows His gift (Ephesians 2:8–9). See the difference?

Because of our free will, that is our ability to choose, our faith is not immutable, nor is it maintained solely by God. The faith that comes from God is entrusted to us, but we are responsible to maintain and apply it (of course, with the Holy Spirit's help). Scripture reinforces this view.

But because of what is taught in the vast majority of today's Modern Churches, many in the Christian community can only see black and white. They believe God does everything, and if man has any part in his salvation, then salvation is of man ("works-based salvation"). We see this more and more as today's evangelical churches slide further and faster down the slippery slope of Calvinism as discussed in Chapter 13, "Calvinism and its Impact on the Modern Church." But this binary view is a false equivalency. Such simplifications are dangerous. Christians who believe they are under no obligation to obey God's commandment are in for a rude awakening.

Much of the reason for the increasing acceptance of this doctrine of OSAS is that it fulfills man's need to have a simple recipe for salvation. It also fulfills man's desire to live in the flesh and not have to worry about the eternal consequences. But the doctrine is contrary with the overall view of scripture.

In his preaching, Paul reasoned from the entire work of scripture that Jesus (Yeshua) was the Messiah. God did not provide this irrefutable stated evidence that Jesus was the Messiah. Paul was forced to reason with people, using scripture, to prove Jesus of Nazareth was in fact, the Messiah. We are to do the same thing about doctrine - that is, reason from the larger context of scripture, not simply take sound bites of scripture. We must set aside our preconceptions to be able to truly understand the Bible. And we must trust God that His Word is true. We must verify in scripture, with the guidance of the Holy Spirit (John 16:13) everything we hear from the pulpit, Sunday school, Bible studies, television and radio, and everything we read that is not scripture.

Key Thoughts

It is the OSAS (Once Saved, Always Saved) doctrine, a doctrine of men, which has built the lukewarm (Laodicean) Modern Church. It is a doctrine that fully engages the flesh, because it teaches believers that they may do whatever they want through their freedom in Christ and remain saved. This is exactly what perceptive adults hear, and too often put into practice. A large percentage of the Modern Church congregation therefore focuses on the temporal rather than the eternal. They are, as one church leader put it, "Too earthly minded to be any heavenly good."

It is an incorrect understanding of scripture to suggest that we have already been saved. Although some scripture may suggest this, the only understanding that can make all scripture true is that eternal life is realized in the future (Philippians 3:7–14). We who believe in Jesus Christ and are trusting in Him have entered "in at the strait gate" (**Matthew 7:13**). Those who are obeying His commandments are in the process of being saved. We are on the narrow way, "which leadeth unto life" (**Matthew 7:14**). It is vitally important that we understand that we have the *hope* (Hebrews 11:1), *not the guarantee*, of our salvation (eternal life with God), because it is we who must endure (aided, of course, by the Holy Spirit) with our living and active faith to be able to fully receive that which is promised.

The concept that once we accept Jesus Christ we have fully and permanently achieved everlasting life directly is contradicted by countless passages in scripture. However, accepting Christ is the single most important decision we can ever make; it is the milestone event (the gate) which puts us on the (narrow) path to eternity with our God. Furthermore, the believer who accepts Jesus Christ and seeks to live faithfully by walking with the Holy Spirit need have no fear of what the future holds. To understand Christ's commands and the leading of the Holy Spirit, we must commit ourselves to reading and obeying scripture.

While there is security in Christ, that security is not unconditional. Any representation that salvation is unconditional and guaranteed at the moment a person accepts Christ directly contradicts the bulk of New Testament scripture. We do not fluctuate between being saved and being unsaved on a moment by moment basis. We were designed to be willing participants in our salvation through our demonstrated faith in Jesus Christ.

After we have accepted Jesus Christ as our Savior through faith given by God (Ephesians 2:8–9), we must be willing to submit ourselves to the Holy Spirit and try to walk faithfully with the Holy Spirit. God knows our hearts, and we are unable to fool Him. Scripture specifically states that, "For as many as are led by the Spirit of God, they are the sons of

God" (**Romans 8:14**). Being led by the Holy Spirit (the Spirit of God) means we must follow where the Holy Spirit leads, not simply be indwelt (Romans 8:1,4). True disciples (followers) of Christ strive to maintain consistency between their life and true Bible doctrine. As God told Paul to tell Timothy, "Take heed unto thyself, and unto the doctrine; continue in them: for in doing this *thou shalt both save thyself,* and them that hear thee" (**1 Timothy 4:16**).

We were bought at a great price. God paid that price. God will not give up on us without exerting great effort to bring us safely into His kingdom. What He will not do is violate our free will, even if we use it to reject both the Holy Spirit's leading and the Father's discipline. Through our free will, we determine whether we will submit to or reject the Holy Spirit; whether to walk with the Holy Spirit, or to walk away from the Holy Spirit. That is why we are told to examine our faith (2 Corinthians 13:5). God will not force us into obedience.

As a final encouragement, it should be noted that our God is a God of love, mercy and great patience. Scripture tells us that God goes to great lengths to keep His children from being lost. He gives us His Holy Spirit to lead us in all truth (John 16:13). He disciplines us in an attempt to bring us back to obedience when we stray from the narrow way (Hebrews 12:4–9). He will provide a way out when we are tempted (1 Corinthians 10:13). He even instructs fellow believers to pray for us when we are committing a sin (1 John 5:16). He is not willing that any of His children should perish, and has patience toward us as He tries to lead us back to Him (2 Peter 3:9).

Chapter 12

The Temporal versus the Eternal: the Prosperity Gospel

Errant Doctrine: No decision we make in this world has any consequence to our salvation except the decision to believe in God's Son, Jesus Christ. God wants us to be prosperous. God promises prosperity in the form of wealth, health and happiness to His children who have enough faith to "claim" His promise.

Although the Prosperity Gospel is preached front and center in some places in the Modern Church, elements of the Prosperity Gospel appear in many churches. We are often taught that once we have accepted Christ, God wants us to enjoy all the good things in this life because He wants the best for His children.

Some church leaders teach that if we do not have wealth, health and happiness, it is because we lack sufficient faith. The focus on the next life is often set aside as we are taught there is no need to be concerned with eternity because our place in heaven was guaranteed when we accepted Christ; now God wants you now to be about enjoying this life. The prosperity gospel teaches that God will provide those things that indulge our worldly desires. It is an insidious and damaging doctrine because it appeals directly to the flesh. Who doesn't want wealth, health and happiness? It makes the greed of American materialism seem respectable by dressing it in (so-called) Christian clothing. The Prosperity Gospel is not one of eternal perspective, but temporal perspective. It is not of God, but of man. Consequently, its focus is on serving ourselves and our pleasures, not serving our Lord and Savior.

Even related errant doctrines affirm the prosperity gospel. As discussed above, the doctrine of OSAS encourages those claiming Christ to live in the flesh, living for this life instead of the next. Elements of the prosperity gospel are preached indirectly through the lack of sermons and Bible studies addressing Christian's accountability to properly use of God's resources. Church-goers are silently encouraged to indulge their fleshly pleasures by not being challenged to use more of God's resources to have an eternal impact.

Which is More Important: Here or the Hereafter?

In this life, we are called to make decisions. While there is no question that the most important decision we will ever make is the acceptance of Jesus Christ as our Lord and Savior, we are faced with other decisions throughout our time in this world.

We often value things in this world that God does not. Jesus challenged the Pharisees of His day where He taught, "And the Pharisees also, who were covetous, heard all these things: and they derided him. And he said unto them, Ye are they which justify yourselves before men; but God knoweth your hearts: *for that which is highly esteemed among men is abomination in the sight of God*" (**Luke 16:14–15**). Abomination (Greek *bdelygma*) means detestable, or of idols.

The idea that wealth is somehow a virtue has become a standard belief in our American culture, and it has seeped into the Modern Church. We highly esteem money in our culture, but what is wealth to God, who literally created everything in the entire universe? The value we assign to money often amounts to idolatry. Our American values esteem too highly that which we should not (wealth) and too little that which we should esteem more (God).

Consider what Paul told the brothers at Philippi, "For many walk, of whom I have told you often, and now tell you even weeping, that they are the enemies of the cross of Christ: Whose end is destruction, whose God is their belly, and whose glory is in their shame, who mind earthly things" (**Philippians 3:18–19**). Paul is directly telling them that there are those who live as enemies of the cross of Christ. The context makes it clear that Paul was not talking about unbelievers, but to some in the Philippian church whose focus was on earthly things.

What does God think of Christians who spend their time and resources first and foremost for their own pleasure? Does this please God when there are so many more worthy investments of an eternal nature we might make? Are we in effect worshipping the idol of money instead of God? Indeed, seeing Christians investing in their pleasures too often may be a part of the reason that non-believers refuse to come to Christ.

They understand that these Christians are putting their worldly pleasures ahead of serving God. Scripture tells us that Christians who put their own wealth and pleasure ahead of obeying God even risk their salvation: "No servant can serve two masters: for either he will hate the one, and love the other; or else he will hold to the one, and despise the other. Ye cannot serve God and mammon" (**Matthew 6:24**). Believers are set apart to serve God (Hebrews 9:14, Romans 6:16–22, and Ephesians 2:10). We neglect our service to God by prioritizing wealth and worldly indulgence at our eternal peril.

Consider a few examples of proper behavior of God's faithful followers from the great faith chapter in the book of Hebrews: "Women received their dead raised to life again: *and others were tortured, not accepting deliverance; that they might obtain a better resurrection*: And others had trial of cruel mockings and scourgings, yea, moreover of bonds and imprisonment: They were stoned, they were sawn asunder, were tempted, were slain with the sword: they wandered about in sheepskins and goatskins; being destitute, afflicted, tormented; (Of whom the world was not worthy) they wandered in deserts, and in mountains, and in dens and caves of the earth" (**Hebrews 11:35–38**). Moses was said to be "Esteeming the reproach of Christ greater riches than the treasures in Egypt: for he had respect unto the recompence of the reward" (**Hebrews 11:26**).

God's servants, spoken of in Hebrews 11:35–38, were looking ahead to their reward with a *focus on the eternal, not the temporal*, even to the degree that they refused to be released from prison or to be freed from torture. When we are able to focus on the next life, it fundamentally changes many of our decisions in this life. Think about those who refused to be released from prison and torture so they might gain a "better

> We must realize and be on guard against the reality that riches can be a horrible distraction from God's kingdom.

resurrection." Is there any question where their focus was? Would not our immediate (temporal) response be to be freed from torture? This is the reason that those who are poor in the eyes of the world are rich in faith: "Hearken, my beloved brethren, Hath not God chosen the poor of this world rich in faith, and heirs of the kingdom which he hath promised to them that love him?"(**James 2:5**). We must realize and be on guard against the reality that riches can be a horrible distraction from God's kingdom.

While these are extreme examples that we may never face, we are constantly faced with the decision of whether to choose the temporal or the eternal. When we decide to invest in ourselves instead of others, when we refuse to share the gospel, when we don't support those suffering for Christ, we are choosing the temporal, not the eternal. God is never pleased when we choose the temporal rather than serving Him.

Think for a moment about the teachings of Jesus regarding worldly things. He said, "Lay not up for yourselves treasures upon earth, where moth and rust doth corrupt, and where thieves break through and steal: But lay up for yourselves treasures in heaven, where neither moth nor rust doth corrupt, and where thieves do not break through nor steal: For where your treasure is, there will your heart be also" (**Matthew 6:19–21**). What is treasure in heaven? Is it not the expending of our time, energy and financial resources on things that have eternal impact?

Why did Christ teach this? He is the one who came from eternity and spoke authoritatively about the importance of an eternal focus. Is there any question where our priority as Christians should be? While none of us can be perfect in this matter, the goal is to strive for the eternal, not the temporal. It's more than just storing up treasure in heaven, although that is a part of it. It is more about our decisions on this earth impacting other people, both spiritually and materially. If our focus is on the eternal, we remember that we are here to serve the Living God. Everything else is secondary.

The apostle Paul wrote to Titus, "For the grace of God that bringeth salvation hath appeared to all men, Teaching us that, denying ungodliness and worldly lusts, we should live soberly, righteously, and godly, in this present world; Looking for that blessed hope, and the glorious appearing of the great God and our Saviour Jesus Christ" (**Titus 2:11–13**). If our focus is on the eternal, we will avoid over-indulging in worldly pleasures. This is the "deny himself" part of Matthew 16:24. That verse makes it clear this is what Jesus expects of his followers. Yet too few Christians do so today. Even worse, the Modern Church has developed doctrine to support this engagement of the flesh. It may get packaged in many forms, but the essence of Jesus' teachings on this matter is that we are to be focused on serving God and avoiding the distractions of worldly pleasures.

Jesus stated it this way: *"And he said to them all, If any man will come after me, let him deny himself, and take up his cross daily, and follow me. For whosoever will save his life shall lose it: but whosoever will lose his life for my sake, the same shall save it"* (**Luke 9:23–24**). Jesus made the point even clearer when He said, "If any man come to me, and hate not his father, and mother, and wife, and children, and brethren, and sisters, yea, and his own life also, he cannot be my disciple" (**Luke 14:26**).

Jesus also said "He that loveth his life shall lose it; and he that hateth his life in this world shall keep it unto life eternal" (**John 12:25**). The apostle John wrote, "Love not the world, neither the things that are in the world. If any man love the world, the love of the Father is not in him" (**1 John 2:15**). Peter records something similar, "Beloved, I urge you as sojourners and exiles to abstain from the passions of the flesh, which wage war against your soul" (**1 Peter 2:11**). Within the Modern Church, there is far too much love of the world. These passages all speak to the need to prioritize the eternal over the temporal by striving to deny ourselves the things of this world and focus on the eternal. The prosperity gospel teaches exactly the opposite of this, demonstrating that it is not a doctrine of God.

The perspective we use to make decisions is important. Not just because of the effect it has on the decisions themselves, but it reveals where our heart really is. This is what God judges. We know that those who are truly in Christ hate this world. If we don't hate the world, we don't see it as God sees it. God sees a world full of persecution, suffering, sickness, and evil. Because we spend so much time pursuing our own pleasures, we insulate ourselves from the harsh reality of most of the world. If we were walking in the Spirit (Galatians 5:25), we would see the world as He sees it.

We want to believe God has a plan for our lives, and indeed there are reasons for that hope (Philippians 1:6). Having said this, God is most concerned with the eternal. Because we are creatures of this world (creatures of the flesh), we make the assumption that many of the statements about God looking after us have to do with His provision in this world rather than the next.

God's view, however, is on our eternal future (If you don't understand this, examine the life of the apostle Paul after he came to Christ). If we are about His business and the eternal, He will provide for our basic necessities (Matthew 6:33 and 1 Timothy 6:6–8), and He will discipline us when we need it (Hebrews 12:4–11), but His focus is always on our eternal destiny. If we are walking with the Spirit as we should be (Galatians 5:25), our focus will be the same as the Holy Spirit.

We know that those who are in Christ and are walking in the Spirit (Romans 8:3–8) consider themselves strangers in this world, "These all died in faith, not having received the promises, but having seen them afar off, and were persuaded of them, and embraced them, and *confessed that they were strangers and pilgrims on the earth*. For they that say such things declare plainly that they seek a country. And truly, if they had been mindful of that country from whence they came out, they might have had opportunity to have returned. But now they desire a better country, that is, an heavenly: wherefore God is not ashamed to be called their God: for he hath prepared for them a city" (**Hebrew 11:13–16**).

We see faithful believers suffering, even to the point of torture and death, in the early church and up to the present day. This fact alone confirms what we see in the scriptures quoted above. God is concerned with our eternal destiny. He doesn't promise His followers peace and prosperity (John 16:2; 33) in this life. This is where the prosperity gospel has left the tracks.

This is part of the essence of faith; we understand that we are here but temporarily and our time here is short when compared to the expanse of eternity. As such, how should we make decisions? Should we not focus on making decisions in a manner that benefit the eternal and not the temporal? We struggle with this in America because of the profound blessings we enjoy. It is ironic that the body of Christ grows stronger under persecution and weaker with prosperity (Revelation 3:17–18).

When we use the time and resources we have for the eternal, lives are saved, lives are changed, people are rescued from the lake of fire, and glory is brought to our God. If we are pursuing our worldly pleasures, are we really being led by the Holy Spirit? We need to listen to the Holy Spirit and not the world.

There is a clever Demotivator® poster aimed at the Prosperity Gospel that shows a picture of a mansion with a caption underneath saying "Why wait for heaven to get your mansion?" It captures the essence of the hypocrisy of the prosperity gospel. This should demonstrate that the world sees Christians as hypocrites. The prosperity gospel is a doctrine that appeals directly to our flesh. It is an insidious teaching that many Americans use to rationalize the relationship between riches and God. But the kingdom of God is not about this world; it is about the next world. The kingdom of God is not about worldly wealth, but spiritual wealth.

James addressed this as well, "Ye ask, and receive not, because ye ask amiss, that ye may consume it upon your lusts" (**James 4:3**). Even if we are not asking for riches, when we receive such blessings, are we raising our standard of living or our standard of giving? Do we recognize the conditions that much of the world lives in? Do we understand how many are lost?

James continued, "Ye adulterers and adulteresses, know ye not that the friendship of the world is enmity with God? *Whosoever therefore will be a friend of the world is the enemy of God*" (**James 4:4**). Rarely do we hear this from the pulpit; indeed we often hear the opposite. We spend so much time on earthly pursuits that we make ourselves worldly, not spiritual. We are strangers here, not citizens. We are here but a short time. Yet many pastors in the Modern Church teach that it is absolutely fine that we live first and foremost in this world. Many more give their assent by silence on the topic.

Which is more important to us, our faith, which is of greater worth than gold, or our possessions? What does scripture teach us about this? Peter wrote, "That the trial of your faith, being much more precious than of gold that perisheth, though it be tried with fire, might be found unto praise and honour and glory at the appearing of Jesus Christ" (**1 Peter 1:7**).

Remember the words that John was inspired to write: "But whoso hath this world's good, and seeth his brother have need, and shutteth up his bowels of compassion from him, how dwelleth the love of God in him? My little children, let us not love in word, neither in tongue; but in deed and in truth" (**1 John 3:17–18**). Almost all Americans can help someone even if only with a very small amount. We need not save the entire world.

How about just starting with a small piece of it? This desire to help the spiritually needy and materially poor more accurately reflects the heart of our God than being selfish with what we have.

How the Focus on the Temporal Affects Teachings

Consider this passage in Romans: "And we know that all things work together for good to them that love God, to them who are the called according to his purpose" (**Romans 8:28**). Far too often, in fact all the times I [Gregg] have heard this quoted from the pulpit save one (Ed Taylor, as I remember), it has been presented as part of the prosperity gospel of comfort on this earth. Many consider this a promise that things will work out in this life.

But this cannot be about primarily about worldly blessings, for the greatest among us are those that suffer the most. Who did Jesus go to? He went to the poor. Who, throughout history, have been persecuted and killed? It is those sharing the gospel and refusing to denounce their faith. Jesus reminded His disciples, "These things I have spoken unto you, that in me ye might have peace. In the world ye shall have tribulation: but be of good cheer; I have overcome the world" (**John 16:33**). Paul wrote to Timothy, "Yea, and all that will live godly in Christ Jesus shall suffer persecution" (**2 Timothy 3:12**). Even in interpreting Romans 8:28, our worldly views have us believing that this is a temporal promise, when history tells us otherwise.

Romans 8:28 is not referring to temporal good as we understand it, but to *eternal good*. That is the true good: eternity with God. Based on scripture, we know what God values and what God does not. Remember that if we are friends with this world, we are His enemies (James 4:4, quoted above). This is not some metaphorical or metaphysical idea; it is a scriptural teaching.

What we as creatures of the flesh value are not necessarily good, and what we view as bad is not necessarily bad. To view the things of this world as God sees them, we must spend time in His Word. The apostles knew this: "And they departed from the presence of the council, rejoicing that they were counted worthy to suffer shame for his name" (**Acts 5:41**). They had God's view, not the world's view. How many of us rejoice in persecution?

Think about those who were beheaded on the beaches or those whose families were killed in front of them in the Middle East. If we look only at the temporal, we would think that God is not fulfilling the promise of Romans 8:28, but if we have an eternal perspective, He is. Those people who refused to deny their Lord are now with Him, in the honored position of being martyrs for Christ. Those who are suffering materially in this world often have great faith. What is more important than great faith?

We are called to weigh our decisions by the eternal, not the temporal. Granted, we are creatures of the flesh. However, our desire should be to make those decisions which honor our God. When we suffer, God uses the things that happen to us to the eternal good, even though those things may not be of temporal (earthly) good. We must keep this in perspective when we suffer, especially if we suffer for the cause of Christ. It is not a hollow philosophy, but the will of God. Paul urged the believers in the church in Rome to, "not be conformed to this world, but be transformed by the renewing of your mind, that you may prove what is that good and acceptable and perfect will of God" (**Romans 12:2**).

So what is good from the eternal perspective? It is becoming more Christ-like. It is coming closer to God. It is doing His will by submitting to the Holy Spirit. It is loving others. It is sharing the gospel and helping others to know God. It is recognizing what God has done for us. It is focusing on Him. It is developing gratitude for what God has blessed us with. These are eternal good, and all demonstrate a true faith through obedience, to our eternal good, eternity with our Savior. In some cases the temporal good must be sacrificed to result in eternal good. Think about our Lord and Savior who prayed, "if thou be willing, remove this cup from me: nevertheless not my will, but thine, be done" (**Luke 22:42**). Jesus Christ sacrificed the temporal good (His health and life) for the eternal good (saving many). Step back and ask yourself, what value does anything in this life have when compared to eternity with Him?

We need to avoid trying to have a foot in both worlds (this temporal world and the eternal world). In most cases, when push comes to shove, we will gravitate to this world and the values of this world. Only a very few are able to effectively divorce themselves from this world to pursue eternal things first and foremost. Praise God for them. That does not mean we shouldn't constantly try to prioritize God and the eternal.

Counting the Cost

The Bible teaches the concept of counting the cost of following Jesus Christ, but this is far too often missing from Modern Church sermons. When was the last time you heard about counting the cost of following Christ from the pulpit? But this is what Jesus taught.

> "And there went great multitudes with him: and he turned, and said unto them, If any man come to me, and hate not his father, and mother, and wife, and children, and brethren, and sisters, yea, and his own life also, he cannot be my disciple. And whosoever doth not bear his cross, and come after me, cannot be my disciple. For which of you, intending to build a tower, sitteth not down first, and counteth the cost, whether he have sufficient to finish it? Lest haply, after he hath laid the foundation, and is not able to finish it, all that behold it begin to mock him, Saying, This man began to build, and was not able to finish. Or what king, going to make war against another king, sitteth not down first, and consulteth whether he be able with ten thousand to meet him that cometh against him with twenty thousand? Or else, while the other is yet a great way off, he sendeth an ambassage, and desireth conditions of peace. So likewise, whosoever he be of you that forsaketh not all that he hath, he cannot be my disciple" (**Luke 14:25–33**).

Before we accept Jesus Christ, we are to count the cost to ensure we are prepared to follow, because there will be costs. We will encounter resistance, rejection, and perhaps even persecution. The more faithful we are in obeying Christ's commands, the more pushback we will get from the world, which is the enemy of God: "Yea, and all that will live godly in Christ Jesus shall suffer persecution" (**2 Timothy 3:12**). But much of the Modern Church has turned the following of Christ into something that promises worldly blessings and no adverse impact on a person's lifestyle.

There is almost always a cost for truly following Jesus. When we submit to what He teaches, this is foolishness in the eyes of the world (1

Corinthians 2:14). There are forces (the evil one and his followers) which are actively opposed to the message of the gospel. So it is not hard to find those opposed to the gospel when we are active in sharing it. We will encounter persecution as we seek to do the will of God. In fact, if you are not encountering any opposition from the world because of the way you are living your faith, you might want to re-evaluate whether you are truly being led by the Spirit. As the old WWII pilot saying goes, "If you are not getting any flack, you are not over the target."

But we must be ever vigilant to ensure that we are not lulled into believing that God wants us to be investing in ourselves and the things of this world first and foremost. Let the Holy Spirit lead you by submitting to His will. He will open doors for you to minister to the needs of others, and provide you the encouragement, time, energy and resources to do so. He is waiting for you to ask. He will help you realign your focus on your eternal home and remove it from your temporal home, while giving you the fruit of the Spirit along the way (Galatians 5:22).

Key Thoughts

The basic premise of the prosperity gospel is an offense to God and directly contradicts the words of Jesus. We should be thankful for what God has blessed us with, but should never seek to maximize our pleasure in this world. Paul himself learned to be content in all situations (Philippians 4:11). In this country we are so greatly blessed that those blessings have often led us further away from God rather than closer to Him. The greatest among us are those that are suffering for the cause of Christ, not those who have the most earthly possessions. Those most blessed are those so suffering, for great is their reward, which will last for all eternity.

Our focus should be on the next life, and that is where we should store our treasure for there our heart will also be (Matthew 6:19–21). While God will provide for us, the idea that God wants us to have everything we want in this life is absurd; in fact the gospels teach exactly the opposite. Prosperity breeds a self-contented, lukewarm church (Revelation 3:17–18), the very thing God hates. We are to deny ourselves. Does that mean we cannot enjoy some things with thanksgiving to God? No, but we must remember that which God provides can always be used to bring glory to

God by helping the poor, spreading the gospel, and helping persecuted brothers and sisters.

If we truly love the Lord, we know that our trials will be used by God to bring about good (Romans 8:28), but not necessarily temporal or earthly good. If we can focus our mind on the eternal and trust God in all things, it will help us to get through these earthly trials. Remember that God is interested in our hearts, not our wallets.

We must count the cost to follow Jesus. Truly following Jesus Christ is not about obtaining access to the best of this world. Indeed, biblically it is just the opposite. The Prosperity Gospel in all its flavors is about adapting Christianity to this world, rather than drawing this world to Christ.

Chapter 13

Calvinism and its Impact on the Modern Church

Errant Doctrine: Everything is preordained by God, including who will be saved and who will be eternally damned. Man has absolutely no choice or influence on God's decisions; nothing man does can ever influence God's decisions

Calvinism is growing; its influence is threatening to further split denominations. In fact, some of the doctrines of the Modern Church essentially embrace elements of Calvinism without formally affirming the religious system of Calvinism. The doctrine is relatively recent; it has only emerged in the last 500 years or so.

Although there were some allusions to parts of the doctrine in the historical church, it is clear that the early church fathers did not believe in Calvinistic theology as embraced today. It would therefore be surprising that the critical doctrines of Calvinism which relate to salvation were not more discussed and embraced during the first 1500 years of the Church Age, *if they were true*.

We would also expect that if that all of the key doctrines of Calvinism were true, we would see more evidence of the nature of predestination repeated over and over in the New Testament (as well as the Old Testament). We do not. What we do see is a few verses that seem to reference predestination supported by attempts to fit other scripture into that view.

It seems that each generation of men want to place their unique stamp on Christian theology, rather than simply submitting to what was inspired of God so many years ago. Here is a trustworthy saying: *the more complex the religious system, the less chance it is truly of God.* What God has done is meant to be understood by all men, not just a few with the deep secrets of the faith. Again, it is the Holy Spirit leads us into truth (John 16:13), not necessarily other men.

Calvinism is the ultimate example of men following men. While there is no need to re-hash all of the issues associated with the group of doctrines associated with the number of Calvinistic variants, let us just consider some of the ways in which Calvinism impacts the Modern Church.

The Bible is written directly to man as a free-will agent who God has expressly told to choose. The entire Bible demonstrates over and over the use of man's free will, often in defiance of God, but also imploring individuals to come to God in obedience through faith. God explicitly reaffirms choice throughout His Word. Indeed there is little need for all the Bible's teachings, commands, admonitions, and warnings if we are nothing more than automatons. Calvinistic teachings conflict with many scriptures and are not compatible with the nature of God as revealed in the Bible.

Even the formal basis of Calvinism, the concept of predestination, is scripturally challenged. Some learned in Greek suggest that the Modern Church linguistically misunderstands the few verses believed to reference the concept of predestination. Their study of Greek would suggest there is no such thing as individual predestination as the Modern Church uses the term. In the Modern Church, predestination (Greek *proorizo*) is most often used to mean someone divinely ordained to a purpose in advance. For example, we have already scripturally dispelled the false notion of Pharaoh not having the choice to submit to God's messenger (Moses).

Unfortunately predestination (again Greek *proorizo*) is a term that was not in general use in ancient Greek and is used very sparsely in the New Testament. The word itself, at least linguistically, does not support how we theologically interpret it. Furthermore, the *tense* of the word is also a concern; it is always rendered in the aorist tense which is timeless. English Bible versions however render the word in the past tense. The remainder of scripture, including specific examples which disprove parts of Calvinistic doctrine, suggests our use of the word may very well be in error. It is why we have the *apparent* number of conflicts between the concept of what God predestines and the freedom to choose as God explicitly tells us in scripture. It is why we end up in epic and pitched battles over God's sovereignty and man's free will.

The scriptures that Calvinists often use to support their one-sided doctrines do not provide the necessary proof-texts because in many cases, they rely on misunderstandings of the underlying Greek. The ideas of Calvinism are based largely on assumed meanings, not the underlying language itself. For example, the discussion of Pharaoh in Romans 9 does not lend itself, either linguistically or scripturally, to be understood as some theologians claim. But whatever we may think of Calvinistic doctrine as a whole, the fruit that it produces is unmistakable.

However, for the purposes of our discussion, we will address errors in Calvinism based on what some biblical scholars believe the Greek word to mean. Calvinism seems to confuse foreknowledge and predestination. Predestination without foreknowledge is different than predestination with foreknowledge. It is an important distinction because God can either take action, *making something happen* (predestination), or *allow something to happen* that He knows (foreknowledge) will happen unless He intervenes. We see both in scripture. But we must remember that we do not have foreknowledge. These two (foreknowledge guiding action vs. foreknowledge guiding inaction) are independent of each other yet can produce the exact same results.

One is an explicit action (predestination); the other is the knowing in advance of facts (foreknowledge) without direct action. God *knowing* something is not necessarily God *doing* something (or causing something to happen). One who knows the future (God) can make statements that can be *interpreted* to imply that He is controlling everything when He is not. Again, understanding the context is essential.

For example, consider one of the major passages in Romans 8 upon which Calvinism is based. We are taught, "For whom he did foreknow, he also did predestinate to be conformed to the image of his Son, that he might be the firstborn among many brethren. Moreover whom he did predestinate, them he also called: and whom he called, them he also justified: and whom he justified, them he also glorified" (**Romans 8:28–30**). Let's analyze what the passage is saying.

First, the group is limited by those whom God *foreknew* (not predestined). It modifies everything in the rest of these verses. The set of people we are talking about are those whom God foreknew. Whom did God foreknow? God foreknew the group of people who would accept Jesus Christ of their own free will using the faith God had given them.

Since God exists outside of time, obviously God also knows in advance that He has a group of people who will remain faithful. God predestined the group He foreknew would remain faithful to be conformed to the image of His Son; that is, true followers. He foreknows the group of faithful people will listen to and follow the Holy Spirit. God's foreknowledge is applicable to all "predestined" actions. To us, what is foreknown and what is predestined are indistinguishable, unless we are specifically told in scripture.

Notice we are told God called that group in Romans 8. But nowhere is it stated as an exclusive calling, nor can we exegetically read this from scripture. So it does not in any way imply that God did not call others. In fact, since we are talking about the group of people that God foreknew would remain faithful, it stands to reason that God called others who God foreknew would accept Jesus Christ but not remain faithful. Other scripture confirms this.

But this passage deals only with those whom God foreknew would remain faithful. Since God foreknew that group would remain faithful, they are justified and glorified through that enduring faith. This understanding of the passage reflects more accurately the plain meaning of the scripture than does the Calvinistic interpretation that man has no free will, no ability to choose in the matter.

The Foundational Doctrines of Calvinism

Selective parts of Calvinistic doctrine arose from the writings of Augustine and were later affirmed and expanded by John Calvin and his followers. Like many doctrines, Calvinism uses a small set of scriptures to justify its beliefs but does not take into account the larger body of scripture. Calvinism is often said to embrace five key doctrines arranged using the TULIP acronym. These doctrines are:

- **T**otal Depravity (No one on his own will ever seek God and His salvation)
- **U**nconditional Election (Nothing a person does affects God's decision to choose him)
- **L**imited Atonement (Christ did not die for all men but only for the "elect")
- **I**rresistible Grace (The "elect" are powerless to resist God's call to salvation)
- **P**erseverance of the Saints (Nothing the "elect" will do through their free will (if any), can ever cause him to lose his salvation)

There are various forms of Calvinism, each with its own name and set of differing beliefs, which do not need to be detailed here. You can research these on your own through the Internet or other sources. These variations in doctrine alone should demonstrate how man has taken a base of scripture and created differing sets of "truth." Unfortunately, this is common to the larger umbrella of Christianity as well. Here is another key truth to consider. The more the version of Calvinism tends towards absolute control of everything by God, the more it diverges from scripture.

Men have taken scripture, and based on a limited number of verses, created multiple sets of doctrine embraced by different sets of followers. Calvinists subscribing to all points listed above are considered "five-point Calvinists." Clear Biblical passages indicating that Christ died for the sins of everyone ("the world"), such as John 3:16 and 1 John 2:2 have forced many "five point Calvinists" to renounce the doctrine of limited atonement and become "four-point Calvinists."

Here is a short summary capturing the essence of Calvinism.

> Calvinism says that if I accept Jesus Christ, I was called by God and cannot refuse His call; that is my free will had no impact on my decision for Christ even though God gives us the faith. It teaches that I am so wicked that I could not have sought nor accepted Christ on my own. Only God's will was involved. Furthermore, those who may desire to know Christ (which Calvinism essentially denies is possible), even if they want to know Him of their own free will, cannot unless God has called them, and God only calls a few. I (the Calvinist) was chosen (elected) by God. Nothing I did, nothing I am doing, or nothing I will ever do, has anything to do with my election or salvation. God just decided. God may have had a basis for selection of the elect, but if so, we do not know it.
>
> God does not desire all to be saved, but only those He has chosen. It is only the elect that receive from Him the faith necessary for salvation. Once God has overridden my will to accept or reject Christ, I have become one of the elect. This was predetermined before the foundation of the world. As one of the elect, I am who Christ died for. Christ did not die for all, just for the elect. Finally, once I have come to know Christ, no free will decisions (and some versions of Calvinism deny total free will) I make, including rejecting Christ, can ever separate me from God and my salvation. It does not mean that I may not try to separate myself from God, just that I can't. No matter how much I sin, or even if I later deny Jesus Christ through my free will (assuming I have any), I will still be welcomed into God's kingdom.

As with all errant doctrines, there are some truths and some falsehoods in the doctrine.

Calvinistic Doctrine: God Decides Who Will Be Saved (Unconditional Election)

Calvinists believe God decided before time began, who would and who would not be saved. In Calvinism, the elect are those that have been chosen by God, forced to accept Jesus Christ, and forced to remain faithful. Man has absolutely no choice on whether he will be a member of the elect (the

Calvinists favorite passage to support this view is Romans 9 which has many problems with a Calvinists understanding of it).

In the Calvinist's view, if God made that decision based on some set of criteria, He never tells us in His Word what the criteria is. At the heart of this doctrine is the Calvinist belief that mankind does not have what theologians call "free will," at least in the matter of salvation. Some Calvinists will grudgingly admit that mankind does have some free will to obey or disobey God, but they all deny that whatever free will mankind may have can in any way effect his salvation.

Calvinists often quote verses 15 and 18 of Romans 9 as support for their belief that God, for His own reasons that we do not know, select some people to be saved and others to be lost: "For he saith to Moses, I will have mercy on whom I will have mercy, and I will have compassion on whom I will have compassion" (**Romans 9:15**). "Therefore hath he mercy on whom he will have mercy, and whom he will he hardeneth" (**Romans 9:18**). Yet this hardening is specific to Pharaoh whose heart God hardened *after* Pharaoh had done it himself.

But Paul goes on to explain in the rest of the chapter (and in chapters 10 and 11) that *God makes that selection on the basis of demonstrated faith*, giving examples of unbelieving, disobedient Israel (not saved, even though they were His chosen people), comparing them to both the believing, obedient Gentiles (saved because of their faith, even though they were not His chosen people), and the believing, obedient remnant of Israel. Verse 18, when taken in context of the message of salvation by demonstrated faith (the major theme of the book of Romans) actually refutes Calvinist doctrine of unconditional election.

Moreover, Paul's examples of Pharaoh and the potter and the clay in Romans 9 actually refute, instead of supporting, the Calvinist doctrine of unconditional election, as we explained in Chapter 11, "Once Saved, Always Saved (OSAS)." This is critical; it demonstrates how scripture can be twisted to fit in with the human-centered theology.

The Calvinist doctrine of Unconditional Election (the "U" in Tulip) is growing in the Modern Church sermons as Calvinism becomes more accepted among church leadership. This doctrine goes a long way toward making Modern Church believers ineffective witnesses for God. "Why should I "get out of my comfort zone" to share the gospel if God has already chosen the elect? They may rationalize that "No matter what I do or say, those who are elect will still be saved, and those who are not elect will never be saved." With this reasoning, the Great Commission of Matthew 28:19–20 can be disregarded, because no believer's obedience or disobedience to the Great Commission will have any effect on anyone else's eternal destiny.

Scripture clearly refutes this Calvinistic view of salvation. Paul was referring to God when he wrote, "Who will have all men to be saved, and to come unto the knowledge of the truth" (**1 Timothy 2:4**). The same teaching exists in 2 Peter 3:9. God gives all men a measure of faith (Romans 12:3). Paul wrote, "For the grace of God that bringeth salvation hath appeared to all men" (**Titus 2:11**). Some may receive different levels of faith (see the Parable of the Talents in Matthew 25:14–30), yet the faith given by God is sufficient to salvation even to those who choose to reject God's gift of faith (Matthew 25:27).

In the men's restroom of an Italian restaurant in Denver, Colorado there is a picture of a two year old in a high chair with a bowl of spaghetti upside down (like a hat) on his head, with spaghetti and marinara sauce streaming down his face. The caption reads, "We make the best d&!^ Italian food in the world. Period. What you do with it is your business." In the same way, what a man decides to do with the faith God gives him (Romans 12:3) is up to him. This is what theologians call "free will."

In the Bible, we see free will for mankind beginning in the Garden of Eden, as discussed above. The Garden was designed around the concept of free will; that is why the tree of knowledge of good and evil was placed in the center of the Garden, and Adam was instructed not to eat its fruit. We see man's ability to choose whether to obey or disobey God begin at that point and continue all through the Old and New Testaments. The Bible is full of history, commands, guidance, and examples that make it clear that humans do have free will, something our God granted us. We see the exercise of man's free will over and over throughout the Bible, with both earthly *and* eternal consequences.

If our free will truly has nothing to do with our salvation, then the whole model that God has communicated to us through His word is either misleading or untruthful. Consider what God told the Israelites through Moses, "I call heaven and earth to record this day against you, that I have set before you life and death, blessing and cursing: *therefore choose life, that both thou and thy seed may live*" (**Deuteronomy 30:19**). He offered them a free-will choice. This makes no sense if, as the Calvinists suggest, they had no choice because everything was predetermined (predestined) by God.

We are reminded of the choices given to the Israelites three times is in the New Testament. Is this is a reasonable thing to do if God is controlling the Israelites? No. It would be, in fact, cruel, like torturing a helpless animal. God is a God of love (1 John 4:16), not of cruelty and damnation. Furthermore, if God is controlling (forcing) them to sin, then God would be the source of evil, which we know He is not because He is holy and hates evil (Psalms 5:4 and Psalm 45:7). The message of the whole Bible tells us that evil is a product of the free will God granted to his sentient created beings: (fallen) angels and mankind.

Calvinist Doctrine: The Elect Can Never Lose Their Salvation (Perseverance of the Saints)

The doctrine of Calvinism that has the greatest impact on the Modern Church is the "P" in TULIP: Perseverance of the Saints (the elect cannot lose their salvation, because God chose them for reasons only He knows, and nothing they will ever do can change that choice).

In the Modern Church, the reasoning behind this doctrine is not articulated, but the conclusion is, in the form of the doctrine of OSAS (*unconditional* eternal security), discussed in Chapter 11, "Once Saved, Always Saved (OSAS)." The almost universal message from evangelical pulpits everywhere is that once a person "has truly accepted Christ" (*see* John 1:12–13), he is forever saved, no matter what he does after that moment of first true belief. The Modern Church calls this "Eternal Security," but they present it as *unconditional* eternal security. The appeal of this "easy grace" doctrine to the flesh is obvious. The new believer is taught that he can henceforth lead any lifestyle he pleases, completely indulging his flesh, and still be assured of eternity with God.

There are many, many passages in scripture that teach otherwise. These include Matthew 6:33, Matthew 7:14, Matthew 7:21, Matthew 10:22, John 14:15, John 15:1–10, Romans 6:16, Romans 6:22, Romans 8:12–13, Galatians 5:16–21, and 1 John 2:3–4), *but the mantra of Once*

Saved, Always Saved has been drilled into the heads of almost every evangelical churchgoer for decades, with the predictable result: the lifestyles of many of these people who consider themselves Christians is indistinguishable from that of unbelievers. Even worse, according to many scriptural passages, including those cited above, their eternal destiny is in serious doubt.

Calvinism also has the effect of developing a superiority complex in those who believe they are saved because they *believe* they are one of the elect (There is no known example of a Calvinist who did not believe he or she was one of the "elect"). This belief automatically produces a feeling of supreme superiority, because they "know" they will spend eternity with God, and they "know" that the poor schmucks they look down on will spend eternity in the lake of fire.

Since they "know" that they are the elect ("U") and can never be lost ("P"), it logically follows that any action they take on earth, no matter how disobedient to God's commands, no matter how destructive to others, no matter how evil, can never have any effect on their salvation. In short, it is a doctrine that leads people who believe that they are saved and can never be lost, whether or not they consider themselves Calvinists, to focus first and foremost on satisfying their lusts of the flesh in this world. Unfortunately, the end result of this kind of thinking can be eternally disastrous (Galatians 5:16–21, Hebrews 10:26–27, and many other passages).

Calvinist Doctrine: God is Sovereign and Therefore Controls Everything

The misunderstanding of the implications of God's sovereignty, as discussed in the Chapter 5, "Salvation and Eternal Life," has its roots in Calvinism. As Calvinism becomes more accepted among evangelical church leaders, this idea that God controls everything is producing more and more of the pernicious consequences discussed in the Chapter 10, "The Sovereignty of God."

Calvinist Doctrine: Christ's Death was only for the Elect ("L" Limited Atonement)

Calvinism teaches that Christ died only for the elect, those whose names are written in the Book of Life, the "saved." This doctrine clearly contradicts scripture, and, frankly, insults the character of God. Here are a couple of passages that state that Christ died for everyone:

- "And he is the propitiation for our sins: and not for ours only, but also for the sins of *the whole world"* (**1 John 2:2**).
  - Commentary: Christ paid for every sin ever committed or that ever will be committed by all members of the human race. (Note again that payment does not equal forgiveness).
- "For God so loved *the world* that he gave his only begotten Son, that *whosoever* believeth in him should not perish, but have everlasting life" (**John 3:16**).
  - Commentary: Tells of God's incomprehensible love for all mankind, and the sacrifice He made so some of us would have the opportunity to spend eternity in His presence.

God is a God of justice and love (Psalm 33:5). How can it be then that God sent Jesus Christ just to pay the penalty for the sins of some, but not others? If God truly loves "the world" as He stated, which clearly means *everyone* (John 3:16), why would He die for some but not others? This doctrine of Limited Atonement, like the doctrine of Unconditional Election, contradicts and insults the very character of God.

This doctrine of Limited Atonement may stem from the Calvinists refusal to appreciate the distinction between atonement and forgiveness. Jesus' last words before he gave up His spirit on the cross were, "It is finished" (**John 19:30**). The word translated "finished" (Greek *teleō*) was placed on promissory notes and receipts at that time to mean "paid in full."

As the scriptures quoted above indicate, Christ *paid for* the sins of the world "in full" on the cross. But only those who, "received him" (**John 1:12**), "who believeth in him" (**John 3:16**) have their sins *forgiven* at that moment of acceptance (belief). So although the sins of all mankind were paid for on the cross (atonement), forgiveness is limited to those who believe. The final benefit of that forgiveness is eternal life for those who endure and, "attain unto the resurrection of the dead" (**Philippians 3:11**).

The idea that Christ died only for the elect creates in professing believers, a feeling of exclusivity and entitlement that is neither valuable nor desirable in the Modern Church. Since Calvinists, and those in the pews listening to this Calvinistic doctrine being preached from the Modern Church pulpit, assume they are part of the elect (although they cannot know), they believe Christ died only for them. Examining their faith (2

Corinthians 13:5) never enters their mind. This dangerous Calvinistic doctrine is not only inconsistent with scripture, but also with the nature of God revealed in scripture.

The Modern Church is increasingly creeping toward Calvinism because church leaders don't want to talk about the responsibility and consequences of free will. It is too unsettling and not encouraging enough. Better to put all the responsibility on God. Consequently, we see the messages of many church leaders avoid these "inconvenient truths." After all, a growing church is a "successful" church, right? "We must be doing God's will, because the congregation is growing and the offerings are increasing. He is clearly blessing our work." Meanwhile, we are concerned that their congregations may be receiving an incomplete and misleading picture of the demonstrated faith God expects, placing many in eternal peril.

Key Thoughts

Calvinism is on shaky ground theologically for a variety of reasons. These include the relative absence of all of its tenets throughout the early church, limited support for Calvinistic doctrines within the New Testament, conflicting scripture, and a possible linguistic misunderstanding of the Greek word used to mean predestination.

Calvinism is built around the idea that man's free will (if any) is irrelevant to the entire process of salvation, but the breadth of scripture directly contradicts that idea. Free will (our ability to choose) is specifically stated in scripture and its eternal consequences are evident throughout the Bible. There are numerous Bible passages that directly contradict Calvinistic doctrine as taught from most Modern Church pulpits.

Calvinistic doctrine promotes the idea that man has no responsibility to God: that his beliefs, lifestyle and heart toward God play no part in his salvation. Its growing influence in the Modern Church has created in a dangerous and unwarranted sense of security and entitlement in the professing (and true) believers in the evangelical community. In all too many cases, the lifestyles of those influenced by Calvinism fall far short of what scripture tells us God expects of His faithful followers.

Chapter 14

The Heart for Our God

This is clearly one of the places where the Modern Church has departed from God. What do we believe a heart for God means? Jesus said the greatest commandment was, "And thou shalt love the Lord thy God with all thy heart, and with all thy soul, and with all thy mind, and with all thy strength: this is the first commandment" (**Mark 12:30**). He followed up with, "And the second is like, namely this, Thou shalt love thy neighbour as thyself. There is none other commandment greater than these" (**Mark 12:31**). Fulfilling these two commandments is what is *most important to God*. Loving God is clearly defined in the Bible: although God looks at the heart, He defines love for Him as obedience to His commandments (John 14:15,21–24).

Keeping God's commandments is also a requirement for abiding in God's love, according to Christ's words, "If ye keep my commandments, ye shall abide in my love, even as I have kept my Father's commandments, and abide in his love" (**John 15:10**). The apostle John wrote, "For this is the love of God, that we keep his commandments: and his commandments are not grievous" (**1 John 5:3**).

Loving others includes us helping them, not simply acknowledging them, or as James wrote, "If a brother or sister be naked, and destitute of daily food, And one of you say unto them, Depart in peace, be ye warmed and filled; notwithstanding ye give them not those things which are needful to the body; what doth it profit?" (**James 2:15–16**). God requires our love, both for Him and for our fellow man, *to be demonstrated* *with action*, not just with emotion. Romans 8:12 specifically addresses *our obligation* to live according to the Spirit.

Our God desires a deep and intimate relationship with us. Remember that we have been adopted into His family. How do we treat our family here on earth? God does not want to be an add-on or a second thought to our lives. He does not want to be viewed simply as someone who will save us from hell. We are to be, above all else, *in Him* (Romans 8:1 and John 15:4a). So what does it mean to have a deep and intimate relationship with Him?

It means spending time reading and searching the riches of His Word to get to know Him better. It is also the desire to help others know God in the same way. It is the desire to talk with *and listen to God* through prayer and time spent with Him. It is our desire to share with God what is on our hearts. It is the desire to have Him constantly in our thoughts. It is the desire to help others in their distress. It is the desire to obey God and submit to the Holy Spirit. It is the desire to choose God over the world in our thoughts and actions.

Does a person with a heart for God still sin? Of course! David had a heart for God but still sinned. David's faith in the Lord was strong and when he failed, as we all do, he sought and received the Lord's forgiveness, even for murder. David was not a rebel, nor did he ignore God. David was committed to obeying God, even though he failed at times. He spent time in prayer with God three times a day. He refused to make a sacrifice to God which cost him nothing. David had a heart of integrity towards God.

In fact, we are told God chose David because of Saul's disobedience and because David had a heart after God's own heart, recorded in Samuel's words to Saul: "But now thy kingdom shall not continue: *the Lord hath sought him a man after his own heart,* and the Lord hath commanded him to be captain over his people, because thou hast not kept that which the Lord commanded thee" (**1 Samuel 13:14**).

What made David special? David sinned, but was sorrowful and repented. David had faith, a generally obedient faith. He had a heart of integrity. He was reverent before God. He loved God (which is equated with his desire to obey). When we are told things from the pulpit which interprets scripture in a manner inconsistent with David's heart, we know we are in trouble. A study of David through Psalms, 1st and 2nd Samuel, 1

Kings, and 1 Chronicles help us come to know better the heart of a man that was a "man after His own heart."

But there are plenty of others in scripture who did not have a heart for God. In Jeremiah 15:6 we read about those who kept repenting and God knew their repentance was not sincere; he was weary of people saying they would turn away from sin and did not. What was their destiny? Destruction. Our God knows if we are sincere in anything we do with Him. The Holy Spirit will lead us if we sincerely desire an intimate relationship with our God.

One of the most significant signs of a heart for God is not whether a person sins, but rather how hard a person tries to avoid sin. When we do sin, God is looking for acknowledgement of our failures and our willingness to seek forgiveness (1 John 1:9–10). We are to turn away from sin when we do fail, and against seek to be in obedience to Christ's commands. Failure to do so demonstrates a hard heart before God and lack of understanding of what our Savior went through for us.

Some may term this God-given desire to obey "legalism" but it is nothing of the sort. Who would say that obeying God is legalism? The evil one! Jesus often confronted the legalism of the Pharisees, but on the question of obedience, He told his disciples (the faithful eleven), "If ye love me, keep my commandments" (John 14:15). A sincere desire to obey Him in all things grows out of a true relationship with God.

Our love for God and our obedience are inextricably linked. When we see a child willfully disobeying his father, at some point the child's love and respect for his father will come into question. So does the father's love for the child. It is the same with our Heavenly Father (*See* John 14:15 and John 15:10, quoted above). So when we hear those in the Modern Church espousing errant doctrine to the contrary based more on men's teachings rather than scripture, this is a warning sign. Here are some other warning signs:

- Failing to spend time studying the Word of God
- Refusing to examine the Word of God with others to resolve an issue
- Believing that there are multiple truths in interpreting the Word of God, or that we cannot reach the truth revealed in the Word of God

- Quoting other men as the source of truth instead of the Word of God
- Following other men's teachings instead of God
- Viewing scripture through a single lens, concept, or set of preconceptions including reading scripture and viewing through the lens of what we want it to say
- Using scripture out of context
- Considering traditions or the words of men as having the same authority as the Word of God.

As we discussed earlier, to have a heart for God, we must desire first and foremost to improve our vertical relationship (the one between ourselves and our God) and spend much less time on the relying on horizontal relationships (the words and reasoning of men) when seeking the truth. This is a natural outcome when we have love for our God.

Key Thoughts

Our heart for God is exactly what scripture defines it to be. We are to love God with all our heart, soul, mind, and strength. Think about the person you have loved most on this planet. How often did you think about them? How often did you want to talk to them? Now understand that our love for God should exceed that. But this love is also defined biblically as a commitment to obey God. Will we fail? Yes. However, God is able to discern the heart of those who demonstrate their love by being committed to obedience. He also knows that if there is no obedience, there is no love of Him, and we shouldn't expect His love for us (John 14:15 and John 15:10).

The heart for God seeks to obey God, not subvert, rationalize or make excuses for disobedience. It is never legalism to obey God; in fact, we are called to do our best to obey. The influence of the evil one is most often marked in the Modern Church by an attitude of disobedience or trivializing of sin (*e.g.,* "I sin all the time" or "my salvation is assured, so why worry about sin?"). The heart for God desires to love, serve, and obey. Be on guard against anyone that trivializes sin, whether it is another believer or a church leader.

If we even harbor these thoughts, we are not following the Holy Spirit, we do not appreciate what our Lord and Savior went through for us, and perhaps most important, we are demonstrating that we do not have a sincere love for our God and what He has truly done for us.

We will find that as we spend more time with the God that we love, it becomes more natural to sin less. In fact, the opposite is also true. That is the more time we spend in the world and away from God, the greater tendency we have to sin. It is only natural that we spend time with those we truly love. We do it with our family and friends here on earth. Is it not natural then to spend more time with our eternal family, God the Father, Son and Holy Spirit?

Chapter 15

The Foundation of Faith

It is a good thing to test yourself to see if you are truly in the faith. Understanding the foundation of your faith is critical. As statistics in the introduction show, many struggle with even the basics of their faith. Scripture commands us, *"Examine yourselves, whether ye be in the faith; prove your own selves.* Know ye not your own selves, how that Jesus Christ is in you, except ye be reprobates?"* (**2 Corinthians 13:5**).

What Do You Actually Believe?
Consider the foundational teachings of our faith.

1. Do you believe that God is the Father, the Son, and the Holy Spirit?
2. Do you believe the Bible is the true, inspired Word of God (2 Timothy 3:16)?
3. Is your relationship with God the most important thing in your life (Exodus 20:2–6), and do you love God first and foremost (Mark 12:30), demonstrating that love through obedience (John 14:15)?
4. Do you hate sin as much as Jesus declared in His teachings, both in yourself and others, trying your best to avoid it, and confessing and repenting of sin when you do sin (1 Thessalonians 5:22 and 1 John 1:9)?
5. Do you understand there is one absolute moral framework, the one established by God (2 Corinthians 6:14–18 and Revelation 18:4)?

6. Do you love and warn your brother and sister about his or her sin with a sincere heart and words of love to help them be closer to the Lord (Hebrews 10:24)?
7. Do you have a healthy fear of God (Proverbs 1:7, Proverbs 2:5, Proverbs 3:7, Jeremiah 5:22–24, Matthew 10:28, and 1 Peter 2:17)?
8. Do you praise God for all that He has created, His justness, His holiness, His mercy, and His love for us (Psalms 145–Psalm 150)?
9. Do you spend increasing amounts of time in His Word, seeking the truth as led by the Holy Spirit (2 Timothy 2:15 and 2 Timothy 3:16–17)?
10. Do you understand that our church leaders cannot save us, and that what they tell us must be examined against the truth of scripture (Acts 17:11)?
11. Do you believe in Satan as a literal being who opposes God's will and seeks to lead God's children away from Him (1 John 3:8, Acts 5:3, and Romans 16:20)?
12. Do you believe in hell as a literal place that will be thrown into the lake of fire (Revelation 20:14), and that God allows people the free will to choose the lake of fire as their eternal destination by rejecting Jesus Christ, God's perfect sacrifice for sin (John 3:18 and John 3:36)?
13. Do you believe that Jesus is the only way to God and eternal life (John 14:6 and Acts 4:12)?
14. Do you believe that Jesus Christ is the Son of God, and therefore is God who has always existed (John 1:1 and John 1:14)?
15. Do you believe that Jesus Christ died for the sins of all mankind and rose on the third day (1 Corinthians 15:3–4 and 1 Corinthians 15:20)?
16. Do you understand that your relationship to God is primarily as a bondservant to a master (1 Peter 2:16 and Revelation 22:3–9)?
17. Have you been water baptized as Christ commanded (Matthew 28:19)?
18. Do you believe in unity with other Christians who are committed to acting like Christians (John 17:17–21 and Ephesians 4:13)?
19. Do you understand that everything in this world belongs to God (Job 41:11) and we are but stewards of what God has provided us (1 John 3:17–18)?

20. Do you share the gospel as commanded by Christ (Matthew 28:19)?
21. Do you teach others to obey God as Christ commanded (Matthew 28:20)?
22. Do you love and care about the poor by reaching out and helping them (James 2:15–16)?
23. Do you hate the world (1 John 2:15)?

While this test is not designed to be all encompassing, it is designed to address some of the key foundations of faithful believers identified in scripture. If we fail on these points, we should revisit scripture to build our convictions about these things, and should examine our faith (2 Corinthians 13:5 and 2 Peter 1:10–11).

What is the Source of Your Faith?

If we are honest, we will acknowledge that the vast majority of today's Christians base their beliefs on what they hear from the pulpit. We trust our church leaders to know and faithfully present the truth of God's Word. But men are not perfect. They may rely on the doctrines of other men, misinterpret scripture, or even intentionally mislead their congregation if they have the wrong motives. The Bereans in Acts 17:10–11 had two of the most reliable, Spirit-led men on the planet preaching the gospel to them in the synagogue. But they didn't just accept and believe what they said: "These [Bereans] were more noble that those in Thessalonica, in that they received the word with all readiness of mind, *and searched the scriptures daily, whether those things were so*" (**Acts 17:10**). We're not saying be suspicious of your church leaders. We are saying that they are human, and it is your responsibility to verify from scripture what you hear from the pulpit, *relying on the Holy Spirit as the arbiter of truth.* They cannot save you.

The same standard applies to all sources of information from men, whether it be from church traditions, formal pronouncements or decrees from church organizations (like the Southern Baptist Convention or the Vatican), television or radio preachers, books on spiritual matters (including this one), even friends and family. In the words of a former American president, "Trust, but verify."

Have you ever heard a church leader claim he is being led by the Holy Spirit to say something that clearly conflicts with scripture? He may even make a statement like "If you argue or disagree with me you are arguing or disagreeing with God." We can tell whether a church leader is led by God. If hear them claiming to be led by the Holy Spirit and espousing a spiritual "truth," conflicting with scripture, there is a problem.

This is not new. As many of the epistles reveal, false teachers have plagued Christ's church from its very beginning, often claiming personal revelation from God. But the Holy Spirit will never lead us to believe errant doctrine. The Holy Spirit reinforces scripture; He does not contradict it. We may rest assured the Holy Spirit does not lead us to act inconsistently with scripture. If there are such leadings, they are not of God but from the rulers of darkness (Ephesians 6:12).

The Bible is the Source of All Spiritual Truth

We must get back to scripture. Because of many recent movies, even those such as Star Wars, we often treat the Holy Spirit as the force leading us to act in a certain manner. We may even believe that we have been led in certain ways that are inconsistent with scripture. Jesus reassures us and tells, *"But the Comforter, which is the Holy Ghost, whom the Father will send in my name, he shall teach you all things, and bring all things to your remembrance, whatsoever I have said unto you"* (**John 14:26**).

The vast majority of today's Christians are not spending enough time reading God's word. This is one of the major reasons we felt compelled to write this book. If all Christians were actually seeking the guidance of the Holy Spirit and studying the Word of God daily, the Holy Spirit would guide them into the truth (John 16:13). The errant doctrine and consequential lukewarm and/or sinful lifestyles we see in today's evangelical churches would disappear. We would all become true disciples of Christ (Luke 14:27).

The irony is that scripture reveals its own truth. The vast majority of people who don't believe the Bible is true have never read it. The more a person reads the Bible (guided by the Holy Spirit), the more its truth jumps off the page into the mind of the reader, almost screaming, "It's true, it's true." But if you do not read the Bible regularly, you may never have that experience. It is hard to build a sound faith with an unshakable knowledge of the truth of the Bible if you don't read it regularly.

For many years there have been huge letters painted on a mountainside just across the Rio Grande from El Paso, Texas which read: "LA BIBLIA ES LA VERDAD. LEELA." Translation: "The Bible is the truth. Read it." Nothing else in this world is more important. Everything else will pass away. Jesus told His disciples, "Heaven and earth shall pass away: but my words shall not pass away." Do not let "the tyranny of the urgent" keep you away from God's Word. If you make it your top priority, you will find time to read it. One hundred years from now, nothing else will matter.

"All scripture is given by inspiration of God, and is profitable for doctrine, for reproof, for correction, for instruction in righteousness" (**2 Timothy 3:16**). Friends, do not try to build your faith on anything less. All else is shifting sand including potentially, the teachings of men.

> A true and saving faith is every Christian's hope, for it results in eternal life (Romans 6:22). But a true and saving faith is not one which is based on intellectual acknowledgment alone. It is based on the entirety of spiritual truth found in the Bible. Read it daily and examine yourselves as scripture commands, to ensure that you have a true and living faith which mirrors the attributes of a true and saving faith as described in the next chapter.

Chapter 16

Saving Faith

Throughout this book, we have discussed the scriptural truth that true and saving faith is not simply intellectual faith or faith without action, in spite of what much of the Modern Church teaches. The faith which saves, described in the Bible, is a faith that is living and active, and manifests itself in the lives of believers and those around them. Such faith guided the lives of the gospel writers, the first century church and some today. To this end, we attempt to answer the question posed by the rich ruler: *What shall I do that I might inherit eternal life?*

The New Testament, even more than the Old Testament, makes it clear that we are saved by faith in God, and specifically His plan for our salvation through His Son, Jesus, the promised Messiah, who paid the price for our sin through His death on the cross, and rose again. Scripture details what that faith will look like: it is an *active, life-long faith* given by God that is evidenced by obedience to God's commands set forth in the New Testament by Jesus Himself and by His apostles in their epistles.

> "For God so loved the world, that he gave his only begotten Son, that whosoever believeth in him should not perish, but have everlasting life" (**John 3:16**).

This well-known verse is the essence of the gospel, the good news of a loving God reaching down and paying the ultimate price to redeem a lost and helpless mankind. It is sad that so simple a path to an eternity of joy and gladness with our Creator has been obscured, twisted and misconstrued to mislead so many, beginning almost from the day of Christ's resurrection and continuing to the present day. We must examine scripture as a whole, especially the New Testament, to get the correct answer to the question the rich ruler asked Jesus, *"Good Master, what shall I do that I may inherit eternal life?"* (**Mark 10:17**).

Let's be honest with ourselves here. If we get the answer to that question wrong, we can get everything else in the Bible right and still spend eternity in the lake of fire. Ultimately, the correct answer, the one we can rely on to determine our eternal destiny, must be found in the Bible itself. We may hear our church leaders, TV evangelists, our family or friends explain their understanding of the requirements for salvation, or we may adopt beliefs from tradition or church dogma, but whatever the source, it is too important a matter to accept without verification from scripture itself.

Our greatest barrier to finding the correct answer to that all-important question consists of the *preconceptions* we have formed from sources like those mentioned above. To learn the truth, *we must put aside those preconceptions* and take an honest look at the scriptures *as a whole* with the guidance of the Holy Spirit.

Salvation is Based on Faith Given to Us by God
Where does scripture say faith and salvation come from?

- "For by grace are ye saved through faith; and that not of yourselves: *it is the gift of God*: Not of works, lest any man should boast" (**Ephesians 2:8–9**).

Faith that is from God is faith in God Himself and in God's plan (provision) for your salvation, not some distorted understanding of God and/or His plan. A quick review of that plan is helpful in understanding exactly what God's plan is.

1. God's plan for our salvation was in place before the foundation of the world. (Revelation 13:8). See also Isaiah 49:5–7 and Isaiah 53.
2. God's plan for our salvation was necessary because He gave all of mankind the ability to choose whether to obey Him or disobey Him (what theologians call "free will"). This choice was the whole

point of the Garden of Eden, which had at its center the tree of the knowledge of good and evil, the fruit of which Adam and Eve were forbidden to eat. They disobeyed God, and all mankind (those responsible for their actions) have followed suit.

3. God is holy; He is sinless, and will not endure the presence of sin (Leviticus 44:11 and 1 Peter 1:15–16). Therefore, Adam and Eve were ejected from the Garden and the presence of God (spiritual death) after they disobeyed His command (sinned), and later died physically as well, the very thing God said was the penalty for disobedience in Genesis 2:17. We all have disobeyed God (sinned) (Romans 3:23), and until we receive God's gift of salvation, are also spiritually dead and awaiting our physical death (Ephesians 2:1–3).

4. God is absolutely just. (Romans 9:14, 2 Thessalonians 1:5, and 2 Timothy 4:8). The penalty for sin, which is death (spiritual and physical), had to be paid.

5. God is a God of love-perfect, infinite, selfless (*agape*) love without regard to the merit of the object (Psalm 33:5, John 3:16, and Romans 5:8; 8:37–39). This is probably why He gave all sentient beings we know of, mankind and the angelic hosts, "free will." He wanted beings who could *choose* to love Him, not be forced to love Him. Out of that love came His mercy in providing a way for those who chose to love Him to spend eternity with Him (Ephesians 2:4–7).

6. The only way God's attribute of justice could be satisfied was by someone sinless paying the penalty for our sins. A murderer on death row is not in a position to die in the place of another condemned murderer on death row. That sinless person was the second member of the Trinity (Father, Son, and Holy Spirit) who, in order to die physically and spiritually and be tempted to sin, had to be born as a man. God's love is so overwhelming, that He would demean Himself to the point of being born as a man and then suffer the humiliation and pain of persecution, scourging, mocking, and a horrible death, all to pay the penalty for the sins of all mankind. He came in the human person of Jesus (Hebrew *Yeshua*) of Nazareth, as described in the New Testament. *God*

Himself paid the penalty for your sins and the sins of the whole world (all mankind) (John 3:16 and 1 John 2:2).
7. If the only requirement of God's plan was that mankind's sins be paid for, then every person who ever lived would spend eternity with God, but the Bible tells us that this is not so. Why? *Because payment for sins does not mean forgiveness of sins. Although the sins of the world were all paid for, the Bible tells us there are additional requirements for forgiveness of our sins.* We will examine those requirements below.
8. This brings us back to the requirement of faith first mentioned in John 3:16, quoted above. It is a conscious decision to choose God: to trust Him for your salvation; to trust His plan and His work on the cross of Calvary, not anything we can do ourselves. Don't forget that the faith you need to truly choose God comes from Him, as the quoted passage above from Ephesians 2:8–9 makes clear.

Paul summed up the Gospel he and Silas preached this way: "That if thou shalt confess with thy mouth the Lord Jesus, and shalt believe in thine heart that God hath raised him from the dead, thou shalt be saved" (**Romans 10:9**).

And at that moment you are saved, as was the thief on the cross at Jesus' right side. The thief on the cross had no time left to serve God in this life, but we do.

At this moment of first belief and confession, *you are just barely inside the narrow [strait] gate* as Jesus described, "Enter ye in at the strait gate: for wide is the gate, and broad is the way, that leadeth to destruction, and many there be which go in thereat: Because strait is the gate, and narrow is *the way, which leadeth unto life*, and few there be that find it" (**Matthew 7:13–14**). *After that moment of first belief, you now have in front of you the narrow way that Jesus spoke of that you must follow, the way that leads to eternal life*, as explained in the sections below.

Saving Faith Produces Obedience

"Know ye not, that to whom ye yield yourselves servants to obey, his servants ye are to whom ye obey; whether of sin unto death, or of obedience unto righteousness? But God be thanked, that ye were the servants of sin, but ye have obeyed from the heart that form of doctrine which was delivered you. Being then made free from sin, ye became the servants of righteousness." [**v16–18**], and "But now being made free from sin, and become servants to God, ye have your fruit unto holiness, *and the end everlasting life*" [**v22**] (**Romans 6:16–18, 22**).

"Not every one that saith unto me, Lord, Lord, shall enter into the kingdom of heaven; but he that doeth the will of my Father which is in heaven" (**Matthew 7:21**). How do we know the will of the Father? We have the Holy Spirit to guide us in the paths of righteousness, just as He guided David in Psalm 23.

As Paul so eloquently described in Romans 7, we cannot serve God in our flesh. That is why God gives believers the indwelling Holy Spirit, as Jesus explained to His faithful 11 disciples: "If ye love me, keep my commandments. And I will pray the Father, and he shall give you another Comforter, that he may abide with you for ever; Even the Spirit of truth; whom the world cannot receive, because it seeth him not, neither knoweth him: but ye know him; for he dwelleth with you, and shall be in you" (**John 14:15–17**). "Howbeit when he, the Spirit of truth, is come, he will guide you into all truth: for he shall not speak of himself; but whatsoever he shall hear [from the Father], that shall he speak: and he will shew you things to come" (**John 16:13**). Jesus was talking to His faithful eleven disciples, but in Acts and in the Epistles we learn that all believers are indwelled by the Holy Spirit.

But the indwelling Holy Spirit only leads us to obey God's commands *if we submit our will to His will*: not just be *indwelled* by the Spirit, but be *led* by the Holy Spirit. "For if ye live after the flesh, ye shall die: but if ye through the Spirit do mortify the deeds of the body, ye shall live. For as many as *are led by the Spirit of God*, they are the sons of God" (**Romans 8:13–14**). Note carefully: *Paul is telling us that being led by the Spirit is a requirement for salvation.* This is a sobering thought. How many of today's "Christians" are submitting their will to the leading of the Holy Spirit?

This concept is also expressed as "walking by" or "walking according to" the Spirit. "There is therefore now no condemnation to them which are in Christ Jesus, who walk not after the flesh, but after the Spirit. For the law of the Spirit of life in Christ Jesus hath made me free from the law of sin and death" [**v1–2**], and "That the righteousness of the law might be fulfilled in us, who walk not after the flesh, but after the Spirit" [v4] (**Romans 8:1–2, 4**).

"If we live in the Spirit, let us also walk in the Spirit" (**Galatians 5:25**).

We can do nothing in our flesh to please God. Only by submitting our will to His will, as Jesus did in the Garden of Gesthsemane (Matthew 26:42), can we be obedient to God and pleasing to Him. Consider these words of Jesus:

> "*If ye keep my commandments, ye shall abide in my love*; even as I have kept my Father's commandments, and abide in his love. These things have I spoken unto you, that my joy might remain in you, and that your joy might be full" (**John 15:10–11**).
>
> "Jesus answered and said unto him, *If a man love me, he will keep my words*: and my Father will love him, and we will come unto him, and make our abode with him" (**John 14:23**).
>
> "I am the true vine, and my Father is the husbandman. Every branch in me that beareth not fruit he taketh away: and every branch that beareth fruit, he purgeth it, that it may bring forth more fruit" (**1 John 5:1–2**).

After describing the "deeds of the flesh" in Galatians 5:19–20, Paul tells the Galatians, "I tell you before, as I have also told you in time past, that they which do such things shall not inherit the kingdom of God" (**Galatians 5:21**). *God's plan is not to spend eternity with those who live in rebellion against His commandments. His plan is to spend eternity with those who love Him*: Jesus said, "If ye love me, keep my commandments" (**John 14:15**).

We cannot do this by ourselves; we can only do it by submitting our will to God's will and being led by the Holy Spirit.

We are all familiar with the parable of the talents in Matthew 25:14–30 (discussed in Chapter 11, "Once Saved, Always Saved"). It is important to understand that this parable is one of several ways Jesus explains how he will judge all people alive at His return to determine who are killed and who are left alive to enter the millennial kingdom (killing all the unsaved, who cannot enter the kingdom per John 3:3). He starts explaining this judgment in Matthew 24:36 and ends in Matthew 24:31.

The parable of the talents describes *the basis* for determining who is saved and who is unsaved. In that parable, the master represents Jesus, his time away on a journey represents the time between His ascension and His second coming, the talents represent *faith*, and the servants represent us.

Do not be deceived by the false teaching of some Calvinists that the talents represent the abilities (talent) that God has given us. Webster's Unabridged Dictionary (1970 ed.) tells us that the English word "talent" comes from this parable. This indicates a misunderstanding of what the talents represent in this parable, a misunderstanding which continues to the present day. Talent (Greek *talanton*) literally means "that which is weighed," is used in reference to a weight equal to 3000 shekels of silver (ten years wages for the average laborer), a great deal of money in the first century.

The talents cannot represent special abilities given to us by God (such as those described in Romans 12:6–8), since the whole point of the parable is describing *how* Jesus will separate the saved from the unsaved, as evidenced by the fact that the third slave's failure to invest the master's talent results in him being cast into the outer darkness, representing hell. The entire Bible speaks to the fact that *we are saved by faith, not works*. If salvation were based solely on using the abilities God has given us, then salvation would be based on all on works, not faith. We know this is not true.

We learn several things from this parable which are affirmed in many other scriptures:

- The faith required for our salvation comes from God (Ephesians 2:8–9).
- Everyone is given a sufficient measure of faith from God (Romans 12:3), which can be received, applied and grown to result in salvation.
- We cannot accept the faith given to us by God and assume it is our ticket to heaven (just sit on it or bury it and forget about it until we appear before Him); we have to use and grow that faith if we are to "enter into the joy" of our Master. This gives us our next point:

Saving Faith is Demonstrated Faith

What does scripture teach about demonstrated faith?

> "I am the true vine, and my Father is the husbandman. *Every branch in me that beareth not fruit he taketh away*: and every branch that beareth fruit, he purgeth it, that it may bring forth more fruit" (**John 15:1–2**).
>
> "What doth it profit, my brethren, though a man say he hath faith, and have not works? can [that] faith save him? (**James 2:14**).

James' question is obviously rhetorical; the answer is, of course not. That is apparent from the parable of the talents. The first two slaves *demonstrated* their faith through serving their master. The third did not, and was not saved, but was cast into hell.

James is *not* making the point that salvation is the result of faith plus works. He is stating the truth we find in many other passages: *If you have saving faith, it will result in the obedient submission to the Holy Spirit and be demonstrated in your life*. If your faith does not produce that result, it is time for self-examination, as described below.

Jesus' next explanation of the judgment at His return (Matthew 25:31–46) makes the same point. Jesus tells the saved sheep on His right, "Then shall the King say unto them on his right hand, Come, ye blessed of my Father, inherit the kingdom prepared for you from the foundation of the world: For I was an hungred, and ye gave me meat: I was thirsty, and ye gave me drink: I was a stranger, and ye took me in: Naked, and ye clothed me: I was sick, and ye visited me: I was in prison, and ye came unto me" (**Matthew 25:34–36**).

Notice that Jesus doesn't mention that "you believed in me." Yes, that was the starting point of entering through the narrow gate, but He is talking about those who then walked the narrow way of obedience by submitting their will to the leading of the Holy Spirit. Everything He mentions is *demonstrated faith*.

We see the same thing in Hebrews 11, the great faith chapter in the Bible. Abraham is held up as a great example of faith by his *demonstrated faith in leaving Haran for the Promised Land and later preparing to sacrifice his son Isaac.* His starting point (the narrow gate) was to believe God in Genesis 15:6, but then he *demonstrated* his faith through obedience.

Faith resulting in salvation is not the lukewarm faith we see in Revelation 3:15–17. *Saving faith compels a true believer to submit his will to the leading of the Holy Spirit,* who will direct him to obey and serve his Lord and Savior. As he does, there will be a visible change in his behavior.

Saving Faith Produces a Close Relationship with God Through Obedience

What does scripture teach about obedience and our relationship with God?

> *"Abide in me, and I in you. As the branch cannot bear fruit of itself, except it abide in the vine; no more can ye, except ye abide in me.* I am the vine, ye are the branches: He that abideth in me, and I in him, the same bringeth forth much fruit: for without me ye can do nothing. *If a man abide not in me, he is cast forth as a branch, and is withered; and men gather them, and cast them into the fire, and they are burned"* (**John 15:4–6**).

So how do we "abide in Christ?" He tells us *"If ye keep my commandments, ye shall abide in my love;* even as I have kept my Father's commandments, and abide in his love. These things have I spoken unto you, that my joy might remain in you, and that your joy might be full" (**John 15:10–11**).

> "Jesus answered and said unto him, *If a man love me, he will keep my words*: and my Father will love him, and we will come unto him, and make our abode with him" (**John 14:23**).

We keep His commandments by submitting our will to the leading of the Holy Spirit. "If we live in the Spirit, let us also walk in the Spirit" (**Galatians 5:25**).

Sin separates us from God (See Romans 5:8–11). When we first receive God's gift of salvation, all the sins we have committed before that time are forgiven, like the thief on the cross. But we know from experience that we continue to sin after that moment, even though we may be trying to be obedient to God's will. Whenever we place our will ahead of His will, we sin: "for whatsoever is not of faith is sin" (**Romans 14:23b**). Paul talks about his personal battle with sin in Romans 7. Here are just a couple of verses:

> "For I know that in me (that is, in my flesh,) dwelleth no good thing: for to will is present with me; but how to perform that which is good I find not. For the good that I would I do not: but the evil which I would not, that I do" (**Romans 7:18–19**).

We all deal with this problem. Paul is not talking about the willful, habitual sin of Hebrews 10:26 and Galatians 5:19–21, but "the evil which I would not."

This sin tends to separate us from God, but we have the remedy explained in scripture:

> "If we say that we have fellowship with him, and walk in darkness, we lie, and do not the truth: But if we walk in the light, as he is in the light, we have fellowship one with another, and the blood of Jesus Christ his Son cleanseth us from all sin. If we say that we have no sin, we deceive ourselves, and the truth is not in us. If we confess our sins, he is faithful and just to forgive us our sins, and to cleanse us from all unrighteousness. If we say that we have not sinned, we make him a liar, and his word is not in us" (**1 John 1:6–10**).

When we remove that barrier of sin, we can once again draw close to God and submit to the leading of the Holy Spirit. Searching the heart and confessing any un-confessed sin should be part of every prayer, just as it is mentioned in what we call the Lord's Prayer in Matthew 6:9–13.

Saving Faith Puts God First

What does scripture teach about God's position in our lives?

> "Thou shalt have no other gods before me" (**Exodus 20:3**).

"If any man come to me, and hate not his father, and mother, and wife, and children, and brethren, and sisters, yea, and his own life also, he cannot be my disciple. And whosoever doth not bear his cross, and come after me, cannot be my disciple" (**Luke 14:26–27**).

"And he said to them all, If any man will come after me, let him deny himself, and take up his cross daily, and follow me. For whosoever will save his life shall lose it: but whosoever will lose his life for my sake, the same shall save it" (**Luke 9:23–24**).

Our willingness and ability to put God first is largely dependent on our perspective. We do not think much about God when we are wrapped up in the cares and pastimes of this world. God is the obvious center point of our thoughts when we are focused on the eternal.

Saving Faith is Enduring Faith

Salvation is not a one-time, instantaneous event. Unless you (perhaps like the thief on the cross) die shortly after believing in Jesus (John 3:16) and receiving Him as your Savior (John 1:12), *salvation is a life-long process.* Jesus referred to as the narrow way in Matthew 7:14. We see an ongoing journey to salvation in the verses quoted in Chapter 5, "Salvation and eternal Life" and in other chapters above.

There is one more requirement given in scripture: we must "endure to the end;" we must "hold fast" to the faith by which we are saved.

"And ye shall be hated of all men for my name's sake: but he that endureth to the end shall be saved" (**Matthew 10:22**).

"For it is impossible for those who were once enlightened, and have tasted of the heavenly gift, and were made partakers of the Holy Ghost, And have tasted the good word of God, and the powers of the world to come, If they shall fall away, to renew them again unto repentance; seeing they crucify to themselves the Son of God afresh, and put him to an open shame" (**Hebrews 6:4–6**).

"Let *us hold fast* the profession of our faith without wavering; for he is faithful that promised" (**Hebrews 10:23**).

"Moreover, brethren, I declare unto you the gospel which I preached unto you, which also ye have received, and wherein ye stand; By which also ye are saved, *if ye keep in memory what I preached unto you"* (**1 Corinthians 15:1–2a**).

"Cast not away therefore your confidence, which hath great recompence of reward. For ye have need of patience, that, after ye have done the will of God, ye might receive the promise. For yet a little while, and he that shall come will come, and will not tarry. Now the just shall live by faith: *but if any man draw back, my soul shall have no pleasure in him.* But we are not of them who draw back *unto perdition*; but of them that believe to the saving of the soul" (**Hebrews 10:35–39**).

"*Stand fast* therefore in the liberty wherewith Christ hath made us free, and be not entangled again with the yoke of bondage" (**Galatians 5:1**).

Key Thoughts

The popular salvation message taught in today's seminaries, books, churches, mission outreach programs, and gospel television and radio broadcasts all mention intellectual faith or "once and done" belief, and downplay or contradict the requirements of obedience, demonstration of faith, close relationship with God, and endurance described throughout the Bible. As a result, many churchgoers may be lulled into a dangerous complacency.

We would all like the popular message to be the true one. If it is, then the passages quoted above, and dozens more like them in the Old and New Testaments are meaningless or, worse, misleading. God is not a God of confusion or deception. Every word in His Word has meaning. He has given all who believe His Holy Spirit to guide them in all truth. It is our prayer for every reader that he or she searches the scriptures to get this right. Every reader's eternal destiny is at stake.

What should we do? We are told to check our own faith:

> "*Examine yourselves, whether ye be in the faith;* prove your own selves. Know ye not your own selves, how that Jesus Christ is in you, except ye be reprobates?" (**2 Corinthians 13:5**).
>
> "Wherefore the rather, brethren, *give diligence to make your calling and election sure*: for if ye do these things, ye shall never fall: *For so an entrance shall be ministered unto you abundantly into the everlasting kingdom of our Lord and Saviour Jesus Christ*" (**2 Peter 1:10–11**).

If you find yourself failing the test, remember that your faith is a gift from God. Ask earnestly, and He will give you what you need so that you can know your eternity will be with Him (Mark 9:24). Submit your will to the Holy Spirit. He will guide you in all truth (John 16:13).

> "These things have I written unto you that believe on the name of the Son of God; that ye may know that ye have eternal life, and that ye may believe on the name of the Son of God" (**1 John 5:13**).

Closing Thoughts

Dear Reader,

As a final encouragement, we encourage you to read God's Word and go to Him, and *Him alone* for the truth. Examine it earnestly, seeking the truth by putting aside what you have been told, your church or family traditions, your preconceptions, and your desires. Scripture is not meant to be screened through any of these filters.

Tell the Lord that you desire His truth and His truth only. Please, let the Lord speak to you through His Word and His Spirit. In this way, you will be able to follow the counsel of God, "I beseech you therefore, brethren, by the mercies of God, that ye present your bodies a living sacrifice, holy, acceptable unto God, which is your reasonable service. And be not conformed to this world: but be ye transformed by the renewing of your mind, that ye may prove what is that good, and acceptable, and perfect, will of God" (**Romans 12:1–2**).

Remember the words of our Lord and Savior: "Let not your heart be troubled: *ye believe in God, believe also in me*" (**John 14:1**).

May God bless you and your families as you seek Him first and foremost.

Gregg Powers and Ed Nolan

About the Author

Gregg and Ed are followers of Jesus Christ who both seek a deeper relationship with the Lord through study of scripture and through trying to walk with the Holy Spirit. Gregg has spent the last 10 years facilitating his community's Bible Study and was responsible for the Children's Programs at his prior church. Ed has led home and church Bible studies since 2000. He currently leads a Sunday school class at his church on end times prophecy based on his book, The Day of the Lord (2nd Edition). They are committed to relying on the Word of God, not the words of men, for spiritual truth.